Metacognition

Charles Seale-Hayne Library
University of Plymouth
(01752) 588 588
LibraryandITenquiries@plymouth.ac.uk

Metacognition

Cognitive and Social Dimensions

edited by Vincent Y. Yzerbyt,
Guy Lories and Benoit Dardenne

SAGE Publications
London • Thousand Oaks • New Delhi

First published 1998

SAGE Publications Ltd
6 Bonhill Street
London EC2A 4PU

SAGE Publications Inc
2455 Teller Road
Thousand Oaks, California 91320

SAGE Publications India Pvt Ltd
32, M-Block Market
Greater Kailash – I
New Delhi 110 048

British Library Cataloguing in Publication data

A catalogue record for this book is available from the British Library

ISBN 0 7619 5258 6
ISBN 0 7619 5259 4 (pbk)

Library of Congress catalog card number 98–060527

Typeset by Mayhew Typesetting, Rhayader, Powys
Printed in Great Britain by Redwood Books, Trowbridge, Wiltshire

Contents

Notes on Contributors

Mahzarin R. Banaji received her PhD at Ohio State University, spent a year as NIAAA postdoctoral fellow at the University of Washington and has been at Yale University since 1986. Her research on social cognition has focused on the role of unconscious processes in social judgment, on the role of emotion in memory, and the development of self in social context. She served as Associate Editor of the *Journal of Experimental Social Psychology* and is currently Associate Editor of *Psychological Review*. In 1991 she received the Lex Hixon Prize for Teaching Excellence from Yale College and is a 1997 Fellow of the John Simon Guggenheim Memorial Foundation.

Herbert Bless received his PhD from the University of Heidelberg. He is now Professor of Social Psychology at the University of Trier. His research interests focus primarily on social judgment and information processing. In particular, his work addresses the role of subjective experiences and metacognitions that accompany information processing, including affective states and ease of retrieval. Other central aspects of his interests relate to the emergence of assimilation and contrast effects in social judgment, and how communication rules influence cognitive processes.

Benoit Dardenne received his PhD in 1995 from the Catholic University of Louvain (Louvain-la-Neuve, Belgium). He was a research fellow at the University of Massachusetts, Amherst. He is now a postdoctoral fellow at the Belgian National Science Foundation. He is teaching social psychology and methods at the Catholic University of Louvain and the University of Liège. His research interests focus primarily on social judgment and social cognition. In particular, his current research interests include hypothesis confirmation process, impression formation, mood and stereotypes.

Nilanjana Dasgupta is currently a postdoctoral fellow at the University of Washington. She received her PhD in 1997 at Yale University. Her dissertation is entitled "Pigments of the imagination: The role of perceived skin color in stereotype maintenance and exacerbation". In this research she investigates the relative accuracy of skin color perception and its influence on stereotypic psychological judgments. Her research interests include beliefs and attitudes toward groups and individuals with a special focus on the unconscious operation of prejudice and stereotypes in social judgments. She is a recipient of a SPSSI dissertation research award.

Meghan Dunn received her BA in psychology from Williams College (1995) and is now a graduate student in the social psychology program at Yale University. In addition to her work on correction processes guided by naive theories of bias, her research examines the interface of psychology and the law (in collaboration with Saul Kassin at Williams College and Peter Salovey at Yale University).

Daniel T. Gilbert received his PhD from Princeton University in 1985. He is currently Professor and Chair of the Program in Social Psychology at Harvard University. He is the recipient of research grants from the National Institute of Mental Health and the National Science Foundation, the recipient of the National Institute of Mental Health's Research Scientist Development Award, a Fellow of the American Psychological Association and the American Psychological Society, and the winner of the APA's Distinguished Scientific Award for an Early Career Contribution to Psychology. He is co-editor of the *Handbook of Social Psychology* (4th edn, 1998) and a Faculty Fellow of Harvard University's Mind-Brain-Behavior Fellowship. His research interests include ordinary personology (how people make inferences about the internal states and traits of others), human credulity (why people tend to believe what they should not), and affective forecasting (how and how well people predict their emotional reactions to future events).

Michael J. Gill received his BA in Psychology from the University of North Carolina at Charlotte and is currently working toward his PhD in social/personality psychology at the University of Texas at Austin. His research interests concern how and how accurately people make inferences about both themselves and others.

John T. Jost received his PhD in social psychology from Yale University in 1995 under the supervision of William J. McGuire. After working as a postdoctoral researcher with Arie W. Kruglanski at the University of Maryland and as a Visiting Assistant Professor in the Department of Psychology at the University of California at Santa Barbara, he joined the faculty in the Graduate School of Business at Stanford University, where he is presently Assistant Professor of Organizational Behavior. His research interests include social cognition, stereotyping, intergroup relations, political psychology, and the theory of system justification.

Asher Koriat is a Professor of Psychology at the University of Haifa, and the Director of the Institute of Information Processing and Decision Making. He received his PhD from the University of California, Berkeley. He has taught at the Hebrew University of Jerusalem, and at the University of Haifa, and has spent periods of time at the University of Oregon, the Institute of Advanced Studies in Jerusalem, the University of Toronto and the Rotman Research Institute. His current research interest is in monitoring and control processes in memory, memory for action, reading processes, and the representation and transformation of spatial information.

Arie W. Kruglanski received his PhD in 1968 at UCLA under the guidance of Harold H. Kelley. He has been Professor of Psychology at Tel-Aviv University (1969–1987) and now holds a similar position at the University of Maryland (1987–). Kruglanski is a Fellow of the American Psychological Society and of the American Psychological Association, and a recipient of the NIMH Senior Scientist Career Award. He has served as Editor of the *Personality and Social Psychology Bulletin* and is now Editor of the *Journal of Personality and Social Psychology*; "Attitudes and Social Cognition" section. His research interests include attribution theory, knowledge acquisition processes and the motivation–cognition interface.

Jacques-Philippe Leyens is Professor of Social Psychology at the Catholic University of Louvain. He is President of the European Association of Experimental Social Psychology and has served as Chief Editor of the *European Journal of Social Psychology*. His research interests include media violence, social cognition and impression formation. Among other books, he is the author of *Stereotypes and social cognition* (1994) with Vincent Yzerbyt and Georges Schadron.

Guy Lories is currently Professor at the Catholic University of Louvain (Louvain-la-Neuve, Belgium) where he teaches cognitive psychology, learning and memory. He received his PhD in cognitive psychology from the Université catholique de Louvain, where he had specialized in psychology and philosophy. His research interests are in memory, metacognition and problem solving.

Leonard L. Martin received his PhD in social psychology from the University of North Carolina at Greensboro in 1983. His dissertation dealing with correction processes in concept priming won the 1984 SESP dissertation of the year award. Dr Martin then spent a year and a half at the University of Illinois as a postdoctoral fellow working with Professor Wyer. In 1985, Dr Martin took a position at the University of Georgia, where he is currently Professor.

Thomas O. Nelson received his PhD from the University of Illinois in 1970, then held a postdoctoral fellowship with Gordon Bower at Stanford University before joining the faculty at the University of Washington, where he was an Assistant, Associate, and Full Professor from 1971 to 1995, when he joined the faculty at the University of Maryland. Nelson's research is on human memory and metacognition. He is a Fellow of the American Psychological Association, American Psychological Society, and the American Association for the Advancement of Science.

Adisack Nhouyvanisvong received his BS from the University of California, Davis (1994) and his MS in cognitive psychology from Carnegie Mellon University (1996). His current research interests concern the application of theories of human learning and memory. He spent a year at the Educational Testing Service developing a computational model of problem solving in the domain of mathematics. He is currently a doctoral student at Carnegie Mellon University where he continues to develop the computational model for his dissertation.

Richard E. Petty received his BA from the University of Virginia (1973), and an MA (1975) and PhD (1977) in social psychology from Ohio State University. After beginning his academic career at the University of Missouri, he returned to Ohio State in 1987. His research on social influence processes (funded largely by the National Science Foundation) has resulted in seven books and about 150 chapters and articles. He is past Editor of the *Personality and Social Psychology Bulletin*, a Fellow in various professional organizations, and recently served as Chair of the social psychology review panel at NIMH.

Lynne M. Reder is a Professor of Psychology at Carnegie Mellon University. She received her Bachelor's degree from Stanford University in 1972, her PhD from the University of Michigan in 1976 and an NIH post-doctoral fellowship at Yale University from 1976 to 1978. She joined the faculty at Carnegie Mellon in 1978. Her research activities include understanding the mechanisms underlying strategy selection and developing a general, computationally specified, memory model that accounts for a broad range of cognitive phenomena, including individual differences in adaptivity. The computer simulations are developed within a unified cognitive architecture that captures the details of behavioral data and enables her to refine her theorizing. She has published over 50 journal articles and book chapters, and has recently edited a volume entitled *Implicit memory and metacognition*.

Marie-Anne Schelstraete received a degree in psychology in 1989 and a degree in speech therapy in 1991, both from the Université catholique de Louvain (UCL), Louvain-la-Neuve, Belgium. Since 1991 she has worked in the laboratory of cognitive psychology in the Department of Experimental Psychology of UCL where she received her PhD Up to 1996 she was Research Assistant and she is now Scientific Collaborator of the Belgian NSF at UCL, and invited Assistant Professor. She is mainly interested in reading strategy and developmental difficulties in language comprehension.

Diederik A. Stapel is a research fellow of the Royal Dutch Academy of Sciences at the University of Amsterdam, the Netherlands. In 1997 he received his PhD in social psychology from the University of Amsterdam. His main research interest concerns the ways in which fleeting characteristics of social situations affect people's perceptions of others as well as their perception of themselves.

Fritz Strack received his PhD in 1983 from the University of Mannheim and was a Postdoctoral Fellow at the University of Illinois. He held the position of Senior Researcher at the Max Planck Institute for Psychological Research in Munich and was Associate Professor of Psychology at the University of Trier. At present he is a Professor of Psychology at the University of Wuerzburg. His research interests are in the field of social cognition. Specifically, he is interested in the role of judgments and inferences in various psychological domains.

William B. Swann, Jr., received his PhD from the University of Minnesota and is currently Professor of Psychology at the University of Texas at Austin. He has been a Fellow at Princeton University and at the Center for Advanced Study in the Behavioral Sciences and is the recipient of multiple research scientist development awards from the National Institutes of Mental Health. His research has focused on the interplay between beliefs about others and the self in interpersonal relationships. He has authored numerous articles on these topics and also a book entitled *Self-traps: The elusive quest for higher self-esteem.*

Duane T. Wegener received his BA in psychology from the University of Missouri (1989) and an MA (1991) and PhD (1994) in social psychology from Ohio State University. After three years as an Assistant Professor of Psychology at Yale University, he became an Associate Professor at Purdue University. His research interests include social judgment, mood management and attitude change. He recently served as Guest Editor (with Richard Petty) of a special issue of the journal *Social Cognition* on the role of naive theories in social judgment and behavior and currently serves on the board of consulting editors for the *Personality and Social Psychology Bulletin.*

Thalia P. Wheatley received her BA from the University of Texas (1993) and is currently a graduate student in the social psychology program of the University of Virginia. Her research interests include people's perceptions of what motivates their behavior and the accuracy of these perceptions.

Timothy D. Wilson has been a member of the faculty of the University of Virginia since 1979 and is currently Professor of Psychology. He received his PhD from the University of Michigan in 1977. His research has focused on affective forecasting, attitudes, and the limits and consequences of introspection. A common theme in his research is that people's theories about their own mental states and processes are important predictors of their feelings and behavior. His research has been supported by grants from the National Science Foundation and the National Institutes of Mental Health.

Vincent Y. Yzerbyt received his "licence" from the University of Louvain in 1984 then spent one year at the University of Massachusetts, Amherst. Back home, he completed his PhD in 1990. After five years as a Research Fellow of the Belgian National Fund for Scientific Research, he took a position as an Associate Professor at the University of Louvain where he teaches social cognition, intergroup relations, attitudes and statistics. His research interest is in intergroup relations and stereotyping. Vincent Yzerbyt won the 1994 Early Career Award for Psychology of the Belgian University Foundation. He is currently Associate Editor of the *British Journal of Social Psychology* and of the *Personality and Social Psychology Bulletin*. Among other books, he is the author of *Stereotypes and social cognition* (1994) with Jacques-Philippe Leyens and Georges Schadron.

Preface

This book addresses one of the most intriguing questions of contemporary psychology, namely, that cognitive activities can apply to themselves. Are metacognitive activities similar to standard cognitive processes or is there something special to metacognition as opposed to cognition? How do people reflect on their cognitive processes? What are the differences and the similarities between self and other regarding the evaluation of cognitive products? Do people rely on naive theories about their judgments and what is the impact of these theories on subsequent correction strategies? Does our metacognitive knowledge affect our behavioral choices? These are only some of the questions addressed in this book.

In the past several years, cognitive as well as social psychologists have become increasingly aware that metacognition is a fundamental aspect of human cognition. Clearly, in order to understand human reasoning and behavior, psychologists should understand both cognitive and metacognitive activities. This book, the first to bring together social and cognitive pschologist, offers a striking illustration of the benefits of confronting and comparing current knowledge in social and cognitive psychology. The contributions reveal not only that there are a fair number of theoretical and methodological concerns common to both fields, but also that the cognitive and social viewpoints can greatly benefit from looking at one another.

In the early 1990s, the idea that cognitive and social psychologists might learn from each other in order to study metacognition was not that obvious. Trapped in the comfort of our respective disciplines, the editors of this book were working on similar things but without knowing that colleagues on another floor were also doing research on metacognition. When it was realized that we were all referring to metacognition to shed new light on people's cognition and behavior, we decided to organize a scientific meeting with the specific aim of cross-fertilizing our knowledge on the topic. We sent out invitations to a dozen colleagues whom we regarded as experts on the issue of metacognition in cognitive and social psychology. Their reaction was extremely positive and the resulting conference on Metacognition: Cognitive and Social Dimensions, held in Louvain-la-Neuve in May 1995, will be remembered as a most exciting scientific event. In fact, the project of the present book crystallized during the conference. Along with a few additional contributors, our invited speakers all agreed to write up their talks in a chapter format. Ziyad Marar, from Sage, immediately accepted the project.

We would like to thank all the people who helped us to produce this book. Our gratitude first goes to the participants of the symposium and to the authors of the chapters for their patience and cooperation. We also want to thank our students who helped us organize the symposium. We acknowledge the financial contribution from various institutions: the Catholic University of Louvain, the Belgian National Science Foundation, the Catholic University of Lille, and the Communauté Française de Belgique. Finally, we thank Lucy Robinson from Sage for her constant support and her thoughtful advice.

Vincent Y. Yzerbyt
Guy Lories
Benoit Dardenne

From Social Cognition to Metacognition

Guy Lories, Benoit Dardenne and Vincent Y. Yzerbyt

Metacognition is a fundamental characteristic of human cognition. Not only do we have cognitive activities but it would seem that they can apply to themselves: we have cognitions about cognition. The possibility of meta-cognition seems typical of the human species and may be related to our being linguistic animals. It stands as one of the important differences between animal and human cognition and the very existence of psychology is proof of our interest in our own mental processes.

Interestingly, however, metacognition has long been neglected as a valid object of scientific inquiry. This state of affairs may have something to do with the disappointments – if not the trauma – that accompanied the historical attempt to use introspection for scientific purposes. It may also have to do with the early preeminence of behaviorism. Last but not least, it may have to do with a healthy defiance regarding some of the philosophical problems involved. Whatever the actual reasons may be, what is now commonly known as metacognition has not been at the center of preoccu-pations until recently. Worse, metacognition was long considered a nuisance. As noted by Nelson (1993), one usually prefers to short circuit most self-reflective mechanisms through experimental control. Still, this may hurt the ecological validity of psychological research. Many interesting cognitive activities are accompanied by rich contents of consciousness. It is necessary to wonder whether these contents are epiphenomenal or whether they play a role in the organization and functioning of our cognition. The present volume was born from the idea that all social interactions fall into the category for which the self-reflective character of cognitive activity is essential.

Social psychologists very often use devices that require at least some interest and confidence in self-reflectivity (e.g. rating scales). As Banaji and Dasgupta (Chapter 9 of this volume) note, however, they also investigate a number of phenomena in which awareness or, rather, the lack of awareness plays a central role. For instance, a large portion of stereotype research attempts to explain when and why perceivers remain largely unaware of the impact of their stereotypic biases. If people were able to detect these biases spontaneously, the biases would probably not have existed in the first place. Moreover, if warning people that some unwanted influence may bias their judgment was enough to allow them to detect that influence and adjust for its effects, the whole field would disappear. So, while social psychological approaches acknowledge the importance of self-reflective elements, they also recognize and even claim that there are limits to what metacognitive or self-reflective activity can do. There are limits to what people know about themselves as well as to what people know about their fellow human beings. Social psychological approaches even suggest that these limits may be quite similar.

The differences and similarities between metacognitive knowledge of the self and metacognitive knowledge of the other are examined in great detail by Nelson, Kruglanski, and Jost in Chapter 5. The clear message that emerges from this review is that the various sources of information made available when people attempt to assess their knowledge of themselves and others only provide the raw material, indications that require interpretation in the light of more or less implicit theories. This perspective stands in sharp contrast with the idea that we are in complete control of our behavior and cognitive activity. It also stresses the fact that what we know about others and ourselves is the result of a complex construction process. But why do we need such a complex process in the first place? What is metacognition good for?

The problems of reflectivity

One prominent idea is that metacognitive activities may monitor and control other cognitive activities. This seems to imply a distinction between levels. The processes belonging to a metacognitive level would control and monitor the activities of the processes at a cognitive level. Yet, such a formulation almost immediately evokes the specter of infinite regress: If we need one level to control our cognitive functioning, why not another to control the previous one, and so on.

The conceptual difficulty is made even worse if we consider that meta-cognitive processes are often thought to be conscious while many other cognitive processes certainly are not. Because the notion of a process being "conscious" or not may seem obscure – it depends on a report by the subject – other distinctions have been developed. A process can be considered, for instance, as semantically penetrable or not (see Pylyshyn, 1984, for a complete discussion). A penetrable process is a process that can be affected by specific instructions or by giving the subject some explicit information. To give a specific example, the Müller-Lyer perceptive illusion is not cognitively penetrable. This means that the illusion is not affected by the knowledge that there is an illusion and that no form of experimental instructions can alter the impression produced by the stimulus. There is a general feeling that a large number of so-called automatic processes (memory access, spreading of semantic activation, etc.), that are not cognitively penetrable are also not conscious.[1]

A distinction can then be made between unconscious and automatic processes on the one hand and conscious and controlling (and themselves uncontrolled?) metacognitive processes on the other. In some areas of cognitive psychology, researchers even suggested that the most reasonable object of study was the "module," a non-penetrable, encapsulated, automatic psychological function. A large enough number of modules would make up the cognitive architecture and whatever process is cognitively penetrable might be left for philosophy to study. As already noted above, this leads us to investigate situations in which experimental control is easier, which is a valuable advantage. One difficulty, however, is that this may tell us only part of the story.

From a philosophical point of view, this conception of the mind very strongly resembles a picture of consciousness as a unique place where mental life "happens," the so-called "Cartesian theater" conception strongly opposed by Dennett (1991). The "modules" just build a model of the world on the stage of the "Cartesian theater" in which the mind is the audience and where conscious processes will apply to themselves, indefinitely. This would indeed be a very convenient solution to the infinite regress conundrum: Ignore it and leave it to philosophy.

A different and maybe more valuable strategy is to address the problem directly. Nelson (1996, p. 105, note 5) indicates very clearly that "it would be a mistake to suppose that there must be different physical structures for object-level cognition and for meta-level cognitions. . . . For example, we do not need special structures for looking at our eyes – just a mirror. Feedback loops could play the role of the mirror for metacognition." The basic idea here is that the same architecture must be responsible for both cognitive and metacognitive processes simultaneously. At the same time, the meta level and the object level are no longer defined as parts of the mental architecture but are seen as a distinction applied to behavior by the observer. We now have to consider the usual cognitive architecture in order to identify the "mirror" postulated by Nelson.

One should note that whatever appears in the mirror must have been put in front of it by some process that is, in a sense, more elementary. So there is a problem of levels after all, but it is a different one. It has to do with the fact that the cognitive level itself emerges from more elementary levels. For instance, Newell (1990) describes the levels of biological, cognitive, rational, and social functioning as shown in Figure 1.1.

Figure 1.1 depicts the basic scheme that underlies the computational metaphor in cognitive psychology. Each level of description is independent in the sense that it has its own laws or principles that can be described independently of the levels below it. Each is nevertheless implemented using relatively simple operations that belong to a lower one. One original aspect added by Newell (1990) is to assign a time band to each level. Loosely speaking, significant social processes such as those that involve interactions between a great many individuals, seem to require days, while a neuron operates on the millisecond scale. Starting from the bottom, the 10 milliseconds assigned to the operation of a neural circuit correspond to the time it takes for a couple of neurons to conclude a transaction of some sort (they

Duration	Action	Temporal band
month		
week		social band
day		
hour	task	
10 min	task	rational band
1 min	task	
10 sec	unit task	
1 sec	cognitive operation	cognitive band
100 msec	deliberation	
10 msec	neural circuit	
1 msec	neuron	biological band
100 μsec	organelle	

Figure 1.1   *Time bands and levels (adapted from Newell, 1990)*

need to integrate action potentials over at least a short period). This is what Newell takes as the lower limit of cognition because it would be the time to access a simple symbol. The 100 millisecond level is the level of an elementary deliberation, i.e. an elementary choice between two possible – automatic – mental operations. The typical cognitive act takes about one second and may be something like uttering the sentence "Pass the salt please!" At the next level, the unit task is described by Newell as the first level of full cognitive functioning; it is an assembly of simple cognitive operations and takes about 10 seconds. Newell cites reasons to believe that the unit task level is indeed meaningful. Newell argues that the time spent by an expert chess player to consider a move (6 to 8 seconds) is indicative of this level of complexity and that, in most verbal (think aloud) protocols, the elementary steps take about that long. Above this limit, the behavior observed with these protocols is essentially rational and obeys some explicit algorithm that the subject obviously learned or developed with experience. This is why think aloud protocols are a nice way to investigate problem solving: They give us access to the appropriate level and allow us to identify the subject's strategies in terms that enable us to determine whether they are rational or not and what their limitations are.

The methodology of think aloud protocols is based on the idea that these protocols allow access to the products of cognitive activities, that is, to the contents of a working memory (Ericsson & Simon, 1984); they can be used to describe large scale, non-automatic, quasi rational behavior provided that the experimenter keeps in mind the possibility that the verbal report of these contents may be incomplete. The difficulty is to make sure, through proper experimental instructions, that the participants do not start introspecting but stick to the description of the contents of working memory.

The above analysis suggests that we may consider metacognition *as the processing of the contents of (working) memory by standard cognitive processes*, and forget the idea of any direct and mysterious access by people to the intricacies of their own mental functioning. In cognitive architectures like Newell and Simon's "physical information systems", Newell's SOAR or Anderson's ACT* and ACT-R, the general processing principle is the matching of productions with the content of working memory. There is nothing to prevent specialized productions from applying to these contents and implementing effective metacognitive abilities, thereby providing a measure of monitoring and control. It is exactly here, to use Newell's words, that "cognition begins to succeed" and begins to apply to its own products. We believe that this is also where metacognition emerges. Although the social band, where interactions between individuals belong, is the upper one in Newell's hierarchy, the durations we meet in social cognition suggest that cognitive social psychology is concerned with the upper part of the cognitive band and maybe also the lower part of the rational band.

Because social behavior and metacognition rely on general cognitive processes, metacognition must also rely on approximations, limited capacity processes, arguable heuristics, intrusion of naive theories, and so forth. The interesting question is whether this explains why our judgments about others and ourselves cannot be better and how they go wrong. The various chapters in this book analyze simple cognitive tasks and a number of problematic social situations. The cognitive analysis seems to converge on a small number of principles that may not be completely understood yet but that seem to agree with what has been observed in social cognition. As such, they hold great promise for future research and the possibility of an integrated approach to social cognition.

Familiarity, availability, accessibility, representational richness, etc.

The idea

The general idea to provide some ground for metacognitive processes is to use the contents of working memory. We will imagine that according to these contents and depending on the circumstances, people reach a judgment concerning their cognitive situation. Consider a person trying to remember something. What will the content of working memory be? It may be something like a name or a place evoked by a cue but it may also be something more like a feeling. It may be an impression that some memory trace has been easily accessed, that some face is familiar, that a pattern has already appeared. In any case there will be the problem of making appropriate inferences from that evidence.

This can be done in several ways. It may involve a fairly explicit and rational line of reasoning or it may be done in a more automatic manner, some of the heuristics may be appropriate and some not, the conclusions reached may or may not be followed by an action, the whole process may come to be more or less automatized with practice and so on. Eventually, a decision will be reached that whatever is shown is familiar because it has been seen already, that information retrieved by memory search indicates that more information can and will be retrieved, etc. The trouble, of course, is that, as for any heuristic, things can go wrong. An unknown face may seem familiar because it simultaneously resembles a lot of other faces that we do know, information retrieved from memory on a given topic may actually be wrong, the impression that something studied has been mastered and is more easily accessed after a learning trial may indicate only that we have not let enough time go by, etc. In other words, the contents of memory in the broad sense indicated above may mislead because it is difficult to determine exactly why they are what they are and what produced them in the first place.

This may be considered as a classical attribution problem. A given response has been evoked in a subject, for instance a feeling of familiarity, and a causal attribution is required. If the correct attribution is made, it will identify a mental state and provide information regarding the functioning of the mind at the moment. It will actually monitor a state of mind. According to standard attribution theory, attributions are made by people about themselves, as they could be made about others if the same kind of information were available. This introduces a fundamental similarity between self and others but also agrees with the idea that there is nothing especially mysterious about metacognition (but see Jones & Nisbett, 1972).

The analysis is similar to the analysis of the source problems in cognitive psychology. In various memory tasks it will often appear that the subjects will erroneously identify a stimulus as having been presented in some context while it has been presented in another. A similar problem is to make the difference between what has been imagined and what has been actually presented (Johnson & Raye, 1981). The question here apparently bears on some external attribution (was the stimulus presented?), but the alternative is internal generation. It has recently become apparent that the mechanisms involved may be especially brittle and among the first to go when there is neurological damage to the memory system.

The problem is made complex by the fact that some memory contents may result from priming. The presentation of one stimulus in the context of another may lead to the automatic retrieval of more or less relevant information and/or to an easier retrieval of the relevant information. This may lead to an impression of greater familiarity. Most heuristics do not take into account automatic activation effects and do not make the distinction between whatever content has been evoked by the stimulus and some aspect of the context. In other words, the source identification problem (the attribution problem) is especially difficult because of the presence of automatic (non-penetrable) activation phenomena.

The feeling-of-knowing example

The above line of thinking pretty well matches what has been discovered in feeling-of-knowing (FOK) research. The FOK is a rating made by people about the probability that they will be able to recognize an element of information they have just been unable to recall. In most experimental operationalizations, participants answer general information questions and make a FOK rating when they fail to remember. A recognition test is given at the end of the session to assess whether their predictions are valid.

The FOK has an intuitive similarity with the well-known tip-of-the-tongue situation, but the FOK does not occur spontaneously and it is not as intense. In the case of the FOK, the theory evolved from a relatively mysterious "partial access" process to a two-process theory based on cue familiarity and amount of material retrieved. As suggested by Nhouyvanisvong and Reder (Chapter 3 in this volume), it seems necessary to distinguish between a fast and a slow FOK. The first type of FOK would be automatic, would rely on cue familiarity and would be involved in pre-retrieval decisions (as, for instance, whether to search memory or not). This fast FOK requires an interpretation of a feeling (familiarity) that is open to errors. Nhouyvanisvong and Reder develop a complete theory of how attribution errors are possible in this context and suggest that, from a cognitive point of view, the problem stems from a confusion of sources. Some forms of cognitive processing, especially fast assessments like this FOK judgment, would allow for more source confusions because they allow the contributions of various cues to add up.

The slow FOK depends on the results of the retrieval activity itself (see Koriat, Chapter 2 in this volume). It is slower because it requires that at least some retrieval attempts take place before an evaluation of what has been retrieved can be made. It is essentially a rating based on the contents of working memory and subjective norms of knowledgeability but it is less clear how it could be very effective as an adaptive strategy (at least at the beginning of the search process). It may not be sensitive to the same source misattribution effects as the fast form of the FOK judgment but it is, in any case, a construction. Koriat describes how this construction takes place and introduces the concept of *accessibility* as the cornerstone of the FOK rating. The idea is that whenever a cue is effective in retrieving a lot of material from memory, this high accessibility indicates that still more material can be retrieved and, presumably, the correct answer also. The problem is that some cues may be deceptive in the sense that retrieving a lot of material when attempting recall does not guarantee that the correct item will be retrieved in due time. What will be retrieved or recognized later on may just be an error. This is why, according to Koriat, the FOK accuracy depends on *output-bound accuracy*, the probability that an answer is correct, once it is actually given. Some items will be essentially deceptive and will produce commission errors that the accessibility heuristic cannot forecast. The absolute FOK level, however, depends on accessibility as defined above.

Although accessibility is defined by the amount of information memory search retrieves and very much resembles informational richness, it does not follow that only internal cues are used to determine the FOK rating. As Lories and Schelstraete (Chapter 4 in this volume) argue, accessibility is a good basis on which to make the FOK judgment because it summarizes, but also confounds, information from a number of different sources. Because of the general laws of human memory, accessibility is bound to correlate with numerous contextual cues like domain familiarity, the existence of related episodic traces, etc. A number of sources that may be described as "meta-informational" are potentially involved.

As a result, recognition performance, these sources, accessibility and, of course, the rating will all correlate. So the very reason why accessibility is a sound heuristic also makes it likely that accessibility will correlate (be confounded) with other cues and it is difficult using a correlational design to make sure that causality goes one way or the other.

On the other hand, whether the answer is well known or not, the information retrieved during memory search will usually decrease recognition uncertainty. For instance, it may make some distractors less plausible and guessing more likely to succeed. This will increase recognition performance for precisely those items that have led to the retrieval of large amounts of information. Whether this specific characteristic of the recognition test leads to a bias or to an appropriate assessment of FOK accuracy is debatable. In any case, it means that a specific class of items may yield higher FOK accuracy if this mechanism is made more effective for that class.

The conclusion is, as in Koriat's view, that the FOK, as a rating, will have a significant accuracy, because of the way human memory works in general and that it will correlate with accessibility for the same reasons, but Lories and Schelstraete stress the constructed aspect of the rating a little more. The analysis shows that the accuracy of the FOK will be constant only in a given experimental context, with a specific type of items and specific recognition alternatives. Things are worse for the absolute level of the rating. It will not be very stable from one item list to another because there is no principled way to set it.

Generalizing: availability and representational richness

Bless and Strack (Chapter 6 in this volume) investigate the idea that people have metacognitive theories about the memorability of objects and events. When these theories lead people to feel uncertain about the occurrence of an event, the situation is set up for the impact of social influence on memory. At this point, and in line with Festinger's social comparison theory, perceivers can decrease or increase their confidence by relying on other people.

Uncertainty is particularly high, and so is social influence, when there is no memory trace, because the absence of such a trace could indicate either that the event has not appeared or that it has occurred but could not be recollected.

A simple example may illustrate the above reasoning. Naive theories about memorability hold that some events are more memorable and thus would not have been forgotten had they happened. These theories could be right or wrong, the fact is that people hold them. Imagine that you want to hide something. You probably hold firm beliefs about what could be a highly memorable place, such as the water tank or the refrigerator for hiding your jewels. Later on, your partner tries to convince you that you probably put the jewels in the water tank. If you did not, you would ridicule your partner because you will be confident that the water tank could not be the place. In contrast, if your partner suggests a location which is much less memorable (i.e. salient), you might end up checking. In their own paradigm, this is exactly what Bless and Strack found (see Chapter 6).

This provides a conceptualization of social influences on memory: Because memory itself is a reconstructive process, there is a always the potential for manipulation after the fact. This is what the misinformation paradigm is all about and the constructive nature of memory has been long known, but the critical fact is that the process is cognitively penetrable. This is not just a matter of automatic inference and automatic – if erroneous – reconstruction. Low salience, hence *perceived* suboptimal encoding, or *perceived* suboptimal retrieval conditions are necessary for the effect to be obtained. The reconstruction is penetrable, the error is sensitive to properly informational influences.[2]

Bless and Strack's chapter deals with a case in which metacognition is inaccurate because it rests on limited information, e.g. when memory is empty. Swann and Gill (Chapter 7 in this volume) further explore the problem of accuracy and more precisely the overconfidence – high confidence with low accuracy – we often display in intimate relationships. Based on the daily observation that we come to feel we know and trust our partner well even in the absence of true accuracy gains, these authors consider several mediators for this overconfidence effect. They suggest that *representational richness* is at the heart of overconfidence. Representational richness is defined as the amount of information available – increasing with relationship length – and the degree of its integration – increasing with involvement in the relationship. Richness does not mean accuracy because, for instance, any information will increase richness but only truly diagnostic and pertinent information can increase accuracy.

Interestingly, because accessibility (probability of retrieval) is a matter of memory organization and coherence, representation richness is very much like accessibility in FOK research. Like accessibility, it is independent of the accuracy of the representation. The information may be rich and integrated but non-diagnostic and, in this case, representation richness may increase confidence without increasing accuracy. Availability as a strategy for estimating probability has similar properties. Our capability to retrieve examples may be taken as a probability estimate but the problem is that an increase in the number of retrieved examples may result from many different causes. For instance, recency will increase the probability of retrieval but this indicates only that one case occurred recently. Swann and Gill found strong support for their conception in several correlational as well as experimental investigations that are reviewed in their chapter.

People receiving information on a given topic may or may not become aware that it is relevant and important depending on a number of cues that may be present. To take a trivial example, participants may be warned that they will be given this information by an experimenter. A less trivial example is the subjective – but purely apparent – availability of individuating information. Such cues are obviously not part of the relevant information themselves but they should be expected to increase confidence in a judgment compared to a situation in which the person is *not* made aware of the available information. Because the information provided is actually held constant in this design, this suggests that confidence increases whether information has actually been provided or not.

According to Swann and Gill, this type of overconfidence can be generated without increasing representational richness. In other words, meta-informational cues do not seem to increase confidence via representational richness. The specific mechanism involved in this case could be that meta-information simply increases the accessibility of the information, which does not affect richness but nevertheless increases confidence.

Judgment construction and correction: metacognition and naive theories

Judgment construction

Meta-informational cues as well as overconfidence are at the heart of Yzerbyt, Dardenne, and Leyens' chapter (Chapter 8 in this volume). According to the social judgeability model (e.g. Yzerbyt, Schadron, Leyens, & Rocher, 1994), (over)confidence is a function of a variety of non-diagnostic aspects of the information and of the judgmental context. The extreme situation is one in which meta-information only influences people's evaluation of confidence. As a special case, the judgeability model foresees that the link between confidence and meta-information may be indirect: Some additional richness may be derived from the meta-informational cues granting appropriate inferences.

In the eye of any social perceiver, a judgment is loaded with meaning: It involves some personal commitment. Because people are to a certain degree committed to their judgment, they want to respect a number of criteria. One is accuracy, but social norms and the framing of the information provided are also important to the perceiver. These additional criteria are the focus of the chapter. The point is that people take social and identity concerns into account to estimate the validity of their judgments, which they proceed to do by relying on naive theories about judgment process.

Yzerbyt, Dardenne and Leyens begin with a description of the social judgeability model and then provide several studies that assess the impact of the naive theories that proceed from social norms. In one of these experiments, the subjective availability of individuating information contributes to the expression of stereotyped judgments. The authors further show that naive theories are truly affecting private beliefs and are not used simply for the purpose of impression management. In another investigation, they present evidence that implicit rules of judgment can have an impact from the beginning of the impression construction, and not only at the end of the process.

In the work reviewed by Yzerbyt and colleagues, metacognitive processes have an impact on social judgments without the perceiver being aware of that influence. Banaji and Dasgupta (Chapter 9 in this volume) present some other non-conscious ways in which beliefs, attitudes, and behaviors are influenced. Based on Johnson-Laird's view of consciousness, the authors focus on spontaneous, uncontrolled, and unconscious beliefs about social groups. They review several experiments in which people display no awareness of and are not able to consciously control the impact of their naive beliefs on the judgments. For instance, among a list of potentially familiar criminal names, black names will be (mis)identified more often than white names as perpetrators of criminal acts (which fits the stereotype linking blacks and criminality). In that case, people are confident that their judgments were based on genuine memory for criminal names. Moreover, they hold explicit egalitarian and non-racist values!

The authors then explore the concepts of responsibility and intention. They clearly dissociate intention as fair and egalitarian on the one hand from discriminatory act and prejudice on the other hand. They discuss this issue with regard to the law. The problem can be summarized in the following manner: Are people responsible for a discriminatory judgment if they are not aware of it and cannot control their reaction (Fiske, 1989)? To make things even more difficult, the very same discriminative act can have intentional as well as unintentional causes.

The need for correction

Although they may not be aware of the details of automatic activation effects, most subjects are aware that aspects of the context can have an impact on their judgment. For instance, they will correctly suppose that a stereotype can influence their perception of others, although they may not understand that the activation of the stereotype and the priming of the features consistent with it are automatic. They will make conscious attempts to determine whether a source confusion may have taken place and will take measures to adjust for these effects. The difficulty is that they will not have much information to work with. Some external aspects of the situation may signal that an error is possible. People may have become familiar, for instance, with the general contrast or assimilation effects that occur when a stimulus is presented in a given context and they may try to discard the part of their impression that they know must be related to the context. Several theories have been proposed to describe this phenomenon. Three chapters in this book deal with people's naive theories of biases and unwanted influences and contribute to our knowledge concerning the ways people try to remove biases guided by their naive metacognitive theories.

Wilson, Gilbert and Wheatley (Chapter 10 in this volume) investigate the role of lay beliefs in protecting our minds against unwanted influences on our own beliefs and emotions – what the authors call mental contamination. People's naive theories about how and when their beliefs and emotions could change determine the specific strategy they follow in order not to be contaminated. The authors suggest that we distinguish between an implicit level of psychology which operates largely outside of awareness (people's use of schematic knowledge) and an explicit level of psychology (meta-beliefs about cognitive processes). Explicit psychology very much corresponds to metacognition.

Wilson and colleagues present an extensive version of their general model, from *exposure* control – whether the person allows the stimulus to enter their mind or not – to *behavior* control – acting as if our mind was not contaminated. Between these extremes, people can use different strategies. Whereas the best way not to be contaminated is simply not to be exposed to the stimulus, the authors speculate that people do not always prefer that strategy, at least in the case of mental contamination. According to the authors, people believe that mental (but not affective) contamination does not necessarily have detrimental effects. Moreover, people seem to think that they can control their beliefs (more easily than their emotions); in other words, according to the authors, people would feel that their beliefs are not "penetrable" by external and unwanted information. As a consequence, they do not systematically avoid exposure to mental contamination. For instance, whereas people think they can freely decide whether to accept a proposition as true, they do seem to understand and believe a proposition at once. The authors review indirect support for their model, bearing on studies conducted for other purposes. They then present recent and more direct data.

Wegener, Petty and Dunn (Chapter 11 in this volume) offer another look at the naive theories of bias. They discuss some of the alternative models of correction and present the unique features of their flexible correction model under the form of several postulates. The model is based on the idea that correction is highly flexible. Corrections are driven by highly context-dependent naive theories of how a given factor can influence judgment. This is why appropriately chosen information will produce adjustments, again making the correction process a "penetrable" one. They suggest that naive theories can be stored in long-term memory but are also likely to be generated on-line (see also Yzerbyt, Dardenne & Leyens, Chapter 8 in this volume). The correction is also flexible in that it depends on the level of motivation and ability. Clearly, thus, correction is costly.

The authors review several initial tests of the flexible correction model and present new data. As predicted by their model, they find opposite corrections for the same target, depending on the specific naive theory people entertain concerning the potential biasing effect of the context. For instance, participants may consider that, if context involves an extremely violent person (vs. an extremely non-violent person), people would judge a target as less (vs. more) violent than if such a context was not present. In the main study, participants were confronted with an extremely violent or non-violent context and were asked either to rate the target immediately or to first correct for the context. Results show that participants obey their naive theory and correct their judgments away from the perceived bias, even when no bias has actually occurred.

In the last chapter of this trilogy (Chapter 12 in this volume), Martin and Stapel begin with a critique of theory-based models of correction. In their eyes, a critical aspect is that those models are guided by a priori and verbalizable naive theories. The authors do not dispute the fact that people have naive theories about their judgment processes. However, they argue that these conscious and naive theories are generally not the causal factor in people's judgmental correction processes. They then discuss the view that people's accuracy attempts are guided by non-conscious processes initiated by features of the general judgment setting (i.e. the implicit processing objectives activated by features of the setting).

In line with Martin's earlier set/reset model, the authors thus accord a much smaller role to naive theories than the two preceding models. Martin and Stapel's model is based instead on a production system that is not open to awareness – not penetrable. Correction, or "reset" in the model jargon, as well as assimilation, or "set," can lead people to experience conscious thoughts and feelings as outputs of the production system. In that way, people's theories come after the judgment and stand as post-hoc explanations or rationalization.

Conclusion

The theme of metacognition is inextricably related to problems of awareness, verbalization, penetrability and to the paradoxes of reflectivity. It is necessary to determine how the mind may actually deploy effective metacognitive abilities without postulating mysterious powers or generating infinite regressions. One way to do this is to conceive metacognition as ordinary cognition applied to its own products in a standard cognitive architecture. The present volume is born from the idea that cognition becomes social at the very moment when metacognition becomes possible, that both social cognition and metacognition depend on the possibility of using the products of cognitive activity in self and others to monitor the cognitive processes themselves.

Yet, this possibility requires an inductive step: Because we go back from the products to the processes, metacognition is a reconstruction and our representation of our own mental functioning is not exact. In the language of social psychology, the inductive step can be described as an attribution process. Attributional work is necessary if we are to go back from the products of cognition to their source and to the conditions that produced them, to bridge the gap between content and process (see Nisbett & Wilson, 1977). Familiarity, accessibility of information or representational richness all play a similar role in this sense; they are used as data that require an interpretation. Metacognition (as well as consciousness?), from this point of view, is woven by a complex set of inferential processes using a variety of elements and there may be holes in the fabric. What we reconstruct may even be plainly wrong.

The main reason for this is that cognitive activity involves automatic processes that we are not aware of. This has been known since Helmholtz and clearly appears, for instance, in our short discussion of verbal protocols. These automatic, non-penetrable, processes will alter the contents of working memory without leaving any perceptible trace of their action. For instance, various contextual cues may prime a stereotype. Hence, an attribution problem occurs: The source of working memory modifications may not be identified properly and errors will follow. Of course, people are not completely naive regarding the whole matter. We usually suspect, for instance, that stereotypes can be primed by contextual elements. Although we may not be aware of the effect of automatic cognitive processes we do know, from education or experience, that influences do occur in specific conditions and may lead to judgment errors. We entertain naive theories regarding these conditions that allow us to call for corrections when "meta-informational" cues indicate that it may be appropriate. We may even decide to protect ourselves from such situations by eliminating some sources of information. Unfortunately, these theories and the corrections they prescribe may not be perfectly correct or effective. There is no guarantee that they will exactly describe the actual influences we undergo.

Naive theories are built and applied "from the outside." They apply to everybody, self and other, in the same way. They rely on the idea that context will have an effect on your judgment. The cues to that effect are in the context, so naive theories can be expected to work in the same way for self and other. Interestingly, it is also a characteristic of the standard theory of attribution that attribution works the same way in self and others. Although the contents of working memory may not always be open to verbalization, and although some of these contents may be privileged in the sense that they are accessible only to ourselves, they nevertheless require the same kind of interpretation that would be required if similar information was available regarding others. So, the information that is available for making inferences regarding self and other may be different, but the process is similar in the sense that this information requires an interpretation, an inductive step. Hence, for most purposes, the lesson of our social approach to metacognition agrees with the poet: "Je est un autre".

Notes

1. Although the distinction between cognitively penetrable and cognitively non-penetrable processes is most useful, it should be mentioned that declarative knowledge used in a controlled and cognitively penetrable manner may be compiled during learning and eventually become automatized and inaccessible to conscious observation.

2. In other words, not only does memory not work like a recording module but data even show that committing oneself to an interpretation has a definite effect on subsequent retrieval attempts.

References

Dennett, D.C. (1991). *Consciousness explained.* Boston, MA: Little, Brown & Company.

Ericsson, K.A. & Simon, H.J. (1984). *Protocol analysis: Verbal reports as data.* Cambridge, MA: MIT Press.

Fiske, S.T. (1989). Examining the role of intent: Toward understanding its role in stereotyping and prejudice. In J.S. Uleman & J.A. Bargh (Eds), *Unintended thought: Limits of awareness, intention, and control* (pp. 253–283). New York: Guilford Press.

Johnson, M.K. & Raye, C.L. (1981). Reality monitoring. *Psychological Review, 88*, 67–85.

Jones, E.E. & Nisbett, R. (1972). The actor and the observer: Divergent perceptions of the causes of behavior. In E.E. Jones, D.E. Kanouse, H.H. Kelley, R.E. Nisbett, S. Valins, & B. Weiner (Eds), *Attribution: Perceiving the causes of behavior* (pp. 79–94). Morristown, NJ: General Learning.

Nelson, T.O. (1993). Judgments of learning and the allocation of study time. *Journal of Experimental Psychology: General, 122*, 269–273.

Nelson, T.O. (1996). Consciousness and metacognition. *American Psychologist, 51*, 102–116.

Newell, A. (1990). *Unified theories of cognition.* Cambridge, MA: Harvard University Press.

Nisbett, R.E. & Wilson, T.D. (1977). Telling more than we can know: Verbal reports on mental processes. *Psychological Review, 84*, 231–259.

Pylyshyn, Z.W. (1984). *Computation and cognition: Toward a foundation for cognitive science.* Cambridge, MA: MIT Press.

Yzerbyt, V., Schadron, G., Leyens, J.-Ph. & Rocher, S. (1994). Social judgeability: The impact of meta-informational rules on the use of stereotypes. *Journal of Personality and Social Psychology, 66*, 48–55.

2

Illusions of Knowing: The Link between Knowledge and Metaknowledge

Asher Koriat

One puzzling observation about metacognition is that people are generally accurate in monitoring their knowledge. The present chapter focuses on the feeling of knowing (FOK) often experienced when people fail to retrieve a solicited target from memory. It is argued that the FOK does not monitor directly the underlying memory trace, but is based on the overall amount of partial information accessed about the target, and on the ease with which it comes to mind. Evidence from conditions that precipitate an illusion of knowing, i.e. a strong FOK which turns out to be unwarranted, supports these assumptions. This evidence suggests that the accuracy of metaknowledge derives from the accuracy of knowledge itself, and that illusions of knowing occur when the accessibility of information is not diagnostic of its accuracy.

Monitoring and control processes in memory

Most cognitive processes are normally accompanied by metacognitive operations that supervise and control various aspects of these processes. Thus, when we make an appointment, we often have to take precautions not to miss it, and these precautions depend on our assessment of their effectiveness as well as on our assessment of the chances of missing the appointment if these precautions are not taken. After performing a planned action (e.g. locking the door) we may wonder whether we have done so, and if we are not sure, we may go back to double-check. When we learn a new text, we normally monitor our comprehension of the material, and can generally monitor the future recallability of the acquired information. In attempting to retrieve a piece of information from memory, we can often tell whether it is indeed in store and worth searching for, and when we finally do succeed in retrieving the solicited information, we can generally assess the likelihood that it is the correct information.

What is important about the subjective feelings that ensue from monitoring operations is that they generally have measurable effects on our behavior (see Koriat & Goldsmith, 1996b; Nelson & Narens, 1994). For example, the stronger my feeling of knowing about an elusive name, the more time I am likely to spend searching for it before giving up (e.g. Costermans, Lories, & Ansay, 1992; Gruneberg, Monks, & Sykes, 1977; Nelson & Leonesio, 1988; Nelson & Narens, 1990). The urge to bring the search to an end is all the more intense when I feel that the name is on the "tip of the tongue" and is about to emerge into consciousness (Brown, 1991; Brown & McNeill, 1966).

The accuracy of the subjective monitoring of knowledge

In view of the possible causal role played by metacognitive judgments, it is important to inquire into their dependability. Curiously, divergent views can be discerned in the literature regarding people's ability to monitor their knowledge. For example, there are those, particularly in the area of judgment and decision, who seem to take this ability for granted, focusing on explaining systematic deviations from perfect accuracy (e.g. Lichtenstein, Fischhoff, & Phillips, 1982; see Juslin, 1994; Koriat, Lichtenstein & Fischhoff, 1980). Thus, a great deal of evidence has accumulated, testifying to people's tendency to be overconfident in the correctness of their knowledge. Others still, particularly in social psychology, have stressed the general fallibility of metacognitive judgments. Ross (1997), for example, emphasized the problems involved in validating one's own memories. Nisbett and his associates (Nisbett & Bellows, 1977; Nisbett & Wilson, 1977) went as far as claiming that people have little direct introspective access to the actual determinants of their behavior: When asked to report on the reasons for their behavior, people simply report those reasons that according to their a priori theory constitute plausible determinants of their behavior.

A similar view has been emerging among cognitive psychologists as a result of the upsurge of research on implicit information processing. This research has yielded many demonstrations indicating that knowledge and metaknowledge may be dissociated (Umilta & Moscovitch, 1994). Jacoby and his associates, in particular, have elaborated on the implications of these dissociations for engendering illusions of memory (see Jacoby and Whitehouse, 1989; Whittlesea, Jacoby, & Girard, 1990).

Traditionally, however, there has been a common belief among cognitive psychologists that as far as explicit knowledge is concerned, there is a general correspondence between subjective and objective indices of knowing: People are able to monitor their knowledge. This ability, however, has generally been treated as something of a mystery. Consider, for example, the following characterization of the tip-of-the-tongue (TOT) state by William James:

> Suppose we try to recall a forgotten name. The state of our consciousness is peculiar. There is a gap therein; but no mere gap. It is a gap that is intensely active. A sort of wraith of the name is in it, beckoning us in a given direction, making us at moments tingle with the sense of our closeness and then letting it sink back without the longed-for term. If wrong names are proposed to us, this singularly definite gap acts immediately so as to negate them. They do not fit into

its mould. And the gap of one word does not feel like the gap of another, all empty of content as both might seem necessarily to be when described as gaps. (1893, p. 251)

This phenomenological description implies that there is something unique about the subjective monitoring of one's memory. A similar attitude is disclosed by Tulving and Madigan's (1970) oft-cited review of the verbal learning literature:

Why not start looking for ways of experimentally studying, and incorporating into theories and models of memory, one of the truly unique characteristics of human memory: its knowledge of its own knowledge. No extant conceptualiza- tion . . . makes provisions for the fact that the human memory system cannot only produce a learned response to an appropriate stimulus or retrieve a stored image, but it can also rather accurately estimate the likelihood of its success in doing it. (p. 477)

It is clear that both of the excerpts cited above take for granted the validity of TOT and feeling-of-knowing (FOK) judgments. What is mys- terious is not that people experience FOK and TOT states, but that these subjective states are diagnostic of actual knowledge. Indeed much of the work since Brown and McNeill's (1966) classic study of the TOT, and Hart's pioneering studies of the FOK (Hart, 1965, 1967a, 1967b) has attempted to establish the validity of subjective judgments of knowledge.

Furthermore, both of these excerpts imply that there is something special about the subjective monitoring of knowledge. As Tulving and Madigan stressed, this monitoring represents "the most important and the least understood aspect of human memory." The implicit assumption is that both the prediction of recall imminence that occurs in the TOT state, and the prediction of recognition performance that occurs in the FOK state are not intellectual judgments like those possibly underlying the assessment that a certain candidate is likely to win the election, or that it will rain the next day. The latter judgments are generally based on an educated inference that takes into account a variety of considerations. Instead, the TOT and the FOK states are seen to involve a direct, unmediated *feeling* that the target is in the memory store and is about to emerge into consciousness. Perhaps, then, the subjective monitoring of knowledge is based on some *special module* that allows the person to monitor directly the availability in the memory store of a target that is not accessible. Such direct access to the underlying memory trace may explain why people can sometimes have a strong feeling that they "know" the answer to a question even when they are unable to retrieve it.

The idea of a specialized monitoring module

The idea that the FOK is based on direct access to memory traces has been incorporated into a model of the FOK put forward by Hart (1965, 1967a, 1967b), and implicitly endorsed in many discussions since (see, e.g. Yaniv &

Meyer, 1987). Hart's model postulates the existence of a special monitoring module that has privileged access to memory traces, and can detect the *availability* in the memory store of an otherwise inaccessible target. Thus, whenever a person is required to recall a target, the monitoring module is activated to make sure that the target is present in memory before the attempt is made to retrieve it.

The assumption of the trace-access model that FOK judgments occur at a pre-retrieval stage implies that monitoring is independent of retrieval. Indeed, according to Hart, the functional value of having a built-in monitoring module derives precisely from the fact that such a module can inform us whether the solicited target is stored in memory *before* we attempt to search for it. In that way we can save the effort of searching for something that is not there.

The assumption that monitoring precedes retrieval is also shared by proponents of the cue-familiarity account of the FOK. According to this account, the FOK monitors the mere familiarity of the question, not the retrievability of the answer. Thus, Reder (1987; Reder & Ritter, 1992), for example, observed that the time for making FOK judgments about the recallability of an answer was faster than that of retrieving the answer itself, suggesting that the FOK could not rely on the output of retrieval.

Another assumption underlying the trace-access model is that FOK judgments monitor the availability of the *correct* target in store, even when incorrect targets are retrieved, or when the partial information accessed during retrieval actually stems from an *incorrect* target (see Koriat, 1994). In fact, this assumption has guided some of the experimental practices in the study of the FOK, for example the practice to solicit FOK judgments both when subjects fail to retrieve any answer (omission error) and when they retrieve what the experimenter considers to be a wrong answer (commission error). Thus, even though a subject may insist that the capital of California is San Francisco, the experimenter still asks for FOK judgments, because such judgments are implicitly assumed to monitor the trace of the *correct* target (see Koriat, 1993). In sum, the trace-access model assumes that the FOK has privileged access to information that is beyond the reach of retrieval.

An elegant feature of this model is that it also offers a straightforward explanation for the accuracy of the FOK, because the FOK is assumed to directly monitor the presence of the trace in memory. In fact, the implicit endorsement of the trace-access model is sometimes disclosed by the researcher's focus on the question of why FOK judgments are *not* perfectly correlated with actual memory performance.

The accessibility account of the feeling-of-knowing

The accessibility account that I have proposed (Koriat, 1993, 1994, 1995), challenges the assumptions of the trace-access model. According to this account, there is no separate monitoring module that has privileged access to information that is not already contained in the output of retrieval. Rather, the cues for the FOK reside in the products of the retrieval process itself. Whenever we search our memory for a name or a word, many clues often come to mind (Brown, 1991; Gardiner, Craik, & Bleasdale, 1973; Lovelace, 1987; Read & Bruce, 1982), including fragments of the target, semantic attributes, episodic information, and a variety of activations emanating from other sources. Such clues are often not articulate enough to support an analytic inference, but can still give rise to the subjective feeling that the target is available in memory and will be recalled at some later time. Thus, FOK monitors the overall *accessibility* of partial information pertaining to the target, primarily the amount of information retrieved and its ease of access. Importantly, it is assumed that people cannot directly monitor the accuracy of the retrieved partial clues. Therefore, both correct and incorrect clues contribute to the enhancement of the FOK.

According to this view, then, monitoring does not precede retrieval but follows it: It is by attempting to retrieve a target from memory that one knows whether the solicited target is "there" or not. Therefore if retrieval goes wrong, so will monitoring. In fact, retrieval may be fooled by a variety of clues deriving from many sources, such as neighboring targets, priming, misleading postevent information, and so on. In that case monitoring too will go wrong.

Explaining the accuracy and inaccuracy of the feeling-of-knowing

The major problem with the accessibility account, of course, concerns the explanation of the *accuracy* of the FOK: If the FOK monitors the overall accessibility of information regardless of whether it is correct or wrong, why is it nevertheless quite accurate in predicting actual memory performance? After all it is because of its validity in predicting actual performance that the FOK has attracted so much attention among students of memory.

The answer to this question derives from a basic postulate of the accessibility account: The accuracy of metamemory stems directly from the accuracy of memory itself. To clarify this point, it is necessary to distinguish between input-bound and output-bound measures of memory performance (see Koriat & Goldsmith, 1994, 1996a, 1996b). For example, suppose a person is presented with 100 words, and remembers 27 words. His input-bound performance, reflecting the percentage of words remembered out of the number of input words is only 27%. However, what matters for FOK accuracy is the output-bound performance, i.e. the percentage of correct words out of those reported by the person. This is generally much higher than the input-bound measure. For example, the person might make three commission errors in addition to the 27 correct words, in which case his output-bound accuracy will amount to 90%. Indeed, in free-recall tests, most of the items that a person reports are correct, and only a few constitute extra-list intrusions. The same is true with regard to partial recall:

When a person fails to retrieve the full target, most of the partial clues that he does access are correct (see Koriat, 1993).

In sum, what matters for the accuracy of subjective monitoring of knowledge is the output-bound accuracy of what comes to mind. This is generally very high. Of course, a memory question may fail to precipitate any information at all, but if it does activate a complete or partial recall, that recall stands a better chance of being correct than of being wrong. Therefore a monitoring mechanism that is based solely on the accessibility of information, as such, is bound to be predictive of actual recall and recognition performance (see also Lories, 1994).

Some evidence in support of the accessibility model of the feeling-of-knowing

Some support for the accessibility account comes from a series of studies using episodic memory for artificial stimuli. In one experiment (Koriat, 1993, Experiment 1) subjects studied a four-letter nonsense string on each trial (e.g. *BKRN*), and following a filler task, they were asked to recall the full target or as many letters as they could remember from it. Then they indicated their FOK judgments about the probability of recognizing the target among distractors, and their recognition memory for the target was finally tested.

The results disclosed the following pattern: FOK judgments increased systematically and significantly as a function of the amount of correct partial information accessed, that is, the number of correct letters retrieved. However, these judgments also increased significantly and systematically with the amount of *incorrect* partial information accessed, that is, the number of incorrect letters reported. Thus, both correct and wrong partial information seemed to contribute to the enhancement of the FOK. Recognition memory, on the other hand, disclosed a different pattern: The likelihood of correct target recognition increased with the amount of correct partial information, but decreased with the amount of incorrect partial information accessed. This pattern of results suggests that correct partial information contributes to the accuracy of FOK in predicting recognition performance, whereas incorrect partial information contributes to its inaccuracy, fostering an illusion of knowing.

Nevertheless, despite the conflicting contributions of correct and wrong partial recalls to the validity of the FOK, the overall correlation between the FOK and recognition was positive and high. Why was that so? The reason is simply that the partial information accessed was correct by and large: The output-bound accuracy of a reported letter was 0.9, i.e. 90% of all reported letters were correct. Therefore even though subjects could not monitor directly the accuracy of the information retrieved, the total amount of information retrieved could serve as a sufficiently good predictor of recognition memory.

In sum, these results indicate that by focusing on the wrong information that comes to mind we can unravel the connection between knowledge and metaknowledge. Although subjects are generally successful in monitoring the availability of inaccessible information, this is not because they have privileged access to the underlying memory trace. Rather, the FOK monitors the accessibility of partial information regardless of its correctness, and its accuracy derives from the fact that most of the information that comes to mind is correct. In this sense the accuracy of metamemory can be said to constitute a by-product of the accuracy of memory itself.

These ideas are illustrated by the following observation: In the experiment just described, subjects' FOK judgments were found to have no greater predictive validity than the mere amount of information retrieved. Thus, the within-subject correlation between number of letters recalled (regardless of their correctness) and recognition memory was 0.58, which is about the same as the correlation between FOK and recognition: 0.55. A similar pattern was observed in another experiment (Koriat, 1993, Experiment 2), the respective correlations being 0.56 and 0.47. Thus, FOK judgments do not appear to have privileged access to information that is not already contained in the output of the retrieval attempt.

Additional cues for the FOK: ease of access

The amount of information accessed about a nonrecallable target represents only one aspect of accessibility, possibly the most influential determinant of the FOK. The other aspect is the *intensity* of the information retrieved, e.g. the ease with which the information comes to mind, its vividness, specificity or persistence. Indeed, the results of one experiment that focused on ease of access (Koriat, 1993, Experiment 2) suggested that this cue makes a contribution to FOK over and above that of the amount of partial information retrieved. The procedure was the same as that described above except that the latency of initiating recall of the string or part thereof was also measured, and was used as an index of ease of access.

The results disclosed three findings. First, correct information was retrieved with shorter latency than incorrect information even when the number of letters recalled was held constant. Thus, ease of access is diagnostic of the accuracy of the information retrieved. Second, ease of access appeared to affect FOK judgments independent of the amount of information retrieved (see also Costermans et al., 1992; Nelson & Narens, 1990). Finally, FOK judgments were diagnostic not only of the likelihood of recognizing the correct target, but also of the accuracy of the partial information retrieved.

These results suggest that the ease with which information comes to mind can serve as a valid cue for the accuracy of that information, and that FOK judgments do in fact monitor ease of access. The reliance on ease of access, then, can also contribute to FOK validity in predicting memory performance. In this manner FOK judgments can function in two capacities, as predictors of the future recognition of the full target (prospective monitoring), and as postdictors of the accuracy of the partial information that has already been accessed (retrospective monitoring).

Dissociations between knowledge and metaknowledge

Because the feeling of knowing is assumed to rely on the mere accessibility of information, systematic differences may be expected between predicted and actual memory performance. Indeed in an earlier study we demonstrated that knowledge and metaknowledge can be dissociated. In that study we examined in detail the nature of memory pointers that contribute to the accuracy and inaccuracy of the FOK (Koriat & Lieblich, 1977). A "memory pointer" was defined as any cue that is intended to specify a particular memory entry, for example a word definition, a general information question calling for a one-word answer (e.g. a name or a concept), or a stimulus word in a paired-associate task. Subjects were presented with word definitions and were asked to signal whether they knew the answer, didn't know it, or were in a TOT state. Then they were asked to recall the target or produce partial information about it. The data allowed us to classify the responses into nine "memory states," such as "Know – Incorrect" (the subject announces that he knows the answer, but provides an incorrect answer), "TOT – Got it – Correct" (the subject announces that the target is on the tip-of-the-tongue, but before the trial is over he succeeds in retrieving the correct answer). An analysis of the memory pointers in terms of the likelihood of precipitating each of these memory states indicated that they differ reliably along two dimensions: (a) the likelihood of eliciting or suggesting the correct target ("knowledge"), and (b) the likelihood of precipitating a FOK or a TOT state ("metaknowledge"). Importantly, these two dimensions were *orthogonal*, suggesting that the properties of pointers that give rise to a strong FOK are not the same as those that contribute to the retrieval or recognition of the correct target. Thus, for example, some pointers consistently produced a strong feeling of knowing that proved unjustified. Other pointers, on the other hand, led to relatively accurate metacognitive judgments. For these pointers subjective and objective indices of knowing were in general agreement.

These results suggest that perhaps some insight into the determinants of the FOK and its accuracy could be gained by investigating the nature of different memory pointers. Furthermore, they seem to indicate that different memory properties are responsible for the FOK than those responsible for its accuracy. Indeed a recent study carried out within the framework of the accessibility model (Koriat, 1995) explored these ideas, and also provided some clues regarding the conditions that produce a dissociation between knowledge and metaknowledge.

That study distinguished between properties of pointers that are pertinent to the FOK and those that are pertinent to its accuracy in predicting actual memory performance. As far as the *determinants of the FOK* are concerned, it was proposed that pointers which bring to mind many clues should result in a stronger FOK than those eliciting only a few clues regardless of whether these clues are valid or not. A simple index of the amount of accessible information elicited by a pointer is the percentage of subjects who produce an answer to that pointer in recall, regardless of whether the answer is correct or wrong. This was called the accessibility index (ACC). The hypothesis is that high ACC pointers will result in relatively high FOK judgments even among subjects who fail to recall any answer. This is because such pointers are assumed to leave behind a large number of clues when recall fails.

What should determine the *accuracy of FOK judgments*? This is assumed to depend on the correctness of the clues that come to mind. When these clues are predominantly correct, FOK will be a valid predictor of actual memory performance. However, if most of the clues that come to mind are incorrect, the pointer should be likely to engender an illusion of knowing, i.e. a strong but unwarranted FOK. The proper index then is what we called output-bound accuracy (OBA; see Koriat & Goldsmith, 1994, 1996b), that is, the percentage of correct answers out of all the answers elicited by a pointer. For example, assume that a pointer (e.g. a general-information question requiring a one-word answer) is presented to 100 subjects, 60 of whom give the correct answer and 15 give a wrong answer. For such a pointer ACC will be 60%, and OBA will be 80%. This pointer is likely to evoke a high FOK even among the 25 subjects who failed to come up with any answer (because of the high ACC), and this FOK is likely to be warranted (because of the high OBA). On the other hand, if the frequencies of correct and incorrect responses are reversed (so that OBA is only 20%), then the pointer should produce an illusion of knowing, i.e. it should evoke an unwarranted high FOK following recall failure. Thus, the assumption is that the critical determinant of FOK accuracy is the conditional probability that an answer that comes to mind is correct.

As noted earlier, memory is generally correct in the sense that information that comes to mind is more likely to be correct than wrong. Hence for the great majority of memory pointers OBA will exceed 50%. Such pointers will be labeled "Consensually Correct" (CC) because they elicit more correct than incorrect answers across subjects. However, there are many atypical pointers which, for one reason or another, elicit more incorrect than correct answers across subjects (i.e. OBA < 50%). These can be called "deceptive" (Fischhoff, Slovic, & Lichtenstein, 1977) or "Consensually Wrong" (CW; Koriat, 1976; see Gruneberg, Smith, & Winfrow, 1973; Nelson, Gerler, & Narens, 1984). One example is the question "What is the capital of Australia?", which tends to elicit Sydney more often than Canberra. Such pointers should be particularly informative regarding the reason for FOK accuracy. If the accuracy of metacognitive judgments derives from the accuracy of memory, then the FOK should be valid for the CC pointers, but not for the CW pointers.

To examine these predictions, a series of general-information questions was compiled which included a heavy representation of deceptive questions. All called for a one-word answer. A typical FOK procedure was used: Subjects attempted to recall the answer, then they provided FOK judgments, and finally were tested on a four-alternative recognition test.

Consider first the question of the basis of FOK judgments. All questions were divided into a high-ACC and a low-ACC class. In general, FOK judgments were markedly higher when an answer was reported than when no answer was reported, and this was true whether the answer reported was correct or wrong. This finding suggests that the mere accessibility of an answer serves as a potent cue that the person will be able to recognize the *correct* answer among distractors (see Nelson & Narens, 1990). However, high-ACC pointers produced higher FOK judgments than low-ACC pointers even for omission trials, i.e. trials in which the subject failed to reach an answer. Thus, if we consider only those questions for which a given subject could not recall an answer, that subject reported higher FOK judgments for questions that elicited many answers than for those that elicited fewer answers among *other* subjects. Presumably the former questions leave behind a larger amount of partial clues and activations even when recall fails, as was indeed confirmed in a separate experiment (Experiment 3). Importantly, high-ACC pointers evoked higher FOK judgments than low-ACC pointers even among CW pointers, i.e. pointers that elicited mostly incorrect responses. Again, it would seem that the FOK depends on the overall accessibility of partial clues regardless of the correctness of these clues.

Consider next the question of *FOK accuracy*. When only CC pointers were taken into account, FOK accuracy was found to be quite high: The within-subject correlation between FOK judgments and recognition memory was +0.50 (Experiment 1), and +0.31 (Experiment 2). In contrast, for the CW pointers the respective correlations were −0.05 and −0.18. Thus, in Experiment 2, for example, recognition memory for the CW pointers *decreased* significantly as FOK increased: For this class of pointers, the more one feels that one knows the answer, the less likely it is that one actually knows it!

The lesson from deceptive pointers

The somewhat atypical results observed for the deviant CW pointers are quite instructive: Although FOK judgments are generally predictive of actual memory performance (see Schwartz, 1994; Schwartz & Metcalfe, 1994), it is particularly those pointers for which knowledge and meta-knowledge are in disagreement that provide insight into the processes underlying the FOK and its accuracy. First, the increase in FOK with increasing ACC was observed for both the CC and CW pointers. This is consistent with the idea that FOK judgments do not have access to the accuracy of the information retrieved, but simply monitor the overall accessibility of information regardless of its correctness.

Second, the CC pointers yielded the expected positive correlation between FOK and recognition memory: FOK judgments following recall failure were predictive of recognition memory performance. This result could be seen to support the assumption of the trace-access model that people can directly monitor the contents of their memories. The results with the CW pointers, however, clearly argue against this interpretation. Instead, they suggest that people have no privileged access to information stored in memory beyond that which becomes available as a result of retrieval attempts. Thus, it would seem that the predictive validity of FOK judgments observed for the typical CC pointers derives simply from the fact that these pointers evoke more correct than incorrect clues regarding the inaccessible target.

Finally, the CW pointers produced a strong dissociation between knowledge and metaknowledge that was disclosed by two aspects of the data: First, as noted above, the within-subject correlation between FOKs and actual memory performance was nil or even negative. Second, the level of FOK judgments associated with these pointers was overly inflated when compared to actual memory performance. For example, for a subset of the CW pointers (those eliciting above median FOK) FOK judgments averaged about 90% (i.e. a 0.9 assessed probability of choosing the correct target from among four distractors), whereas recognition performance averaged only about 35%, barely better than chance! It would seem, then, that the illusion of knowing is associated with the accessibility of a large amount of partial clues that contaminate metacognitive judgments. Thus, an examination of the nature of these pointers can throw some light on the conditions that produce a strong illusion of knowing in general (see also Fischhoff et al., 1977; Glenberg, Wilkinson, & Epstein, 1982; Koriat, 1976; Koriat & Lieblich, 1977; Nelson et al., 1984).

Factors contributing to the illusion of knowing

In Experiment 1 of Koriat (1995), 37 memory pointers were identified which elicited more incorrect than correct answers and also produced strong undue FOKs among those who did not recall an answer. What are the characteristics of these pointers that make them induce a strong illusion of knowing? As I have argued, metamemory goes wrong when memory itself goes wrong, so in what sense does memory go wrong in the case of these pointers?

A simple hypothesis is that a pointer that elicits an illusion of knowing is one for which people consensually hold the wrong answer in memory. However, very few of the deceptive pointers conform to this characterization. For example, all of the subjects who produced an incorrect response to the question "What is the capital of Uganda?" mentioned Entebbe (rather than Kampala) as the answer. In this case, it is the incorrect memory entry that possibly serves as the effective target (see Brown & McNeill, 1966), and FOK judgments following a recall failure possibly monitor the partial activations emanating from that target. However, the great majority of CW pointers turned out to evoke more than one incorrect answer across subjects, and in fact, about 50% of them elicited four or more different incorrect answers across subjects (two elicited as many as nine different incorrect answers each!).

Thus, the key to the illusion of knowing must lie not only in the inaccessibility of the correct target, but also in the inflated accessibility of contaminating clues that cannot be readily discredited. This is what distinguishes between two classes of pointers, in both of which the subject does *not* "know" the correct answer (i.e. in both of which the correct target tends to be unavailable or inaccessible): The CW pointers, which apparently evoke a great deal of associations and activations even when recall fails, and the low-accessibility (LA) pointers that leave behind few activations or a "blank" feeling (Koriat, 1995). Compare the following two questions: "In which US state is Yale University located?" and "In which US state is the College of William and Mary located?". Whereas the former tends to produce more incorrect than correct responses among (Israeli) subjects, and to precipitate an unduly strong FOK among subjects who fail to produce an answer, the latter tends to yield no answers at all, and to appropriately evoke a feeling of not knowing.

In comparing the nature of the pointers representing the CW and LA pointers, three general factors emerge which seem to contribute to the inflated accessibility of contaminating information that is associated with the CW pointers. The first is cue familiarity (see Reder, 1987). Apparently, in order for a pointer to produce a high FOK, it must evoke a sense of familiarity that leads us to interrogate our memory for the answer, and, perhaps explore possible candidates. This exploration increases the overall accessibility of information that is left behind when we fail to find an answer. When the pointer initially leaves us completely blank, we experience a feeling of not knowing even if later on we do succeed in retrieving the target (see Koriat & Lieblich, 1974, 1977).

In fact, several researchers argued that FOK judgments are due primarily to domain familiarity or cue familiarity (see Metcalfe, 1993; Metcalfe, Schwartz, & Joaquim, 1993; Nelson et al., 1984; Reder, 1987; Nhouy-vanisvong & Reder, Chapter 3 in this volume; Reder & Ritter, 1992; Schwartz & Metcalfe, 1992). Thus, it has been argued that the FOK is strictly based on the familiarity of the pointer. Support for this view comes from findings indicating that advance priming of the elements of the pointer can enhance FOK judgments without correspondingly raising the recall or recognition of the answer.

A second factor is that the memory target has many "close neighbors," i.e. targets that roughly satisfy the pointer. Activations emanating from these pointers enhance the FOK regarding the availability of the *correct* target. It would seem that during the early stages of the search for a solicited target, the FOK monitors the overall accessibility of information from a broad region around the target. The more "populated" that region is, the stronger the FOK. Thus, Koriat and Lieblich (1977) observed that FOK judgments were higher when the solicited word could be readily confused with other alternative words that roughly satisfied the definition. The results suggested that activations from other words in the vicinity of the target affects the FOK even when the subject ultimately succeeds in zeroing in on the correct target.

In fact, in discussing the processes leading to the TOT state, several researchers emphasized the role of neighboring candidate targets. They argued that the TOT state results from the interfering effect of "interlopers" or "blockers" that come to mind when one is attempting to search for the target, and that activations stemming from such compelling but wrong candidates must first be suppressed before the correct target itself can be retrieved (see Brown, 1991; Jones, 1989; Reason & Lucas, 1984). Note that these discussions focus on explaining one aspect of the FOK: the failure to retrieve the target. However, they might also be relevant to the explanation of a second aspect of the TOT: The accompanying subjective conviction that the target is "there" and is about to emerge into consciousness. It would seem that the activations emanating from neighboring memory entries exert two conflicting effects: They interfere with accessing the correct target and at the same time enhance the subjective conviction that the target is about to emerge into consciousness (see Koriat, 1994). These conflicting effects are perhaps one of the reasons for the feelings of frustration accompanying the feeling of knowing (see Smith, 1994).

The foregoing discussion emphasized contaminating activations arising from neighboring targets, but activations from other sources may also enhance the FOK. For example, Koriat and Lieblich (1977) reported findings suggesting that pointers that contain redundant or repetitive information tend to increase the FOK, possibly by enhancing overall accessibility. Also, Brown and Bradley (1985) reported that FOK judgments about the recognition of a state capital are increased by advance exposure to other cities from the same state. As noted earlier, studies conducted in the context of the cue-familiarity account of the FOK (see Chapter 3 in this volume) also indicated that FOK judgments are increased by priming parts of the pointer. Prior exposure to correct or incorrect answers to general information questions has also been found to increase the speed, frequency and confidence with which subjects subsequently gave those answers (Kelley & Lindsay, 1993; see Nelson & Narens, 1990).

In addition to the factors mentioned above, there is another factor that must be considered in explaining the illusion of knowing: The special difficulties involved in escaping the influence of contaminating activations on the FOK. A great deal of research in both cognitive and social psychology indicates that subjects can often avoid the effects of irrelevant activations by attributing them to their source. However, they can do so only under some conditions (see e.g. Bless & Strack, Chapter 6 in this volume; Jacoby & Kelley, 1987; Jacoby, Kelley, Brown, & Jasechko, 1989; Jacoby and Whitehouse, 1989; Jacoby, Woloshyn, & Kelley,1989; Lombardi, Higgins, & Bargh, 1987; Strack, Schwarz, Bless, Kübler, & Wänke, 1993). Strack et al. (1993), for example, observed that the prior exposure to relevant trait categories affected subsequent impression formation judgments (assimilation). However, when subjects were reminded of that prior exposure, they were able to escape its influence, and showed overcorrection (contrast). Similarly, in the study of Jacoby and Whitehouse (1989), a word presented just before a recognition memory test produced an illusion of memory among subjects who were unaware of that word, but a reduced recognition when subjects were aware of it.

Why then cannot people discount the effects of contaminating activations in the case of the FOK? Why, for example, cannot they escape the polluting effects of the partial clues originating from other entries at the vicinity of the target, and thus avoid the illusion of knowing associated with the CW pointers? The problem apparently derives from some of the conditions that are specific to the computation of FOK judgments. Thus, FOK and TOT judgments are prospective in nature, occurring prior to the retrieval of the target. Before knowing what the target is, it is often difficult to tell whether the clues that come to mind originate from the target itself or from other sources. In fact, it is only after a TOT state has been resolved that a person can sometimes discover the potential source of the contaminating clues that emerged during the search for the target (Koriat, 1994). In any case, the cues for the FOK often consist of partial clues and activations that are not sufficiently articulated to be traced to their source. Furthermore, according to the accessibility account, the *feeling* of knowing is based on a nonanalytic process (see Jacoby & Brooks, 1984; Jacoby & Kelley, 1987; Kelley & Jacoby, in press) that considers the mere accessibility of information without regard to its content. Only when the process becomes more analytic and deliberate is the content of the information taken into account as in the judgment that one "ought to know" the answer (see Costermans et al., 1992), and then the various clues can be deliberately pitted against each other to allow evaluation of their credibility or relevance.

A final word

The present chapter has focused on the feeling of knowing that is often experienced when one searches for a solicited information in memory. It was proposed that although the subjective experience associated with the TOT and FOK states accords with a trace-access model according to which the trace of the sought-for target is directly monitored, the FOK actually rests on an accessibility heuristic. Examination of the conditions giving rise to unwarranted FOKs is particularly informative because it suggests that indeed the FOK is based on the mere accessibility of information without regard to its accuracy, and that the accuracy of the FOK in predicting actual memory performance depends heavily on the accuracy of the partial clues retrieved.

The position advocated here with regard to the FOK has much in common with many discussions in both cognitive psychology and social psychology which emphasize the importance of internal cues as a basis for a variety of judgments (see, e.g. Schwarz & Clore, 1996). In the area of memory research, Jacoby and his associates have advanced the notion of a fluency heuristic as a basis for the subjective experience of familiarity (e.g. Jacoby & Kelley, 1991; Jacoby, Kelley & Dywan, 1989; Jacoby, Lindsay, & Toth, 1992; Kelley & Jacoby, 1990). They provided evidence suggesting that the experience of remembering itself relies on an inferential process, and that illusions of memory can result from the misattribution of fluency to past experience (see Jacoby & Whitehouse, 1989; Whittlesea, 1993; Whittlesea et al., 1990). The misattribution of fluency has also been seen to underlie such phenomena as illusory knowledge (Begg, Robertson, Gruppuso, Anas & Needham, 1996), illusory truth (Begg, Anas, & Farinacci, 1992; Begg, Needham & Bookbinder, 1993), illusions of difficulty (Kelley & Jacoby, in press), and a variety of perceptual illusions (Jacoby, Allan, Collins, & Lawrill, 1988; Mandler, Nakamura, & Van Zandt, 1987; Whittlesea et al., 1990; Witherspoon & Allan, 1985). Fluent processing and accessibility have also been seen to influence judgments of learning (Begg, Duft, Lalonde, Melnick, & Sanvito, 1989), subjective confidence (Kelley & Lindsay, 1993; Nelson & Narens, 1990), and judgments of comprehension (Morris, 1990).

The accessibility account of the FOK is also consistent with findings in social psychology indicating that subjective experiences and social judgments are affected by the fluency with which stimuli are processed, and by the ease with which information comes to mind. These findings too suggest that under some conditions judgments are based on a nonanalytic, inferential process rather than on direct access to the judged attribute, and that people are not always capable of monitoring the validity or relevance of the associations that come to mind (Schwarz, Bless, Strack, Klumpp, Rittenauer-Schatka, & Simons, 1991; Schwarz & Clore, 1983; Strack, Schwarz, & Gschneidinger, 1985; Strack, et al., 1993).

Acknowledgment

I am grateful to Ravit Levy-Sadot for her comments and assistance in the writing of this chapter.

References

Begg, I., Anas, A., & Farinacci, S. (1992). Dissociation of processes in belief: Source recollection, familiarity and the illusion of truth. *Journal of Experimental Psychology: General, 121*, 446–458.

Begg, I., Duft, S., Lalonde, P., Melnick, R., & Sanvito, J. (1989). Memory predictions are based on ease of processing. *Journal of Memory and Language, 28*, 610–632.

Begg, I.M., Needham, D.R., & Bookbinder, M. (1993). Do backward messages unconsciously affect listeners? No. *Canadian Journal of Experimental Psychology, 47*, 1–14.

Begg, I.M., Robertson, R.K., Gruppuso, V., Anas, A., & Needham, D.R. (1996). The illusory-knowledge effect. *Journal of Memory and Language, 35*, 410–433.

Brown, A.S. (1991). A review of the tip-of-the-tongue experience. *Psychological Bulletin, 109*, 204–223.

Brown, A.S. & Bradley, C.K. (1985). Semantic prime inhibition and memory monitoring. *Bulletin of the Psychonomic Society, 23*, 98–100.

Brown, R. & McNeill, D. (1966). The "tip of the tongue" phenomenon. *Journal of Verbal Learning and Verbal Behavior, 5*, 325–337.

Costermans, J., Lories, G., & Ansay, C. (1992). Confidence level and feeling of knowing in question answering: The weight of inferential processes. *Journal of Experimental Psychology: Learning, Memory, and Cognition, 18*, 142–150.

Fischhoff, B., Slovic, P., & Lichtenstein, S. (1977). Knowing with certainty: The appropriateness of extreme confidence. *Journal of Experimental Psychology: Human Perception and Performance, 3*, 552–564.

Gardiner, J.M., Craik, F.I.M., & Bleasdale, F.A. (1973). Retrieval difficulty and subsequent recall. *Memory & Cognition, 1*, 213–216.

Glenberg, A.M., Wilkinson, A.C., & Epstein, W. (1982). The illusion of knowing: Failure in the self-assessment of comprehension. *Memory & Cognition, 10*, 597–602.

Gruneberg, M.M., Monks, J., & Sykes, R.N. (1977). Some methodological problems with feeling of knowing studies. *Acta Psychologica, 41*, 365–371.

Gruneberg, M.M., Smith, R.L., & Winfrow, P. (1973). An investigation into response blockaging. *Acta Psychologica, 37*, 187–196.

Hart, J.T. (1965). Memory and the feeling-of-knowing experience. *Journal of Educational Psychology, 56*, 208–216.

Hart, J.T. (1967a). Memory and the memory-monitoring process. *Journal of Verbal Learning and Verbal Behavior, 6*, 685–691.

Hart, J.T. (1967b). Second-try recall, recognition and the memory-monitoring process. *Journal of Educational Psychology, 58*, 193–197.

Jacoby, L.L., Allan, L.G., Collins, J.C., & Lawrill, L.K. (1988). Memory influences subjective experience: Noise judgments. *Journal of Experimental Psychology: Learning, Memory and Cognition, 14*, 240–247.

Jacoby, L.L. & Brooks, L.R. (1984). Nonanalytic cognition: Memory, perception, and concept learning. In G.H. Bower (Ed.), *The psychology of learning and motivation: Advances in research and theory* (Vol. 18, pp. 1–47). New York: Academic Press.

Jacoby, L.L. & Kelley, C.M. (1987). Unconscious influences of memory for a prior event. *Personality and Social Psychology Bulletin, 13*, 314–336.

Jacoby, L.L. & Kelley, C.M. (1991). Unconscious influences of memory: Dissociations and automaticity. In D. Milner & M. Rugg (Eds), *The neuropsychology of consciousness* (pp. 201–233). London: Academic Press.

Jacoby, L.L., Kelley, C.M., Brown, J., & Jasechko, J. (1989). Becoming famous overnight: Limits on the ability to avoid unconscious influences of memory by dividing attention. *Journal of Experimental Psychology: General, 118*, 115–125.

Jacoby, L.L., Kelley, C.M., & Dywan, J. (1989). Memory attributions. In H.L. Roediger & F.I.M. Craik (Eds), *Varieties of memory and consciousness: Essays in honour of Endel Tulving* (pp. 391–422). Hillsdale, NJ: Erlbaum.

Jacoby, L.L., Lindsay, S.D., & Toth, J.P. (1992). Unconscious influences revealed: Attention, awareness, and control. *American Psychologist, 47*, 802–809.

Jacoby, L.L. & Whitehouse, K. (1989). An illusion of memory: False recognition influenced by unconscious perception. *Journal of Experimental Psychology: General, 118*, 126–135.

Jacoby, L.L., Woloshyn, V., & Kelley, C.M. (1989). Becoming famous without being recognized: Unconscious influences of memory provided by divided attention. *Journal of Experimental Psychology: General, 118*, 115–125.

James, W. (1893). *The principles of psychology* (Vol. 1). New York: Holt.

Jones, G.V. (1989). Back to Woodworth: Role of interlopers in the tip-of-the-tongue phenomenon. *Memory & Cognition, 17*, 69–76.

Juslin, P. (1994). The overconfidence phenomenon as a consequence of informal experimenter-guided selection of almanac items. *Organizational Behavior and Human Decision Processes, 57*, 226–246.

Kelley, C.M. & Jacoby, L.L. (1990). The construction of subjective experience: Memory attributions. *Mind & Language, 5*, 49–68.

Kelley, C.M. & Jacoby, L.L. (in press). Adult egocentrism: Subjective experience versus analytic bases for judgment. *Journal of Memory and Language.*

Kelley, C.M. & Lindsay, D.S. (1993). Remembering mistaken for knowing: Ease of retrieval as a basis for confidence in answers to general knowledge questions. *Journal of Memory and Language, 32*, 1–24.

Koriat, A. (1976). Another look at the relationship between phonetic symbolism and the feeling of knowing. *Memory & Cognition, 4*, 244–248.

Koriat, A. (1993). How do we know that we know? The accessibility model of the feeling of knowing. *Psychological Review, 100*, 609–639.

Koriat A. (1994). Memory's knowledge of its own knowledge: The accessibility account of the feeling of knowing. In J. Metcalfe & A.P. Shimamura (Eds), *Metacognition: Knowing about knowing* (pp. 115–135). Cambridge, MA: MIT Press.

Koriat A. (1995). Dissociating knowing and the feeling of knowing: Further evidence for the accessibility model. *Journal of Experimental Psychology: General, 124*, 311–333.

Koriat, A. & Goldsmith, M. (1994). Memory in naturalistic and laboratory contexts: Distinguishing the accuracy-oriented and quantity-oriented approaches to memory assessment. *Journal of Experimental Psychology: General, 123*, 297–315.

Koriat A. & Goldsmith, M. (1996a). Memory metaphors and the real life/laboratory controversy: Correspondence versus storehouse views of memory. *Behavioral and Brain Sciences, 19*, 167–188.

Koriat A. & Goldsmith, M. (1996b). Monitoring and control processes in the strategic regulation of memory accuracy. *Psychological Review, 103*, 490–517.

Koriat, A., Lichtenstein, S., & Fischhoff, B. (1980). Reasons for confidence. *Journal of Experimental Psychology: Human Learning and Memory, 6*, 107–118.

Koriat, A. & Lieblich, I. (1974). What does a person in a "TOT" state know that a person in a "don't know" state dosen't know? *Memory & Cognition, 2*, 647–655.

Koriat, A. & Lieblich, I. (1977). A study of memory pointers. *Acta Psychologica, 41*, 151–164.

Lichtenstein, S., Fischhoff, B., & Phillips, L.D. (1982). Calibration of probabilities: The state of the art to 1980. In D. Kahneman, P. Slovic, & A. Tversky (Eds), *Judgment under uncertainty: Heuristics and biases* (pp. 306–334). Cambridge, UK: Cambridge University Press.

Lombardi, W.J., Higgins, T.E., & Bargh, J.A. (1987). The role of consciousness in priming effects on categorization: Assimilation vs. contrast as a function of awareness of the priming task. *Personality and Social Psychology Bulletin, 13*, 411–429.

Lories, G. (1994). Partial knowledge, distractor elimination, and FOK accuracy. *Current Psychology of Cognition, 13*, 833–844.

Lovelace, E. (1987). Attributes that come to mind in the TOT state. *Bulletin of the Psychonomic Society, 25*, 370–372.

Mandler, G., Nakamura, Y., & Van Zandt, B.J.S. (1987). Non-specific effects of exposure on stimuli that cannot be recognized. *Journal of Experimental Psychology: Learning, Memory, and Cognition, 13*, 646–648.

Metcalfe, J. (1993). Novelty monitoring, metacognition, and control in a composite holographic associative recall model: Implications for Korsakoff amnesia. *Psychological Review, 100*, 3–22.

Metcalfe, J., Schwartz, B.L., & Joaquim, S.G. (1993). The cue-familiarity heuristic in metacognition. *Journal of Experimental Psychology: Learning, Memory, and Cognition, 19*, 851–861.

Morris, C.C. (1990). Retrieval processes underlying confidence in comprehension judgments. *Journal of Experimental Psychology: Learning, Memory, and Cognition, 16*, 223–232.

Nelson, T.O., Gerler, D., & Narens, L. (1984). Accuracy of feeling of knowing judgment for predicting perceptual identification and relearning. *Journal of Experimental Psychology: General, 113*, 282–300.

Nelson, T.O. & Leonesio, R.J. (1988). Allocation of self paced study time and the "labor-in-vain effect". *Journal of Experimental Psychology: Learning, Memory and Cognition, 14*, 676–686.

Nelson, T.O. & Narens, L. (1990). Metamemory: A theoretical framework and new findings. In G. Bower (Ed.), *The Psychology of Learning and Motivation, Advances in Research and Theory*, Vol. 26 (pp. 125–173). New York: Academic Press.

Nelson, T.O. & Narens, L. (1994). Why investigate metacognition? In J. Metcalfe & A.P. Shimamura (Eds), *Metacognition: Knowing about knowing* (pp. 1–25). Cambridge, MA: MIT Press.

Nisbett, R.E. & Bellows, N. (1977). Verbal reports about causal influences on social judgments: Private access versus public theories. *Journal of Personality and Social Psychology, 35*, 613–624.

Nisbett, R.E. & Wilson, T.D. (1977). Telling more than we know: Verbal reports on mental processes. *Psychological Review, 84*, 231–279.

Read, J.D. & Bruce, D. (1982). Longitudinal tracking of difficult memory retrievals. *Cognitive Psychology, 14*, 280–300.

Reason, J. & Lucas, D. (1984). Using cognitive diaries to investigate naturally occurring memory blocks. In J.E. Harris, & P.E. Morris (Eds), *Everyday memory, actions and absentmindedness* (pp. 53–69). San Diego, CA: Academic Press.

Reder, L.M. (1987). Strategy selection in question answering. *Cognitive Psychology, 19*, 90–138.

Reder, L.M. & Ritter, F.E. (1992). What determines initial feeling of knowing? Familiarity with question terms, not with the answer. *Journal of Experimental Psychology: Learning, Memory, and Cognition, 18*, 435–451.

Ross, M. (1997). Validating memories. In N.L. Stein, P.A. Ornstein, B. Tversky, & C. Brainerd (Eds), *Memory for Everyday and Emotional Events* (pp. 49–81). Mahwah, NJ: Erlbaum.

Schwartz, B.L. (1994). Sources of information in metamemory: Judgments of learning and feeling of knowing. *Psychonomic Bulletin Review, 1*, 357–375.

Schwartz, B.L. & Metcalfe, J. (1992). Cue familiarity but not target retrievability enhances feeling-of-knowing judgments. *Journal of Experimental Psychology: Learning, Memory & Cognition, 18*, 1074–1083.

Schwartz, B.L. & Metcalfe, J. (1994). Methodological problems and pitfalls in the study of human metacognition. In J. Metcalfe & A.P. Shimamura (Eds), *Metacognition: Knowing about knowing* (pp. 93–113). Cambridge, MA: MIT Press.

Schwarz, N., Bless, H., Strack, F., Klumpp, G., Rittenauer-Schatka, H., & Simons, A. (1991). Ease of retrieval as information: Another look at the availability heuristic. *Journal of Personality and Social Psychology, 61*, 195–202.

Schwarz, N. & Clore, G.L. (1983). Mood, misattribution, and judgments of well-being: Information and directive functions of affective states. *Journal of Personality and Social Psychology, 45*, 513–523.

Schwarz, N. & Clore, G.L. (1996). Feelings of phenomenal experiences. In E.T. Higgins & A. Kruglanski (Eds), *A handbook of basic principles* (pp. 443–465). New York: Guilford Press.

Smith, S.M. (1994). Frustrated feelings of imminent recall: On the tip of the tongue. In J. Metcalfe & A.P. Shimamura (Eds), *Metacognition: Knowing about knowing* (pp. 27–45). Cambridge, MA: MIT Press.

Strack, F., Schwarz, N., Bless, H., Kübler, A., & Wänke, M. (1993). Awareness of influences as a determinant of assimilation versus contrast. *European Journal of Social Psychology, 23*, 53–62.

Strack, F., Schwarz, N., & Gschneidinger, E. (1985). Happiness and reminiscing: The role of time perspective, affect, and mode of thinking. *Journal of Personality and Social Psychology*, *49*, 1460–1469.

Tulving, E. & Madigan, S.A. (1970). Memory and verbal learning. *Annual Review of Psychology*, *21*, 434–437.

Umilta, C. & Moscovitch, M. (Eds). (1994). *Attention & performance 15: Conscious and nonconscious information processing*. Cambridge MA: MIT Press.

Witherspoon, D. & Allan, L.G. (1985). The effects of prior presentation on temporal judgments in perceptual identification task. *Memory & Cognition*, *13*, 101–111.

Whittlesea, B.W.A. (1993). Illusion of familiarity. *Journal of Experimental Psychology: Learning, Memory, and Cognition*, *19*, 1235–1253.

Whittlesea, B.W.A., Jacoby, L.L., & Girard, K. (1990). Illusions of immediate memory: Evidence of an attributional basis of feelings of familiarity and perceptual quality. *Journal of Memory and Language*, *29*, 716–732.

Yaniv, I. & Meyer, D.E (1987). Activation and metacognition of inaccessible stored information: Potential bases for incubation effects in problem solving. *Journal of Experimental Psychology: Learning, Memory and Cognition*, *13*, 187–205.

3

Rapid Feeling-of-Knowing: A Strategy Selection Mechanism

Adisack Nhouyvanisvong and Lynne M. Reder

The topic of feeling-of-knowing has received increasing attention (e.g. Hart, 1965; Koriat, 1993, 1994, 1995; Metcalfe, 1994; Metcalfe, Schwartz, & Joaquim, 1993; Miner & Reder, 1994; Nelson, Gerler, & Narens, 1984; Nelson & Narens, 1990; Reder, 1987, 1988; Reder & Ritter, 1992; Schwartz, 1994; Schwartz & Metcalfe, 1992). This growth in interest has focused on the accuracy of this feeling-of-knowing judgment and the variables that influence it. There has been much less concern with the purpose or functionality of the process. Most research that looks at feeling-of-knowing uses a paradigm that asks for a judgment following a memory retrieval failure.

This approach is reminiscent of the tip-of-the-tongue phenomenon (Brown & McNeill, 1966; Smith, 1994), although there are important differences. In the tip-of-the-tongue experience, a person who cannot retrieve the answer to a question is nonetheless confident that at some later point, the answer will come to mind. The person in a tip-of-the-tongue state wants very much to retrieve the almost-available answer. In contrast, the subject in a feeling-of-knowing experiment is merely asked to rate the likelihood of being able to recognize the answer at some later time. Although subjects' judgments are far better than chance when judging feeling-of-knowing, they are typically not in a state of "I must keep searching! I know, I know this answer." Why then are subjects able to estimate the probability of recognizing the answer? It does not exist merely to keep memory theorists employed, and surely it does not exist solely for the tip-of-the-tongue experiences. What is the function of this process?

Feeling-of-knowing as part of a rapid strategy selection mechanism

Reder (1987, 1988; Miner & Reder, 1994) recently speculated that feeling-of-knowing is part of a more general process that occurs automatically when a question is asked. The purpose of this process is to help regulate strategy selection, and this operates for all questions, not just those for which answers are currently inaccessible. This view evolved from earlier findings that implicated a *rapid* initial process that directs allocation of resources to search memory or to calculate an answer or to otherwise respond "I don't know" (e.g. Reder, 1982).

Reder's (1982) subjects answered questions based on short stories they had read. One group of subjects was asked to decide whether a particular sentence was in a story (direct retrieval), while the other group was asked to judge whether a particular sentence was plausible given the story they had just read (plausible reasoning). Using the direct retrieval strategy meant searching memory for a close match to the queried target, whereas plausible reasoning meant constructing a plausible answer to a question, given a set of facts stored in memory. Half of the plausible test probes had been presented in the story. It might be reasonable to assume that subjects in the recognition group would exclusively use the verbatim or direct retrieval strategy whereas the plausibility group would use only a plausibility strategy. The data, however, indicated that subjects often first tried the strategy that corresponded to the other task. Specifically, at short delays between reading the story and test, subjects in both groups tended to use the direct retrieval strategy, while at a longer delay, both groups exhibited a preference for the plausibility strategy.

Latency and accuracy differences were used to infer strategy use. The test probes used in both the recognition and plausibility tasks were previously classified as highly plausible or moderately plausible (by other ratings). It is reasonable to assume that subjects should take more time to judge a moderately plausible test probe as plausible than a highly plausible test probe. In addition, subjects should be more likely to judge a highly plausible test probe as plausible than a moderately plausible one. However, when subjects are asked to make a recognition judgment, the time to decide whether a statement was presented should not vary with plausibility unless they are using the plausibility strategy when making recognition judgments. These plausibility effects did occur when subjects were asked to recognize whether or not the test probe was stated in the story. That is, subjects recognized moderately plausible statements more slowly than highly plausible ones, and also they recognized moderately plausible statements less often than highly plausible ones. Thus, latency and accuracy differences due to the plausibility of the test probes provide evidence for the use of the plausibility strategy in both the plausibility and the recognition tasks.

As stated earlier, subjects tended to shift away from using the direct retrieval strategy with an increase in delay between study and test. This shift in strategy is evidenced by the change in the size of the plausibility effects with delay. Differences in reaction time between moderately and highly plausible statements increased with delay for recognition judgments and stated (in the story) plausibility judgments. This suggests that subjects changed strategy preference from the direct retrieval at short delays to the plausibility strategy at longer delays. Additionally, this change in strategy preference for the plausibility strategy at longer delays is revealed by the error rates in the recognition task for not-stated items. Highly plausible test probes that were not presented in the story were more likely to be judged as previously presented, presumably because they were using plausibility as a heuristic.

If strategy preference changes with delay between study and test, then there must be some point at which subjects decide to use a given strategy. Other research (e.g. Reder 1987, 1988) provided additional empirical support for a rapid, pre-retrieval stage during which individuals judge the expected retrievability of a queried piece of information in order to select a preferred strategy. In these series of experiments, Reder again had subjects select between two strategies, direct retrieval and plausible reasoning. Subjects in these experiments also showed a tendency to switch from a direct retrieval strategy to a plausibility strategy as the delay between study and test lengthened, even when they could not anticipate the test delay before getting the question. In addition to delay, subjects were found to be sensitive to the probability of the success of each strategy, altering their strategy preference in accordance with the probability that a given strategy would prove effective.

The above pattern of results suggests that there must be a mechanism which rapidly regulates strategy selection. One component of this appears to be a rapid feeling-of-knowing that is based on the familiarity with the question terms rather than on partial retrieval of the answer (Reder, 1987, 1988; Reder and Ritter, 1992; Schunn, Reder, Nhouyvanisvong, Richards, & Stroffolino, 1997). We review the evidence for this conclusion below. Note that the position that feeling-of-knowing is based on cue familiarity is necessary for this view of its functionality: If feeling-of-knowing were based on a partial retrieval of the target, the decision to use the retrieval strategy would have already been initiated prior to the feeling-of-knowing process. Since we believe that a *rapid* feeling-of-knowing functions to guide strategy choice, it cannot be influenced by retrieval products. This is because retrieval is a strategy, whereas feeling-of-knowing is a strategy choice mechanism.

Two paradigms and views of feeling-of-knowing

The aim of this chapter is to clarify the difference in perspective among the various researchers working on the topic of feeling-of-knowing, and especially to clarify the differences in methodologies and the implications for differences in results. Briefly, the standard methodology has been to assess feeling-of-knowing *following* a memory retrieval failure. Reder (1987, 1988; Reder & Ritter, 1992; Schunn, et al., 1997), on the other hand, has assessed feeling-of-knowing prior to any retrieval attempt. The claim of this chapter is that feeling-of-knowing is used primarily to guide strategy use, and to regulate the length of search before unsuccessful termination once retrieval has been initiated. The standard feeling-of-knowing paradigm has explored a phenomenon that is much less prevalent in the real world. That is, people routinely decide how to answer a question and how long to search. With the exception of the tip-of-the-tongue state, people do not typically gauge their likelihood of recognizing an answer later.

Below, we explore the differences between the two types of paradigms, namely the *rapid* feeling-of-knowing vs. the post-retrieval failure paradigm. We review the differences in findings from these two paradigms and try to make clear the greater functionality of rapid feeling-of-knowing. More importantly, we want to distinguish the two paradigms and to reconcile their theoretical differences and seemingly contradictory findings.

Early work on feeling-of-knowing

In his dissertation, Hart (1965) explored whether the tip-of-the-tongue phenomenon generalized to other failed recall experiences. Hart was struck by the strong sense of knowing the answers that people had in tip-of-the-tongue experiences, and wondered whether in other situations people might also have an inkling of whether they really knew the answer. In this seminal work, Hart used a three-phase paradigm to assess feeling-of-knowing. First, the subjects were given a recall test. Second, for those items that were not correctly recalled, subjects were asked to give a feeling-of-knowing rating. Third, a recognition test was administered to determine the accuracy of subjects' feeling-of-knowing judgments.

Interestingly, Hart found that subjects were significantly above chance in predicting correct recognition and recognition failure for those items which they were not able to recall. When subjects gave a low feeling-of-knowing rating, indicating that they did not know the answer, their performance on the recognition test was at chance level. However, when subjects gave a high feeling-of-knowing rating, suggesting that they knew the answer, their performance on the recognition test was three times the level of chance.

Since Hart's seminal work, other researchers have extended these findings. Nelson and his colleagues have shown a negative correlation between feeling-of-knowing and perceptual identification latencies for tachistoscopically presented answers to previously unrecalled general knowledge questions. That is, as feeling-of-knowing judgments increased, identification latencies decreased (Nelson et al., 1984). This result suggests that the metacognitive system is more sensitive to perceptual information than to a high-threshold task such as recall. However, this conclusion was qualified by a later study. Jameson, Narens, Goldfarb, and Nelson (1990) found that feeling-of-knowing ratings were not influenced by the perceptual input from a near-threshold prime. However, if the information had been recently learned, that same perceptual input increased recall for previous recall failures. This finding is consistent with earlier results of Nelson, Leonesio, Shimamura, Landwehr, & Narens (1982), who reported that feeling-of-knowing judgments were not accurate for word pairs learned to a criterion of one successful recall, while accuracy for overlearned word pairs increased significantly beyond chance. One can conclude from this line of research that the accuracy of feeling-of-knowing judgments is well above chance yet "far from perfect" (Leonesio & Nelson, 1990).

In addition to prediction of accuracy, feeling-of-knowing has been shown to be correlated with search duration. Nelson et al. (1984) presented subjects with general information questions, then asked them to make feeling-of-knowing judgments for the first 21 questions that they could not recall. The researchers used a perceptual-identification task and a multiple-choice recognition test as the two measures of knowledge for the unrecalled item. They found that latencies to commit an error of commission (give the incorrect answer) were not correlated with either recognition or perceptual identification. However, the latency to say "don't know" was significantly correlated with the feeling-of-knowing. That is, when subjects experienced stronger feelings of knowing, they searched longer.

Several researchers exploring the feeling-of-knowing phenomenon have speculated about the underlying mechanisms that are involved in this process. One viewpoint that has received some attention is the *trace access* hypothesis. This presumes that subjects have partial access to, and are able to monitor some aspects of, the target item during feeling-of-knowing judgments (Nelson et al., 1984). The evidence for this hypothesis comes from studies that have shown that, even when subjects cannot recall a target item such as a word, they can still identify information such as the beginning letter or the number of syllables it contains (e.g. Blake, 1973; Koriat & Lieblich, 1977).

An alternative viewpoint to the trace access hypothesis is the *cue familiarity* hypothesis. This position argues that feeling-of-knowing judgments rely on the familiarity of the cues in the questions themselves (e.g. Metcalfe, 1994; Metcalfe et al., 1993; Reder, 1987, 1988; Reder & Ritter, 1992; Schwartz & Metcalfe, 1992). In two arithmetic experiments, Reder and Ritter (1992) showed that subjects' feeling-of-knowing were based on the familiarity with configural features of the arithmetic problems instead of partial retrieval of the answer. Specifically, they trained subjects to know the answer to otherwise novel math problems such as 29 × 32 and found that similar-looking problems for which they did not know the answer were also likely to elicit a feeling-of-knowing. Indeed, the Reder and Ritter study independently manipulated familiarity with configural features of problems and answers and found that only the former predicted feeling-of-knowing. Schwartz and Metcalfe (1992) also provide evidence supporting the cue familiarity hypothesis. In an experiment where subjects were asked to recall the second pair of a rhyme associate, these researchers found that when subjects were asked to generate the second pair during study, their recall of the target item at test improved significantly while their feeling-of-knowing judgments were not affected. On the other hand, when subjects were primed with the cue during a pleasantness rating task, their recall of the target did not improve but their feeling-of-knowing ratings did.

So which hypothesis is correct: Trace access of cue familiarity? There is empirical evidence supporting both views. Thus, one can say that both hypotheses are correct (or wrong). However, we believe that this must be qualified by stating that the accuracy of the hypothesis depends on the methodology one uses to investigate feeling-of-knowing. If the researcher is investigating a feeling-of-knowing process that occurs after a memory retrieval failure, then it is likely that the feeling-of-knowing that is assessed is a by-product of the retrieval attempt. When the methodology is concerned with strategy selection, feeling-of-knowing turns out to be based solely on the cues of the question. Further, when conceptualized as a *rapid initial process* based on familiarity of the cues, feeling-of-knowing has functionality. In addition to the peripheral functions of predicting accuracy on a subsequent test or influencing search duration, conceptualizing feeling-of-knowing as an ongoing, rapid, initial process gives it the real-world functionality of affecting metacognitive behaviors such as strategy selection.

Functionality of rapid feeling-of-knowing

As discussed earlier, Hart (1965) showed that feeling-of-knowing judgments following retrieval failure are a good predictor of future performance on recognition tests. This finding has been substantiated many times by later researchers (e.g. Nelson & Narens, 1980; Nelson et al., 1984). It has also been shown that feeling-of-knowing ratings are correlated with search duration before responding "I don't know". However, these feeling-of-knowing judgments are assessed on only the subset of the items that are not answered correctly.

It seems to us that there is a more central function to feeling-of-knowing than just rating questions after the fact, specifically, to regulate strategy selection. It is important to emphasize that *rapid* feeling-of-knowing, assessed *before* retrieval failure, serves this function; the standard feeling-of-knowing judgment that is made after retrieval failure does not have this function. For example, when presented with a general knowledge question, a person can decide, based on this initial, rapid feeling-of-knowing, whether to try to retrieve the answer from memory or to use another strategy, such as reasoning or looking up the answer in a textbook. Similarly, after presentation of a novel math problem (e.g. 26 × 43), it would be this initial rapid feeling-of-knowing which would help a person decide either to retrieve or to calculate the answer. If the initial feeling-of-knowing for the problem is high, the person tries to retrieve the answer; if the feeling-of-knowing is low, the person computes the answer. Note that it is possible for the person to choose to compute even if the answer is stored in memory, and conversely, it is possible to choose to retrieve when the answer is not known. We will return to this point later.

What causes the feeling-of-knowing?

Given that a person makes an initial decision between retrieval and computation, we can see what underlies the initial rapid feeling-of-knowing process. We have provided evidence suggesting that familiarity with the terms in the question underlies this rapid feeling-of-knowing (Reder, 1987, 1988; Reder & Ritter, 1992; Schunn et al., 1997). Other researchers have also shown empirical support for the cue familiarity hypothesis (Schwartz & Metcalfe, 1992). Our research indicates that this feeling-of-knowing due to cue familiarity is achieved when configural properties, i.e. pairs of terms, have been seen before. Below we review the evidence that the rapid feeling-of-knowing process is based on the familiarity with question terms/pairs.[1]

Reder (1987) devised a game-show paradigm that illustrates the accuracy of this rapid feeling-of-knowing. Subjects were given questions of varying difficulty. In the "game-show" condition, subjects quickly estimated whether or not they could answer the question. Subjects were encouraged to respond as if competing against an imaginary competitor in a game show. When subjects indicated that they thought they knew the answer, they were required to give the answer, or at least try. If they responded that they did not know, the experiment continued with the next question. This provided a measure of how accurate their initial feeling-of-knowing had been. In a control condition, subjects were asked to respond with the answer as quickly as possible, or otherwise to respond "don't know." Note that this paradigm differs from the procedure used by Hart (1965) and other researchers (Nelson & Narens, 1980; Nelson et al., 1984) in two ways: First, subjects do not give their feeling-of-knowing judgments after failing to retrieve the answer; rather, they give a first impression of knowing for all questions. Second, they are never asked to judge how likely it is that they will be able to identify the correct answer on a subsequent recognition test.

Subjects were 25% faster to respond in the game-show condition than those in the rapid question answering control condition, a mean difference of over 700 milliseconds. Subjects in the Estimate (game-show) condition attempted to answer fewer questions than those in the Answer (control) condition; that is, though they attempted to answer fewer questions, they still answered the same absolute number of questions correctly. This meant that they were 10% more accurate in their judgments of what they knew. This is important because it indicates that the greater response speed of subjects in the Estimate condition was not the result of a speed-accuracy tradeoff.

An additional result from this same study further suggests that feeling-of-knowing is an ongoing process preceding all retrieval attempts, not just a by-product of tasks dreamed up by the experimenter. In Experiment 5, Reder (1987) found that the time for subjects in the Estimate condition first to give a strategy choice and then to give the answer was equal to the time for a subject simply to answer the question in the Answer condition.[2] This finding is consistent with the claim that the strategy choice process is a natural process preceding retrieval attempts.

In another set of related experiments using the game-show paradigm, Reder & Ritter (1992) and Schunn et al. (1997) have provided more empirical evidence for the cue familiarity hypothesis of rapid feeling-of-knowing. In these experiments, subjects were presented with novel arithmetic problems (ones for which the answer would not be known initially). They were asked to rapidly choose (in under 850 milliseconds) whether they would retrieve or compute the answer to the arithmetic problem. If they chose to retrieve, they were then required to give the answer within 1500 milliseconds. If they chose to compute, they were given ample time to calculate it.

Subjects were able to perform the task with little practice. To measure the appropriateness of the strategy choice, d' (Swets, 1986a, 1986b) and gamma (Nelson, 1984, 1986) scores were calculated where a hit was defined as selecting retrieval and answering within two seconds and a false alarm as selecting retrieval and not answering correctly within two seconds. Even at the beginning of the experiment, d' was 2.0 and gamma = 0.85, providing further support that rapid feeling-of-knowing is a metacognitive process which occurs prior to retrieval, that can be used with high accuracy to control strategy choice.

The findings just reviewed support the idea that a rapid feeling-of-knowing takes place prior to a retrieval stage. But what about the claim that rapid feeling-of-knowing is due to cue familiarity? Logically it should not be based on the answer if it occurs before retrieval; however this claim would be more convincing with converging evidence that supports cue familiarity. Reder and Ritter (1992) presented subjects with unfamiliar arithmetic problems, such as 29 × 32. At the beginning of the experiment when the problems were novel, subjects realized that their best choice would be to compute. However, over the course of the experiment, the level of exposure to the problems varied from one to 20 times. Thus, as the experiment progressed, subjects were able to learn the answers to the problems and could choose to retrieve. The payoffs were adjusted to encourage selection of the retrieval strategy when the answer could be given correctly in less than one second.

As the subjects began to learn the answers to some of the problems, during the final quarter of the experiment, they were presented with novel problems that resembled earlier problems. For example, if a subject was presented the problem 29 × 32 multiple times, 29 + 32 was presented. If feeling-of-knowing is based on partial retrieval of the answer, subjects should not be inclined to choose retrieval for this problem, since the answer is not already in memory. That is, the subject's feeling-of-knowing should not be any stronger for these test problems than for other genuinely new problems. On the other hand, if feeling-of-knowing is instead based on familiarity with the terms of the question, then subjects should be inclined to choose the retrieval strategy for these test problems because they look familiar. Frequencies of exposure to the entire problem and elements of the problem were varied independently, so it was possible to determine which contributed more to rapid feeling-of-knowing judgments.

As exposure to a given problem increased, subjects' tendency to choose retrieval increased. Over the course of the experiment, subjects were able to learn the answers to problems and could thus select retrieval appropriately, rather than need to compute. For the novel test problems, which consisted of well-practiced operand pairs with a new operator, subjects were equally likely to choose retrieval. In fact, the tendency to select retrieval was strictly a function of how often the operands had been seen together, and did not depend on whether the answer to the problem had been studied.

Although this result seems to provide evidence for a rapid pre-retrieval feeling-of-knowing based purely on cue familiarity, it may be that subjects actually attempted to retrieve the (wrong) answer first, and that their feeling-of-knowing was actually based on an early read of the answer to the problem that looked similar. To rule out this explanation, Schunn et al. (1997, Experiment 1) conducted a conceptual replication of the Reder and Ritter (1992) experiments. In this experiment, a portion of the problems were deemed "special", such that after subjects made the initial retrieve/ compute decision, they were not allowed to actually retrieve or compute an answer. That is, after making the initial decision to retrieve or calculate, they were instructed to move on to the next problem. Importantly, subjects did occasionally give an answer to these "special" problems (specifically, one time out of seven, randomly determined). This was done to insure that subjects could not learn that these problems were never answered. The rationale for using special treatment of these problems was to independently vary exposure to problem and answer.

Given that familiarity with these special problems increased without a comparable increase in familiarity with the associated answers, we can test the target retrievability hypothesis more directly: subjects should be less likely to select the retrieval strategy for these special problems than for comparably exposed normal trials. However, if the cue familiarity hypothesis is correct, then subjects should select the retrieval strategy for these special problems at a rate predicted by the amount of time for which the problem was presented, not the answer. The results revealed that frequency of exposure to the problem rather than exposure to the answer predicted strategy choice.

Given all of the support for familiarity with problem features as the sole determinant of rapid feeling-of-knowing, we can ask how this mechanism might be formally implemented in a cognitive model of behavior. Below, we present a computational model of the tasks just described, fitting the simulation data to the human empirical data.

Mechanistic account of rapid feeling-of-knowing and strategy choice

The model is based on a generic semantic network model of memory called SAC, which stands for Source of Activation Confusion (see also Reder & Schunn, 1996; Reder & Gordon, 1997; Schunn et al., 1997). The model representation consists of interassociated nodes representing concepts that vary in long term strength. Applied to the arithmetic task, nodes represent the numbers, operators, and whole problems. There are links which connect the node for the whole problems to the operand, operator, and answer nodes. For example, for the problem 29 × 32, there would be a 29 × 32 problem node. Connected to this node would be the 29 and 32 operand nodes, the operator node ×, and the answer node 928.

Each node has a base-level or long term strength. The strength of a node represents the prior history of exposure to that concept. The more exposure the system has had to a concept, the greater the node's base-level strength. In the arithmetic game-show experiment, problems were assumed to have no pre-experimental familiarity (unlike problems such as 12 × 12), and problems were assumed to start out with the same low base-level strength.

Base-level strength (also called resting level of activation) increases and decreases according to a power function. This function captures the phenomenon of a quick initial decay of memories and the much slower decay at increasing delays for forgetting. Similarly, for learning, the power function reflects the fact that the first exposure to an item contributes more than do subsequent exposures.

In addition to the resting level of activation, each node also has a *current activation* level. This current level of activation will be higher than the resting level of activation whenever the concept receives stimulation from the environment. However, unlike the resting activation level, the current activation level decays rapidly and exponentially towards the base level, having effects only on the trial in which it was activated, and perhaps the trials immediately following.

The other class of assumptions concerns the links that connect the nodes to one another, e.g. the links connecting the components of the arithmetic problem to the entire problem, and the problem node to the answer node. The strength of a link that connects two nodes will depend on how often the two concepts (nodes) have been stimulated together. Just as link strength grows with stimulation, it decays with disuse, i.e. delay between exposures.

The current activation level of a node can increase as a result of environmental stimulation or if associated nodes send it activation. How much activation a node receives from associated nodes depends on the strength of the sending (source) node and the relative strength of the link from the source node to the receiving node. This relative strength of a link is determined by competition with other links emanating from the same source node.[3] This property also accounts for the data in fan effect paradigms (e.g. Anderson, 1974).

In this spreading activation model, it is the activation level of the problem node that determines feeling-of-knowing. In essence, feeling-of-knowing is a process that monitors the intersection of activation from two source nodes. When two terms of a question send out activation to associated concepts, and an intersection of activation is detected by bringing an intermediate node over threshold, a person will have a feeling-of-knowing response.

Below, we present some comparisons between the simulation of the arithmetic task described above and the empirical data. An aggregation procedure developed by Anderson (1990) was used to compare the model's predictions to subjects' actual retrieve/compute decisions. For each trial, for each subject, the model produced a probability of choosing retrieval based on the calculated activation values resulting from the trial history for that subject. Trials were aggregated based on the predicted probability of selecting retrieval. Those probabilities were compared with the observed proportion of trials where retrieval was selected for that subset.[4]

For the Reder and Ritter data set, the model fits the data quite well, producing a Pearson *r* of 0.990 (see Figure 3.1a). Recall that the model also predicts that subjects would also be as likely to select retrieval for operator-switch problems as for training problems. The model predicts this effect because operators are associated with a large number of problems and, due to the large fan, the model predicts that there will be little impact of switching operators on retrieve/compute decisions because the activation of the problem nodes is not significantly affected. The fit of the model to the operator-switch retrieval data is quite good (*r* = 0.981). Figure 3.1b presents this fit.

Earlier in the chapter, we referred to Experiment 1 of Schunn et al. which showed that rapid first impressions (i.e. rapid decisions to retrieve) were based on familiarity with the problem rather than associative strength of the answer. Using the same parameter values as in the Reder and Ritter simulation, with the exception of the individual subject thresholds parameter,[5] the fit of the simulation for this data set were still impressive (*r* = 0.994). The fit of the simulation's predictions to the subject performance is shown in Figure 3.2.

Reconciling theoretical differences

Koriat (1993, 1995) has argued that feeling-of-knowing is based not on familiarity with the probe, but rather on the accessibility of partial information related to the target. Specifically, he argues that the sum of the information pertaining to the target as a result of a retrieval process determines the judgment.

Koriat presents some empirical findings to support this claim. Koriat (1993) required subjects to learn nonsense letter strings (e.g. TLBN). The procedure basically conforms to the recall–judgment–recognition paradigm introduced by Hart (1965) with the following exceptions. First, feeling-of-knowing judgments were always solicited regardless of the subject's performance on the initial recall test. Second, subjects were not forced to report everything they studied; instead, they were given the option of reporting as many letters as they could remember. Each trial began with four Stroop items followed by the target string. Then subjects did more Stroop items for 18 seconds before being asked to recall the target string. After attempting to recall as many letters as possible, subjects gave a feeling-of-knowing judgment for the presented target string on a 100-point scale. Immediately following this, a recognition test with eight alternatives was administered. A

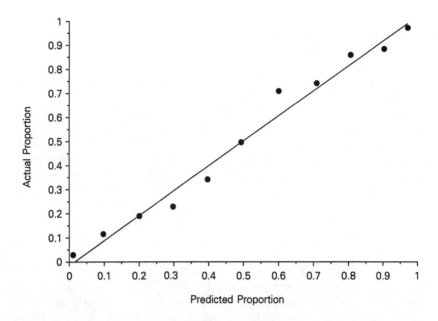

Figure 3.1a *Predicted vs. actual proportion of retrieval strategy selections in Reder and Ritter, grouped by predicted proportion for all problems (from Reder & Schunn, 1996)*

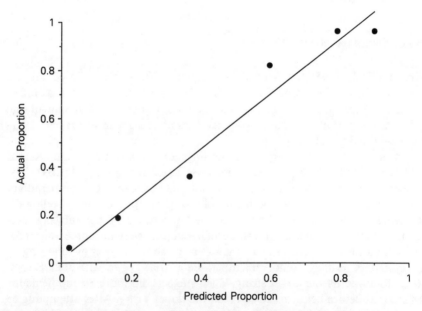

Figure 3.1b *Predicted vs. actual proportion of retrieval strategy selections in Reder and Ritter, grouped by predicted proportion, for the operator-switch problems only (from Reder & Schunn, 1996)*

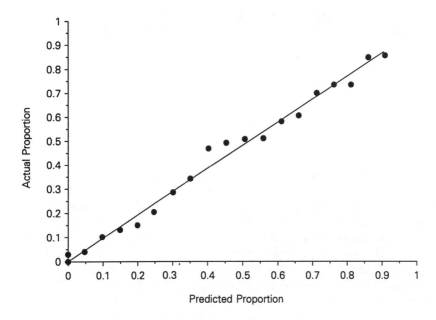

Figure 3.2   *Predicted vs. actual proportion of retrieval strategy selections in Experiment 1 of Schunn et al., grouped by predicted proportion, for all problems (from Reder & Schunn, 1996)*

unique feature of this recognition test was that the correct alternative in the recognition test was a random ordering of the correct four letters (e.g. if target was FKDR, the correct choice could have been RDFK). The results from two nonsense letter string experiments showed that feeling-of-knowing judgments increased with the amount of information recalled regardless of the accuracy of that information. Specifically, feeling-of-knowing judgments were highly correlated with the number of correct and incorrect letters the subjects were able to report.

It is noteworthy that subjects were not encouraged to chunk the letter strings as one item: the letters could come in any order in the recognition test. In our view, this means that subjects were not really asked for a feeling-of-knowing for an *answer*. Instead, they were asked for a feeling of being able to report *all of the letters*. Accordingly, this task seems artificial. Most feeling-of-knowing experiments are concerned with recalling one answer, not four letters in any order. Therefore, the experiment just described does not provide a good test of the target accessibility versus cue familiarity hypotheses. Unlike experiments that use questions and answers or even paired associates, this experiment treated the cue and the target as one and the same. Consequently, it is difficult to say whether the high feeling-of-knowing was due to a strong cue or a strong target.

Koriat (1995) also acknowledged the restrictive nature and artificiality of the letter string recall task. Addressing this problem was one of the goals of his more recent paper. The newer experiments involved asking subjects general knowledge questions, followed by feeling-of-knowing judgments. In the first experiment, subjects were asked general knowledge questions one at a time and were told to write down the answer if they knew it. They were also asked to give a judgment of how likely it was that they would be able to identify the correct answer among four distractors. The recognition test was administered immediately after all of the questions had been presented.

In a second experiment, Koriat (1995) attempted to investigate a preliminary feeling-of-knowing similar to the process investigated in the rapid game-show paradigm used by Reder and her colleagues. In this experiment, subjects were told to provide a *fast, prospective* feeling-of-knowing judgment after each question was read. They were asked to estimate the probability of being able to select the correct answer between two alternatives. They were instructed not to make a deliberate attempt to search for the answer. However, if the answer came to mind within this "fast" estimation period of five seconds, they were to write it down instead. The two-alternative-choice recognition test was given immediately after all of the questions were asked.

To support his argument that feeling-of-knowing judgments are based on the accessibility of the answer, Koriat showed that subjects' feeling-of-knowing judgments in these general-knowledge-question experiments were correlated with the accessibility of the answer. An accessibility index was calculated for each question, where the accessibility index was defined as the percentage of subjects reporting an answer, both correct or incorrect, to each question. Each memory pointer (i.e. answer to a general knowledge question) was then classified as either high or low in accessibility. The main finding from these experiments was that feeling-of-knowing judgments, irrespective of whether solicited prospectively or retrospectively, were highly correlated with the accessibility index. That is, subjects gave a high feeling-of-knowing for highly accessible targets and a low feeling-of-knowing for targets classified as less accessible.

Note that the findings from these experiments are only correlational, i.e. a subject who gives a high feeling-of-knowing is not the same subject who retrieves the answer. However, the pattern of questions producing one or the other is reasonably strong across subjects. These correlational data do not provide as strong evidence as a direct within-subjects experimental manipulation that shows that the frequency of the cues (familiarity) leads to a higher feeling-of-knowing. In the game-show paradigm with either general knowledge questions or arithmetic problems, we can manipulate a subject's feeling-of-knowing through prior exposure or familiarization with compound cues from a query. We can do this without affecting the subject's knowledge base. This random assignment of materials to condition for each subject seems a stronger test than a correlational result that is more vulnerable to alternative interpretations. Even if Koriat's interpretation of his data is correct, his model cannot explain our data.

Assuming that Koriat's data are correctly interpreted, why then are his data, using a similar game-show paradigm, inconsistent with ours? That is, why does he find evidence of partial retrieval influencing feeling-of-knowing? It may be because his subjects have *already attempted* a retrieval. His definition of rapid feeling-of-knowing is not very rapid and we doubt that it is a pre-retrieval estimation. Reder's subjects gave their judgments in under one second, which was not enough time to retrieve (Staszewski, 1988). In contrast, Koriat's subjects were given up to five seconds to make a judgment. Furthermore, by allowing subjects to write down the answer if it came to them, without imposing a quick deadline, there is no insurance that subjects did not attempt to retrieve the answer before giving their feeling-of-knowing judgments. Therefore, considering his subjects' performance as representative of a rapid feeling-of-knowing seems inappropriate.

One stage or two for feeling-of-knowing?

In light of his results, Koriat (1995) proposes that the same continuous stage can account for both rapid pre-retrieval feeling-of-knowing and post-retrieval-failure feeling-of-knowing. This continuous, integrative monitoring and retrieval process is updated on-line, and can influence search duration. Thus, this continuous process of monitoring and retrieving has predictive validity and can influence search duration. Koriat questions why we would need a separate pre-retrieval feeling-of-knowing stage since the continuous accessibility model accounts for both pre-retrieval and post-retrieval feeling-of-knowing. For parsimony's sake, he further questions the value added of a system that first computes feeling-of-knowing before simply attempting to retrieve; he argues that a continuous retrieval process can account for both.

We can respond to this in two ways. First, the value added by a pre-retrieval or pre-strategy execution stage was shown in Reder (1982), and reviewed above. To repeat, it is clear that subjects do not always attempt retrieval, and sometimes they use other strategies. This has also been shown by Lemaire & Reder (under review) and in the other studies reviewed earlier. Given that subjects do not always execute a retrieval strategy, it is reasonable to posit a stage in which such strategy selection decisions are made.

It is also clear from these studies that strategy choice is not simply a competition between two parallel procedures. Rather, subjects exhibit a preference for one strategy. Lovett & Anderson (1996) have reported similar findings. We cannot rule out a parallel, but biased (in terms of allocation of resources) competition; however, there still must be a mechanism that selects this bias from trial to trial. Furthermore, the similar data of Lovett and Anderson seem more difficult to accommodate with an assumption of biased competition (as opposed to a serial execution).

One still might ask, like Koriat, how humans could evolve to inspect memory, i.e. use feeling-of-knowing in order to decide whether to carefully inspect memory, that is, conduct a specific retrieval of an answer. The model that we described briefly above provides an answer to this conundrum: Feeling-of-knowing is automatically represented in the parsing and representation of the problem or question (not the elements, per se). In other words, the rapid, preliminary feeling-of-knowing stage necessarily occurs before the retrieval attempt, because it is a product of parsing the question. Consequently, feeling-of-knowing is a natural precursor to the retrieval process.

Conclusion

The aim of this chapter has been to clarify the different views regarding feeling-of-knowing. We reviewed the work of researchers looking at feeling-of-knowing in the post-memory-retrieval-failure paradigm. There is strong evidence that judgments made after a retrieval failure have predictive validity for subsequent recognition. These judgments are also correlated with length of search before termination. We also reviewed work from our lab that looked at feeling-of-knowing as a judgment that precedes execution of question-answering strategies. Specifically, we believe feeling-of-knowing is a process which utilizes compound cue familiarity to regulate strategy selection. In summary, the difference in perspectives and findings between feeling-of-knowing researchers stems from the fact that two different processes are being compared: post-retrieval-failure feeling-of-knowing, and rapid pre-retrieval feeling-of-knowing.

The predictive validity of feeling-of-knowing judgments in this paradigm is much higher than in the conventional paradigm ($d' = 2.0$ vs. 1.0, and gamma $= 0.85$ vs. 0.62). This is partly due to the non-restricted range of judging all questions (see Reder & Ritter, 1992 for a fuller discussion), but it is also due to the fact that the task is more natural. Our thesis has been that feeling-of-knowing is a typically unconscious judgment that directs strategy use (Reder & Schunn, 1996). In everyday life, people only become aware of these feelings-of-knowing when there continues to be a strong feeling-of-knowing alongside lack of search success, i.e. a tip-of-the-tongue state.

In the context of the rapid assessment of whether to begin search (as opposed to using another strategy, such as reasoning or calculation), only the familiarity of the elements of the query or problem is assessed.[6] In contrast, after retrieval has been selected and search has commenced, other attributes no doubt influence how long search continues. These variables also influence the feeling-of-knowing judgments that are made after memory retrieval failure, e.g. partial products of retrieval attempts.

Notes

1. The Schwartz and Metcalfe (1992) evidence is not from a rapid paradigm and was after a memory retrieval failure. Further, we only find the effect with pairs, so we do not wish to comment on their results.

2. Subjects in both conditions responded by pushing one of two buttons. This manipulation controlled for any possible advantages due to the short binary responses (i.e. "yes" or "no") in the Estimate condition over the word responses (e.g. "baseball") in the Answer condition. Consequently, subjects in both groups made binary decisions prior to giving the answer.

3. Thus, the absolute magnitude of the link strength is irrelevant. It is the strength relative to the total strength of the other links that really matters.

4. Refer to Schunn et al. for detailed description of modeling procedure.

5. Refer to Schunn et al. for all parameters and the values used in simulations.

6. By this we mean a higher-level representation of the integration of the query elements. What we do not mean is the elements in isolation or the answer.

References

Anderson, J.R. (1974). Retrieval of propositional information from long-term memory. *Cognitive Psychology, 6*, 451–474.

Anderson, J.R. (1990). *The adaptive character of thought*. Hillsdale, NJ: Erlbaum.

Blake, M. (1973). Prediction of recognition when recall fails: Exploring the feeling-of-knowing phenomenon. *Journal of Verbal Learning and Verbal Behavior, 12*, 311–319.

Brown, R. & McNeill, D. (1966). The "tip-of-the-tongue" phenomenon. *Journal of verbal Learning and Verbal Behavior, 5*, 325–337.

Hart, J.T. (1965). Memory and the feeling-of-knowing experience. *Journal of Educational Psychology, 56*, 208–216.

Jameson, K.A., Narens, L., Goldfarb, K., & Nelson, T.O. (1990). The influence of near-threshold priming on metamemory and recall. *Acta Psychologica, 73*, 1–14.

Koriat, A. (1993). How do we know that we know? The accessibility account of the feeling-of-knowing. *Psychological Review, 100*, 609–639.

Koriat, A. (1994). Memory's knowledge of its own knowledge: The accessibility account of the feeling-of-knowing. In J. Metcalfe & A.P. Shimamura (Eds), *Metacognition: Knowing about knowing* (pp. 115–135). Cambridge, MA: Bradford.

Koriat, A. (1995). Dissociating knowing and the feeling-of-knowing: Further evidence for the accessibility model. *Journal of Experimental Psychology: General, 24*, 311–333.

Koriat, A. & Lieblich, I. (1977). A study of memory pointers. *Acta Psychologica, 41*, 151–164.

Lemaire, P. & Reder, L.M. (manuscript under review). How do subjects control their strategy selection in arithmetic? The example of parity effects on product verification. *Memory and Cognition*.

Leonesio, R.J. & Nelson, T.O. (1990). Do different metamemory judgments tap the same underlying aspects of memory? *Journal of Experimental Psychology: Learning, Memory, & Cognition, 16*, 464–470.

Lovett, M.C. & Anderson, J.R. (1996). History of success and current context in problem solving: Combined influences on operator selection. *Cognitive Psychology, 31*, 168–217.

Metcalfe, J. (1994). A computational modeling approach to novelty monitoring, metacognition, and frontal lobe dysfunction. In J. Metcalfe & A.P. Shimamura (Eds), *Metacognition: Knowing about knowing* (pp. 137–156). Cambridge, MA: Bradford.

Metcalfe, J., Schwartz, B.L., & Joaquim, S.G. (1993). The cue-familiarity heuristic in metacognition. *Journal of Experimental Psychology: Learning, Memory, & Cognition, 19*, 851–861.

Miner, A. & Reder, L.M. (1994). A new look at feeling-of-knowing: Its metacognitive role in regulating question answering. In J. Metcalfe & A.P. Shimamura (Eds), *Metacognition: Knowing about knowing* (pp. 47–70). Cambridge, MA: Bradford.

Nelson, T.O. (1984). A comparison of current measure of the accuracy of feeling-of-knowing predictions. *Psychological Bulletin, 95*, 109–133.

Nelson, T.O. (1986). ROC curves and measures of discrimination accuracy: A reply to Swets. *Psychological Bulletin, 100*, 128–132.

Nelson, T.O., Gerler, D., & Narens, L. (1984). Accuracy of feeling-of-knowing judgments for predicting perceptual identification and relearning. *Journal of Experimental Psychology: General, 113*, 282–300.

Nelson, T.O., Leonesio, R.J., Shimamura, A.P., Landwehr, R.S., & Narens, L. (1982). Overlearning and the feeling-of-knowing. *Journal of Experimental Psychology: Learning, Memory, & Cognition, 8*, 279–288.

Nelson, T.O. & Narens, L. (1980). Norms of 300 general-information questions: Accuracy of recall, latency of recall, and feeling-of-knowing ratings. *Journal of Verbal Learning and Verbal Behavior, 19*, 338–368.

Nelson, T.O. & Narens, L. (1990). Metamemory: A theoretical framework and some new findings. In G.H. Bower (Ed.), *The psychology of learning and motivation* (pp. 1–45). New York: Academic Press.

Reder, L.M. (1979). The role of elaborations in memory for prose. *Cognitive Psychology, 11*, 221–234.

Reder, L.M. (1982). Plausibility judgments versus fact retrieval: Alternative strategies for sentence verification. *Psychological Review, 89*, 250–280.

Reder, L.M. (1987). Strategy selection in question answering. *Cognitive Psychology, 19*, 90–137.

Reder, L.M. (1988). Strategic control of retrieval strategies. In G.H. Bower (Ed.), *The psychology of learning and motivation* (Vol. 22, pp. 227–259). San Diego, CA: Academic Press.

Reder, L.M. & Gordon, J.S. (1997). Subliminal perception: Nothing special cognitively speaking. In: J. Cohen, and J. Schooler (Eds), *Cognitive and neuropsychological approaches to the study of consciousness* (pp. 125–134). Hillsdale, NJ: Erlbaum.

Reder, L.M. & Ritter, F.E. (1992). What determines initial feeling-of-knowing? Familiarity with question terms, not with the answer. *Journal of Experimental Psychology: Learning, Memory, & Cognition, 18*, 435–451.

Reder, L.M. & Schunn, C.D. (1996). Metacognition does not imply awareness: Strategy choice is governed by implicit learning and memory. In L.M. Reder (Ed.), *Implicit memory and metacognition* (pp. 45–77). Mahwah, NJ: Erlbaum.

Schunn, C.D., Reder, L.M., Nhouyvanisvong, A., Richards, D.R., & Stroffolino, P.J. (1997). To calculate or not to calculate: A source activation confusion model of problem-familiarity's role in strategy selection. *Journal of Experimental Psychology: Learning, Memory, & Cognition, 23*(1), 3–29.

Schwartz, B.L. (1994). Sources of information in metamemory: Judgments of learning and feelings of knowing. *Psychonomic Bulletin and Review, 1*, 357–375.

Schwartz, B.L. & Metcalfe, J. (1992). Cue familiarity but not target retrievability enhances feeling-of-knowing judgments. *Journal of Experimental Psychology: Learning, Memory, & Cognition, 18*, 1074–1083.

Smith, S.M. (1994). Frustrated feelings of imminent recall: On the tip of the tongue. In J. Metcalfe & A.P. Shimamura (Eds), *Metacognition: Knowing about knowing* (pp. 27–45). Cambridge, MA: Bradford.

Staszewski, J.J. (1988). Skilled memory and expert mental calculation. In M.T.H. Chi, R. Glaser, & J. Farr (Eds), *The nature of expertise* (pp. 71–128). Hillsdale, NJ: Erlbaum.

Swets, J.A. (1986a). Form of empirical ROCs in discrimination and diagnostic tasks: Implications for theory and measurement of performance. *Psychological Bulletin, 99*, 181–198.

Swets, J.A. (1986b). Indices of discrimination or diagnostic accuracy: Their ROCs and implied models. *Psychological Bulletin, 99*, 100–117.

4

The Feeling-of-Knowing as a Judgment

Guy Lories and Marie-Anne Schelstraete

The question answering situation

The feeling-of-knowing paradigm

How we answer simple, factual questions involves more complexities than one would expect. We should wonder, for instance, why we keep searching for an answer we do not find immediately, how we know we do not know something (Glucksberg & McCloskey, 1981; Kolers & Palef, 1976), why we start searching at all (Miner & Reder, 1994; Reder, 1987, 1988; Reder & Ritter, 1992) or what makes us confident in some response we have been able to come up with (Koriat, 1993; Koriat, Lichtenstein, & Fischoff, 1980). All the above points are somehow related to metacognition, that is, to the more or less explicit knowledge we have of the way our memory and our mind work.

Research has shown that human subjects can express a number of more or less valid judgments about various aspects of experimental cognitive tasks; they can express, for instance, judgments of learning or judgments of comprehension that correlate under appropriate conditions with actual learning or comprehension. Research also suggests that these judgments are more or less directly related to the optimization of cognitive processes, determining how long one will search for an answer, keep rehearsing when learning, etc. (Miner & Reder, 1994; Reder & Ritter, 1992).

In this chapter, we will only deal with the feeling-of-knowing judgment (see Nelson, 1996 or Schwartz, 1994 for a general review of metacognition). The feeling-of-knowing is a judgment that subjects make regarding their ability to recognize or recall some information that is not accessible at the time the judgment is made. It is somewhat different from the well-known tip-of-the tongue phenomenon because no reference is made to the very specific, phenomenologically strong experience the tip-of-the tongue phenomenon implies (see Smith, 1994 for a discussion of the relationship between the feeling-of-knowing and the tip-of-the tongue). A review of the feeling-of-knowing literature can be found in Koriat (1993; and Chapter 2 in this volume), Nelson and Narens (1990) or Nhouyvanisvong and Reder (Chapter 3 in this volume).

The most common experimental situation is due to Hart (1965, 1966) and has come to be called the RJR (recall-judgment-recognition) paradigm. The subjects are first given a list of questions; whenever they cannot answer a question, a rating is asked on a feeling-of-knowing, Likert-like, scale. Usually the subjects are asked whether they feel they know the answer and whether they think they would be able to recognize it. After all items have been presented in the recall stage, the subjects go through the whole list again but, this time, choose among a number of possible responses. It should be noted that while the recall and feeling-of-knowing rating stages are interleaved, the recognition test is delayed until all items have been recalled or rated. The subjects have no precise notion of what the recognition test will be when they make their ratings; the only elements of information they have are the questions themselves and the only thing they can do is use that information to roughly categorize the questions as more or less useful cues for a later recognition test.

Some form of covariation measure must be used to assess the relationship between the rating and recognition performance. Nelson (1984) recommended the Goodman-Kruskall gamma coefficient. It has become the standard practice to use this because it only requires ordinal scales, is not sensitive to a shift in the feeling-of-knowing scale, does not depend on the marginal correct recognition rates and has a simple and clear probabilistic interpretation.

The RJR design as summarized above typically yields low to moderate but consistent correlations (as measured by a gamma coefficient) between recognition success or failure (a binary variable) and the feeling-of-knowing (treated as an ordinal scale). Most of the literature has been devoted to replicating and explaining this result (Koriat, 1995, and Chapter 2 in this volume; Nelson & Narens, 1990). It essentially deals with the sensitivity or accuracy of the feeling-of-knowing as a predictor of recognition, for which it provides several explanations. These explanations at first seem to fall into two categories.

Theories of the feeling-of-knowing

Trace access theories   A first group of theories, *trace access theories* postulates that some form of partial access to the target trace is possible even though the trace cannot be "fully" retrieved. They have been popular to explain the tip-of-the-tongue phenomenon. In this context, they often involve some hypothesis regarding a blocking of the correct response by a competitor (Meyer & Bock, 1992; Smith, 1994). An extension to the feeling-of-knowing problem may thus seem natural. Here, some specialized process is postulated that can monitor memory activity and can be sensitive to the existing trace even when normal access to that trace has not (yet) taken place.

As pointed out by Koriat (1993, 1994, 1995), trace access theories can explain a positive feeling-of-knowing when access is blocked or delayed, but they do not easily explain *illusions of knowing*: cases in which a high feeling-of-knowing rating is – wrongly – assigned to a question while the correct response is totally unknown. If the feeling-of-knowing is to be generated by a partially accessed trace, it is difficult to imagine how a feeling-of-knowing can be generated when the subject does *not* know the answer. There are a number of other difficulties as well. Partial activation explanations, for instance, do not seem to fit with the fact that priming the answer can increase the probability of a correct response without increasing the feeling-of-knowing (Jameson, Narens, Goldfarb, & Nelson, 1990). A review of the problems involved can be found for instance in Koriat (1995; and Chapter 2 in this volume).

Inferential aspects The feeling-of-knowing may be affected by numerous variables. Cue familiarity, domain familiarity, contextual or normative information, recency of use have all been found to influence the feeling-of-knowing rating (see Metcalfe & Shimamura, 1994, for detailed reviews). It can also be affected by episodic elements like remembering the context in which the response might have been acquired, and even by more social or normative elements like estimates of the probability that the response will be known by people the subject usually interacts with (Costermans, Lories, & Ansay, 1992). Most of these elements are correlated, so it is not easy to determine which has the most important weight. A subject who thinks he/she can remember *when* something was learned, for instance, may be expected to have learned about it from somebody he/she knew but the subject will produce a higher feeling-of-knowing rating in any case. This subject would also have an above average probability of recalling or recognizing the answer, or something related to it, if only because recent traces are usually more easily accessed. As a consequence, the overall *accessibility* of information regarding a domain should correlate with all the above cues and with recognition performance.

Slow and fast feeling-of-knowing From this point, two different theoretical frameworks have developed. One rests on the effect of cue familiarity. The latest developments on this perspective are given by Nhouyvanisvong and Reder (Chapter 3 in this volume). The other rests on the accessibility idea (Koriat 1993, 1995, Chapter 2 in this volume).

The *cue familiarity approach* suggests that the familiarity of the cues (the question terms) can be used to predict subsequent recognition performance. It has been shown that a fast form of the feeling-of-knowing can be computed very rapidly and used to decide, for instance, whether to search memory or not (Reder, 1987, 1988; Reder & Ritter, 1992; Schunn et al., 1997). This specific decision seems to rely on an impression of familiarity and is computed in a preliminary stage of information processing during which extensive checks on the relationship between the various elements of information involved are not possible. It has been suggested that it plays an important role in text comprehension during the first stages of processing (Kamas & Reder, 1995; Miner & Reder, 1994).

Accessibility theory explains the accuracy of the feeling-of-knowing by postulating that the subjects retrieve all sorts of relevant but not completely appropriate traces that justify a high feeling-of-knowing rating. The rating is determined by the amount of information retrieved using the question as a cue. If high amounts of information are retrieved, the domain is presumably familiar and a correct recognition later on is likely. This justifies and validates a high feeling-of-knowing rating.

Both approaches are very different from the trace access approach. For instance, familiarity can be induced by various factors; it provides a first check and does not guarantee a correct response so the cue familiarity approach has no problem explaining illusions of knowing. According to accessibility theory, the feeling-of-knowing would also have only moderate validity because the information retrieved, although relevant, is usually partial and does not guarantee a correct response either: confusions remain possible both at recall and at recognition and erroneous beliefs of all kinds can lead to commission errors.

In this sense, both accessibility theory and the cue familiarity approach are no-magic theories (Nelson & Narens, 1990). No specific metacognitive ability is postulated; common cognitive operations are used to explain why, how and when the feeling-of-knowing can be accurate. The important difference is in the time scale. The mechanisms postulated by accessibility theory are slower; they require more time because the amount of information retrieved cannot be estimated before a number of retrieval attempts have actually been made. This also means that there will be a lot of time available for a large number of intervening processes, inferences, etc. Clearly both forms of feeling-of-knowing are also operationally different. The experiments regarding the fast form of feeling-of-knowing require a rapid decision from the subject, while the slow form is usually approached by having the subject formulate a rating according to the standard RJR procedure. Thus the slow form is the one that actually provides a judgment on a scale. Although the distinction is not absolute, we will only be dealing here with this traditional, slow form of the feeling-of-knowing, expressed as a rating and not as a presumably more automatic choice of cognitive strategy.

Some implications of accessibility theory

Evidence for a single accessibility continuum

The thing that should be expected when asking for a simple rating is that the underlying continuum should also be a single dimension. Although cue familiarity should probably be dealt with separately, accessibility theory offers the advantage of binding the one-dimensional feeling-of-knowing rating to a single "variable" that probably correlates well with *all* the inferential cues we have mentioned above. The amount of information retrieved, which is the accessibility estimate on which the feeling-of-knowing

Table 4.1   *Gamma correlations between the feeling-of-knowing and its various inferential correlates*

	Feeling-of-knowing	Source	Recency	Familiarity
Source	0.67			
Recency	0.38	0.58		
Familiarity	0.49	0.59	0.45	
Notoriety	0.59	0.58	0.30	0.49

Source: Costermans et al., 1992

rating is based, probably summarizes the influence of most of the above-mentioned "inferential" factors. Not only do these factors correlate but they probably add up to increase the amount of information retrieved and the feeling-of-knowing rating. This makes accessibility an interesting concept but predicts that there should be, in fact, one single common factor to the various determinants of the feeling-of-knowing.

Costermans, Lories, and Ansay (1992) provide data that have direct implications regarding this point. The authors had their subjects answer different questions about the inaccessible answer in the standard RJR paradigm. They asked about the *source* of the information (whether the subjects remembered where or when they might have learned the answer), its *recency* (whether the subjects had used that particular element of information recently), its *familiarity* (whether the question domain was familiar to them) and its *notoriety* (whether they thought the question domain was known to others around them). They provide the matrix of gamma coefficients reproduced in Table 4. 1.

Accessibility theory suggests all these variables reduce to one single factor and this seems to be the case. The gamma coefficients are fairly high and homogeneously distributed across the table; this is compatible with a single underlying factor. Unfortunately, due to the nature of the coefficient, the standard factor analysis approach is not appropriate. If we compute the eigenvectors and eigenvalues of this matrix, the first eigenvalue will amount to 61% of the sum of all eigenvalues. This is what would normally be interpreted as attributing 61% of "variance" to the first component. Since the coefficients are not correlations this interpretation is not possible, but the high first eigenvalue nevertheless supports the impression of homogeneity.

Other factors can probably play a role similar to the one played by accessibility and will probably also be correlated with it in most contexts, like ease of access (Koriat, 1993) or familiarity; in other metacognitive tasks other factors still have been considered, like ease of recognition for the judgment of learning (Begg, Duft, Lalonde, Melnick, & Sanvito, 1989). Our point here is not that accessibility is the only factor, it is that in most circumstances there will be an important commonality between a fair number of determinants of metacognitive judgments. Because all these variables predict the retrieval of some elements, when taken together they predict the amount of information retrieved, which is accessibility. Accessibility will thus be essentially determined by this common component.

Feeling-of-knowing accuracy and memory organization

If accessibility theory is correct, accuracy of the feeling-of-knowing rating requires an appropriate organization of memory: the organization must be such that a lot of information will be retrieved for the items on which correct recognition will actually take place.

The very fact that the feeling-of-knowing has some validity shows that this condition is probably met. There must be a clustering of information around domains so that retrieving information from a cue means that a reasonably important memory structure has been tapped. Koriat (1995) defines accessibility as the probability that a given question will elicit some response, correct or not. Accessibility theory predicts that the mean feeling-of-knowing ratings for these items (called *high accessibility* items) should be higher than for low accessibility items and it actually is. It should be the same items that allow for the retrieval of the higher amount of information (even when they are not *actually* retrieved) and generate high feeling-of-knowing ratings (Koriat, 1995). Still, to guarantee feeling-of-knowing accuracy these items should also be recognized correctly. This is not necessarily the case. An item might be such that the subject will retrieve a lot of information using it as a cue, but at the same time be deceptive in the sense that the correct answer will not be strongly associated with whatever is retrieved at first. Hence items that usually give rise to a large number of errors (i.e. that frequently receive an inappropriate answer when they receive one) should also give rise to inaccurate feeling-of-knowing ratings; Koriat (1995) shows that a high probability of a response being correct once emitted (which he calls *output-bound* accuracy) is actually associated, across items, with a higher accuracy of the feeling-of-knowing rating.

Since retrieval is bound to be easier in some domains than in others, the feeling-of-knowing should also increase in some specific domains for specific subjects. Whenever a question is asked that falls within the bounds of the appropriate domain for a given subject, retrieval attempts will yield a lot of information and the feeling-of-knowing rating will increase for that item. Unfortunately, it is difficult to determine in advance which questions are going to be effective memory cues for which subject. This would require that we collect, so to speak, "individual norms," domain by domain. This information is not obtained within the usual RJR paradigm.

Still, although we cannot know how effective a specific cue may be for a specific person, the theory says that whatever information is retrieved using the cue will be used both to determine the feeling-of-knowing rating and to help solve the recognition problem. Retrieving more knowledge on a given topic should allow the subject to rule out some or all of the distractors in the recognition test. This will obviously help the subject to choose the right answer. As a consequence, if we retrospectively group items according to the number of distractors a given subject can rule out for that item, that number provides an approximate measure of the amount of available information in the domain of that item for that subject. Lories (1994) ran an experiment in which the feeling-of-knowing could be correlated with distractor elimination. As in the standard RJR paradigm, subjects completed a questionnaire and expressed a feeling-of-knowing rating whenever they were unable to answer the question. The only difference was in the format of the recognition test. Subjects were asked not only to choose the correct answer but also to cross out any choice that they were sure could not be correct. The number of distractors eliminated in this way varied widely across items. The gamma coefficient between feeling-of-knowing ratings and distractor elimination, averaged across subjects, was about 0.32. Feeling-of-knowing accuracy in this experiment was only 0.18 and fell to 0 when the effect of distractor elimination was partialled out.[1]

Is the feeling-of-knowing adaptive?

The above type of result supports accessibility theory and suggests that the feeling-of-knowing can be a valid predictor of recognition because of a suitable memory organization. Koriat (1993, 1995, Chapter 2 in this volume) develops strong arguments in favor of the theory. We have tried to show above that accessibility is a very interesting concept because it provides a single framework in which a large number of variables can naturally come into play. The rating entirely depends on one single quantity. Yet a price has been paid. Accessibility theory gives a picture of the feeling-of-knowing as a reconstruction. Moreover, a judgment based on the accessibility of information through normal retrieval operations cannot be made before, at least, a few retrieval attempts have taken place. This limits the usefulness of the feeling-of-knowing as described by accessibility theory: it must be a slow judgment that can be used to decide whether to keep searching but less easily to decide whether to initiate search. It is no longer clear how adaptive it can be, or how useful it is to control memory search.

This is not really characteristic of accessibility theory, though. The arguments against the usefulness of the feeling-of-knowing stem from the characteristics of the experimental situation and from empirical results.

First, as pointed by Nhouyvanisvong and Reder (Chapter 3 in this volume) the rating obtained is not the one that can be the most useful. The feeling-of-knowing is computed in most experiments on *omissions*. This is in part a technical problem: if we proceed otherwise, many subjects will find an answer to many questions *before* they come up with a rating and we will end up with a *confidence* rating. Still, the most interesting case for the perspective of adaptation is when you predict success or failure *overall*, not when you predict nuances of recognition performance after failure to recall. Probably, the standard RJR paradigm was designed with something like the trace access theory in mind and not adaptation, but the whole task may now seem a rather artificial task that the subjects manage to accomplish as well as they can by combining a number of factors into inferences or by observing the consequences these factors must have on accessibility. In other words, the subjects probably base their rating on whatever information is available and the general laws of memory retrieval ensure that the most important determinants of retrieval correlate together, which, in turn, guarantees moderate accuracy.

Another problem stems from the fact that accuracy as measured by gamma is usually the main object of interest. The absolute level of the feeling-of-knowing is treated more or less as random variability in scale use. Still, considering only accuracy as it is usually measured, the adaptive value of the feeling-of-knowing rating is limited. It is guaranteed to be useful only to compare items. This follows from the interpretation explicitly – and correctly – ascribed to gamma by Nelson (1984, p. 130). The gamma coefficient is interpreted as a function of the probability that an item that is recognized correctly will receive a higher feeling-of-knowing rating than an item that is not recognized correctly (let P be this probability, $P = 0.5$ gamma $+ 0.5$). The actual form of the functional relationship between the feeling-of-knowing level and the recognition probability remains undefined. What has been demonstrated by using gamma in standard feeling-of-knowing research is the subjects' capability of assigning a higher rating to an item that has a higher recognition probability.[2] This would be useful, for instance, in a task where the subject had to select the items that offer the best chance of correct recognition, but not in general.

Even so, another reason why the feeling-of-knowing cannot be very useful is that the correlations usually observed are very low. Gamma is usually below 0.5 and easily falls below 0.3. If, instead of gamma, we adopt a measure of redundancy (in the sense of information theory) and measure the power of the feeling-of-knowing to predict recognition, it is about 20% in some of our experiments. Considering that the information to be predicted is at most one bit (when recognition success or failure is equally likely), this means that the five-level feeling-of-knowing scale provides approximately 0.2 bits of information. The predictive power of the recognition score regarding the feeling-of-knowing score, on the other hand, is about 10%, meaning that 90% of the actual feeling-of-knowing information (uncertainty) has nothing whatever to do with the result of the recognition test. It is determined by uncontrolled factors and may even be random. This may seem to be an artefact of the procedure because subjects are asked for a rating on a five-level scale to predict a binary issue but the point is that there must be more to the rating than its predictive power, otherwise it would be underdetermined and random.

By using an ordinal statistic, research on the feeling-of-knowing recognizes that there is no principled way for the subject to calibrate the scale. It cannot be done on the basis of the recognition test, because the test has not taken place yet. The subjects have to "calibrate" the scale more or less arbitrarily. The result of that operation is treated as random and an ordinal scale is chosen because the interest is in accuracy.

Yet, the literature on human judgment does not suggest that the scale levels are used randomly. They may not be reliable; there may be biases of all kinds, but scale levels are used according to complex rules that involve, for instance, communication considerations (see, for instance, Schwarz, Hippler, Deutsch, & Strack, 1985, Schwarz, Knäuper et al., 1991, Schwarz, 1996, for a review). Is there evidence that the overall feeling-of-knowing level may not be random?

The feeling-of-knowing as a judgment

Meaning of the feeling-of-knowing level

A result obtained in a recent experiment provides some arguments that the absolute feeling-of-knowing level is not completely random although it is determined by complex processes. The object of the experiment was to compare the feeling-of-knowing obtained with different kinds of items. The material consisted of two lists of 60 items, one list of "general information" items and one "lexical" list; the difficulty with "lexical" items was in accessing a rare lexical label while, for general information items, the information requested was in itself difficult to retrieve but could be expressed by a very simple and common lexical label (for example: "what color is the flag that signals danger in automobile competitions?").

The study used a standard RJR paradigm. The distractor elimination technique was also used. To control for list effects, the subjects were randomly assigned to two experimental conditions. The two subsets of items were either mixed randomly and presented in a single list or presented in two separate lists. Accessibility and output-bound accuracy turned out to be slightly different for the two types of items and there was also a difference in recognition performance, but, first of all, feeling-of-knowing accuracy, as measured by gamma, was significantly higher for lexical items in both experimental conditions. There was no significant interaction between type of list and type of item for feeling-of-knowing accuracy. At the same time, distractor elimination was more effective for lexical items. As a consequence, the probability of a correct recognition response averaged across subjects was also higher. This provides further support for the idea that feeling-of-knowing accuracy depends on bringing retrieved information to bear during the recognition test. What was not completely expected was another result.

Regarding the feeling-of-knowing judgment, an interaction was observed between the type of item and the type of presentation list: although the feeling-of-knowing rating was higher in both cases for lexical items, it was slightly higher still in the mixed condition.

In other words, the feeling-of-knowing is higher for lexical items but the difference (the contrast) between lexical and semantic items seems to

increase in the mixed list condition. It should be noted that this phenomenon is in principle independent of what happens to feeling-of-knowing
accuracy. The gamma statistic loses all absolute level information; as long
as a successful item receives a higher rating than an unsuccessful one, it
does not matter how high that rating is. An overall increase in feeling-of-
knowing level does not affect gamma and two subsets of items may yield a
same feeling-of-knowing accuracy with a different feeling-of-knowing
average. In this case, for instance, the accuracy increase might have
occurred without the change in absolute level. This is certainly not evidence
that the overall feeling-of-knowing could be used safely to control cognitive
processes. It seems to imply a different use of the scale levels for both list
types with a different mapping of the accessibility continuum on the rating
scale in each case. Since the items involved are the same in both cases, it
would not seem that both mappings can be simultaneously optimal.

Still, the result is ambiguous because it shows at the same time that the
overall level of feeling-of-knowing is not fixed randomly. There was enough
information in the absolute level of the feeling-of-knowing to yield consistent (significant) differences between the experimental conditions.

This kind of context effect is not new. An interesting similar case is
reported in the information retrieval literature. Improving information
retrieval systems (e.g. in libraries) requires that users be able to assess the
relevance of the information retrieved by the system as a response to their
query. Eisenberg (1988) shows that the relevance ratings obtained from
end users of information retrieval systems depend on the context in which
the rating is made. In particular the relevance rating assigned to a specific
item for the same query depends on whether other, more or less relevant
items have been retrieved. It has been known for some time that the
overall level of a rating scale may be unstable. This is usually considered
as an artefact but it has also been analyzed in detail as a consequence of
the communication situation in which the subject is placed (Schwartz,
1996).

One way to explain such an effect is to postulate that the subjects
somehow attempt to "optimize" the way they use the scale. In the context
of signal detection theory, Treisman and Williams (1984a) provide an
analysis of criterion setting that can be used to support this view and relies
on three mechanisms. They postulate a long term criterion setting
mechanism that determines the decisions globally and postulate two other
mechanisms that can move the decision criteria according to the stimuli
encountered and the responses given. The tracking mechanism favors the
repetition of the same response on two consecutive items. It is related to the
idea that in a normal environment, perceptive events tend to occur together
and cluster locally.

The theory can be extended to the kind of scales used in feeling-of-
knowing or confidence experiments; it is only necessary to postulate that
there is a separate criterion for each level of the scale (Treisman &
Williams, 1984b). In this case the stabilization mechanism tends to move the

criteria in such a way that the scale is used homogeneously. Clearly such a stabilization process may produce the context effects described above. This analysis is compatible with the previous one. Optimizing the use of the rating scale is optimizing communication. All this suggests that we should start searching for evidence of a long term reference setting mechanism.

Level and accuracy problems

The problems involved in assigning a rating to a dimension like accessibility also appear theoretically similar to the problems involved in Clore's (1992) description of how mood can be used as information. A large amount of research has been devoted to identifying the conditions under which feelings like mood, uncertainty, or even availability can be used directly to build ratings. In particular, a large amount of research in social cognitive psychology deals with the attributional and judgeability problems involved in this process. One typical paradigm involves a judgment on some form of "feeling" like uncertainty or familiarity and manipulates attribution. For instance, Schwarz, Bless et al. (1991) examine the effect of an attribution manipulation on an assertiveness judgment. Subjects are asked to recall 6 or 12 examples of assertive behavior according to experimental condition; this factor is crossed in their design with a second experimental factor: for half of the subjects, background music is played that is said to hinder retrieval. Clearly in this case, the difficulty in finding the examples is an analog to accessibility in the feeling-of-knowing context and indeed, the assertiveness judgment is found to correlate with ease of retrieval: as most of the subjects easily retrieve 6 examples, assertiveness judgments are higher in the conditions where the experimenter asks for 6 events than when 12 events are called for. However, the effect is eliminated when the difficulty in retrieving 12 examples can be attributed by the subjects to the music and not to a paucity of examples in their personal history.

As Clore (1992) himself suggests, the feeling-of-knowing paradigm is obviously similar to the mood information problem except that no manipulation of attribution is usually made in feeling-of-knowing research. Although there is no clear emotional or affective component to the assessment of accessibility, there are important similarities between what Clore describes and the feeling-of-knowing rating situation. In both cases a single continuum is involved and a single intensity value is returned. Just as various events have an influence on our mood, various inferential cues condition accessibility. In both cases this "confounding" of influence sources is usually acceptable from the subjects' point of view because there is a general correlation between the sources, but both cases involve a potential attribution problem that is directly related to this "confounding." In the case of the feeling-of-knowing, high accessibility may be due to a number of factors, some of them related to the existence of an appropriate response, some related to extraneous considerations (inferential aspects), some related, even, to elements of information that do not constitute a proper answer.

Generally speaking it seems convenient to make a distinction here between overall level effects that will be sensitive to attribution problems, context, contrast effects, etc. and accuracy considerations. Interestingly, cognitive research has focused almost exclusively on accuracy considerations by choosing appropriate association measures. There are a few exceptions, though. Schacter (1986), for instance, has shown that the feeling-of-knowing is calibrated differently in subjects who fake forgetting and when forgetting is real. Schacter had subjects read a story and the experimental subjects were instructed to fake forgetting when asked questions about it. All subjects were then asked questions about a detail of the story. The detail had been chosen to keep memory performance very low and the subjects were also asked to make a feeling-of-knowing judgment about their ability to retrieve the information if primed. The mean feeling-of-knowing rating was larger in the control group. This suggests that the subjects figure they know what the feeling-of-knowing level should be, try to reproduce it and fail. They apparently make a systematic error in doing so. An interesting aspect of the results is that Schacter also had a group of judges try to determine from thinking aloud protocols whether forgetting was genuine. The judges were not able to discriminate between control and experimental subjects. Schacter suggests that the judges and the subjects shared a common misconception of the way a forgetful subject would answer. In any case there not only seems to be some regularity in the way the rating is calibrated but there even seems to be a "common knowledge," some kind of implicit theory on the topic, that the subjects rely on, because, without this, there could be no systematic difference. This is typically a kind of effect that would be sensitive to attribution and judgeability manipulations. One should wonder for instance how a subject who actually remembers something will be able to discard what is remembered in order to use the scale in a "neutral" manner.

A more social look at feeling-of-knowing accuracy

According to accessibility theory, feeling-of-knowing rests on an internal accessibility estimate that is apparently privileged information. The amount of information retrieved using the question as a cue is an *internal* response. Does this mean that the feeling-of-knowing is highly individual? Actually we already know it does not. Nelson, Leonosio, Landwehr, and Narens (1986) have shown that normative item difficulty correlates with feeling-of-knowing. Since normative item difficulty is objective information based on the behavior of a number of test subjects, the feeling of knowing cannot be completely individual. On the other hand, the same authors show that feeling-of-knowing accuracy is not explained entirely by normative difficulty. There is an internal source of information that is accurate. It does not seem either that the feeling-of-knowing makes as much use as possible of normative information. Calogero and Nelson (1993) compare subjects who make feeling-of-knowing ratings *with* and *without* normative information on items exhibiting three different levels of difficulty. They show that *both* the overall feeling-of-knowing level and the feeling-of-knowing accuracy (as measured by gamma) change in the prior-information group. Accuracy is higher when the subjects can use the actuarial information provided, just as Calogero and Nelson expected. At the same time, the difference between the feeling-of-knowing ratings for the easiest and for the most difficult items is twice as large in those with prior information in comparison with the no-information condition. This suggests that the subjects combine the actuarial information and their own feeling-of-knowing according to some scheme that we cannot identify but that results in a wider range of ratings. For some reason, the combination of internal responses and actuarial information yields a larger range of scores than the usual procedure. It might be a simple side-effect of the combination heuristic but it may also involve some kind of judgeability phenomenon (the subjects might feel safer because they have the actuarial information). In any case, it suggests that the final rating can be a combination of internally available and more objective information.

Further evidence for that view stems from the results of Jameson, Nelson, Leonosio, and Narens (1993). These authors use the Vesonder and Voss (1985) paradigm to determine the role of internal responses, observable behavior and actuarial information in determining the accuracy of the feeling-of-knowing. They use a trio of subjects: a target, an observer and a judge. The target is a subject placed in the standard RJR paradigm. The observer can only observe the target subject and makes a feeling-of-knowing rating regarding success or failure by the target subject in the recognition test. The judge has access to the question only but still makes predictions. The various feeling-of-knowing ratings are correlated differently with the final performance. The targets make more accurate predictions than the observer, who is him/herself better than the judges.

So, again, the final rating seems to involve elements of internal (privileged) and objective (shared) information, but here there is more. What Jameson et al. show is that the judges can use their *own* assessment of difficulty to make a reasonable prediction. Because they have no access to external information like the time spent searching and because they also have no access to tabulated, objective, actuarial information, the result implies that the judges must be using their *own* internal responses and that the feeling-of-knowing – or accessibility rating – *of the judges* correlates with the subjects' feeling-of-knowing, if only moderately.

There is an intriguing aspect to this use of highly individual information. Their own retrieval rate or some similar index was the only way the judges could assess the knowledge of *others*. The "privileged" source of information actually correlates with and provides a basis for whatever appears to be common to all subjects. Why? One reason for this may be that memory organization is essentially similar in most subjects because it is necessary to the pragmatic organization of communication: one needs to guess at what people know to prepare messages that will easily allow them to connect what they know with what you are about to tell them. From this point of view, the feeling-of-knowing rating is an individual response that must be based on some fundamentally common ground.

Conclusion

A distinction has been proposed between a fast form and a slow form of the feeling-of-knowing. While the fast form essentially corresponds to a feeling of familiarity that can be used to make a decision but is not usually expressed as a rating, the slow form is usually expressed as a rating and can be described as a judgment. According to accessibility theory this judgment is based on the amount of information retrieved using the question as a cue. We have examined a number of aspects of this presentation of the feeling-of-knowing as a kind of one-dimensional judgement. Data confirm that when a set of judgments correlate well with the feeling-of-knowing they are likely to have one single important component.

The accuracy of this judgment rests on the idea that the information clusters in memory in such a way that the information retrieved using the question as cue may be relevant enough to improve recognition performance by constraining the subjects' choice in the recognition test. Still, this validity is low to moderate. This and a number of other arguments suggest that, although the feeling-of-knowing probably can be used adaptively, it is also a construction, a response to the experimenter's demands, a judgment that suffers the ambiguities of any similar rating. The accessibility continuum must be mapped onto the rating scale in a more or less optimal manner. This mapping problem exists for any feeling and the situation is comparable for many ratings, but cognitive research has focused on accuracy problems (across items) rather than on overall rating levels that may exhibit contrast or judgeability effects.

Results of cognitive research show that there is some consensus among subjects on the way the scale should be used and on which items are supposed to be difficult. One aspect of that consensus is the relationship between objective difficulty norms and the feeling-of-knowing, but the fact that entirely "internal" responses to the question cues can be used by a subject to predict the response of another suggests that it is actually more like a social norm. How such a norm may have come to exist is an interesting question. We think that one reason for keeping a reasonable estimate of what is known by others and oneself may be that it is required to organize effective communication.

Notes

1. After the items for one subject are grouped according to the number of eliminated distractors, gamma can be computed within each class and the resulting statistics combined.

2. What has been demonstrated is slightly less than that, because using gamma instead of tau-b postulates that the accuracy observed across scale levels is replicated within scale levels (Quade, 1974).

References

Begg, I., Duft, S., Lalonde, P., Melnick, R., & Sanvito, J. (1989) Memory predictions are based on ease of processing. *Journal of Memory and Language, 28*(5), 610–632.

Clore, G.L. (1992). Cognitive phenomenology: Feelings and the construction of judgment. In L.L. Martin & A. Tesser (Eds), *The construction of social judgment* (pp. 133–163). Hillsdale, NJ: Lawrence Erlbaum.

Calogero, M. & Nelson, T.O. (1993) Utilization of base rate information during feeling-of-knowing judgments. *American Journal of Psychology, 105*, 565–573.

Costermans, J., Lories, G., & Ansay, C. (1992). Confidence level and feeling of knowing in question answering: The weight of inferential processes. *Journal of Experimental Psychology: Learning, Memory, and Cognition, 18*, 142–150.

Eisenberg, M.B. (1988). Measuring relevance judgment. *Information Processing and Management, 24*, 373–389.

Glucksberg, S. & McCloskey, M. (1981). Decision about ignorance: Knowing that you do not know. *Journal of Experimental Psychology: Human Learning and Memory, 7*, 311–325.

Hart, J.T. (1965). Memory and the feeling-of-knowing experience. *Journal of Educational Psychology, 56*, 208–216.

Hart, J.T. (1966). Methodological note on the feeling-of-knowing experiments. *Journal of Educational Psychology, 57*, 347–349.

Jameson, K.A., Narens, I., Goldfarb, K., & Nelson, T.O. (1990). The influence of subthreshold priming on metamemory and recall. *Acta Psychologica, 73*, 55–68.

Jameson, A., Nelson, T.O., Leonosio, R.J., & Narens, L. (1993). The feeling of another person's knowing. *Journal of Memory and Language, 32*, 320–335.

Kamas E.N. & Reder L.M. (1995) The role of familiarity in cognitive processing, In R.F. Lorch and E.J. O'Brien (Eds), *Sources of coherence in reading* (pp. 177–202). Hillsdale, NJ: Lawrence Erlbaum.

Kolers, P.A. & Palef, S.R. (1976). Knowing not. *Memory and Cognition, 4*, 553–558.

Koriat, A. (1993). How do we know that we know? The accessibility model of the feeling of knowing. *Psychological Review, 100*, 609–639.

Koriat, A. (1994) Memory's knowledge of its own knowledge: The accessibility account of the feeling of knowing. In J. Metcalfe & A. Shimamura (Eds), *Metacognition: Knowing about knowing* (pp. 115–136). Cambridge, MA: MIT Press.

Koriat, A. (1995). Dissociating knowing and the feeling of knowing: Further evidence for the accessibility model. *Journal of Experimental Psychology: General, 124*(3), 311–333.

Koriat, A., Lichtenstein, S., & Fischoff, B. (1980). Reasons for confidence. *Journal of Experimental Psychology: Human Learning and Memory, 6*, 107–118.

Lories, G. (1994). Partial knowledge, distractor elimination and feeling of knowing accuracy. *Current Psychology of Cognition, 13*, 833–844.

Meyer, A.S. & Bock, K. (1992). The tip-of-the-tongue phenomenon: Blocking or partial activation. *Memory and Cognition, 20*, 715–726.

Miner, A.C. & Reder, L.M. (1994). A new look at feeling of knowing. Its metacognitive role in regulating question answering. In J. Metcalfe & A. Shimamura (Eds), *Metacognition: Knowing about knowing* (pp. 47–70). Cambridge, MA: MIT Press.

Nelson, T.O. (1984). A comparison of current measures of feeling-of-knowing accuracy. *Psychological Bulletin, 95*, 109–133.

Nelson, T.O. (1996) Consciousness and metacognition. *American Psychologist, 51*(2), 102–116.

Nelson, T.O., Leonesio, R.J., Landwehr, R.S., & Narens, L. (1986). A comparison of three predictors of an individual's memory performance: The individual's feeling of knowing versus the normative feeling of knowing versus base rate item difficulty. *Journal of Experimental Psychology: Learning, Memory, and Cognition, 12*, 279–287.

Nelson, T.O. & Narens, L. (1990). Metamemory: A theoretical framework and new findings. *The Psychology of Learning and Motivation, 26*, 125–173.

Quade, D. (1974). Non parametric partial correlations. In H. M. Blalock (Ed.), *Measurement in the social sciences* (pp. 344–369). Chicago: Aldine.

Reder, L.M. (1987). Strategy selection in question-answering. *Cognitive Psychology, 19*, 90–138.

Reder, L.M. (1988). Strategic control of retrieval strategies. *The psychology of Learning and Motivation, 22*, 227–259.

Reder L.M. & Ritter F.E. (1992). What determines initial feeling of knowing? Familiarity with question terms, not with answer. *Journal of Experimental Psychology: Learning, Memory, and Cognition, 18*,(3), 435–451.

Schacter D.L. (1986). Feeling-of-knowing ratings distinguish between genuine and simulated forgetting. *Journal of Experimental Psychology: Learning, Memory, and Cognition, 12*, 30–41.

Schunn, C.D., Reder, L.M., Nhouyvanisvong, A., Richards, D.R., & Stroffolino, P.J. (1997). To calculate or not to calculate: A source activation confusion model of problem familiarity's role in strategy selection. *Journal of Experimental Psychology Learning, Memory, and Cognition, 23*(1), 3–29.

Schwartz, B.L. (1994). Sources of information in metamemory: Judgements of learning and feelings of knowing. *Psychonomic Bulletin and Review, 1*(3), 357–375.

Schwarz, N. (1996). *Cognition and communication: Judgmental biases, research methods and the logic of conversation.* Mahwah, NJ: Lawrence Erlbaum.

Schwarz, N., Bless, H., Strack, F., Klumpp, G., Rittenauer-Schatka, H., & Simons, A. (1991). Ease of retrieval as information: Another look at the availability heuristic. *Journal of Personality and Social Psychology, 61*, 195–202.

Schwarz, N., Hippler, H.J., Deutsch, B., & Strack, F. (1985). Response scales: Effects of category range on reported behavior and subsequent judgments. *Public Opinion Quarterly, 49*, 388–395.

Schwarz, N., Knaüper, B., Hippler, H.J., Noelle-Neumann, E., & Clark, L.F. (1991). Rating scales: Numeric values may change the meaning of the scale labels. *Public Opinion Quarterly, 55*, 570–582.

Smith, S.M. (1994). Frustrated feelings of imminent recall: On the tip of the tongue. In J. Metcalfe (Ed.), *Metacognition: Knowing about knowing* (pp. 27–45). Cambridge, MA: MIT Press.

Treisman, M. & Williams, T.C. (1984a). A theory of criterion setting with an application to sequential dependencies. *Psychological Review, 91*, 68–111.

Treisman, M. & Williams, T.C. (1984b). The setting and maintenance of criteria representing levels of confidence. *Journal of Experimental Psychology: Human Perception and Performance, 10*, 119–139.

Vesonder, G.T. & Voss, J.F. (1985). On the ability to predict one's own responses while learning. *Journal of Memory and Language, 24*, 363–376.

5

Knowing Thyself and Others: Progress in Metacognitive Social Psychology

Thomas O. Nelson, Arie W. Kruglanski and John T. Jost

The social world requires that we make a staggering number of decisions about the extent and nature of our own knowledge and beliefs as well as decisions about the extent and nature of other people's knowledge and beliefs. We rely continuously upon the advice of friends, family members, experts, colleagues, doctors, therapists, lawyers, accountants, and countless others in deciding how to handle complicated and consequential situations in domains as vitally important to us as health, education, friendship, romance, avocation, law, finance, and politics. In such situations, we are forced to make complicated calculations about the quantity and quality of other people's knowledge. Often, we choose to go it alone, to follow our own feeling or sense of what is appropriate. This, too, requires an assessment about the validity of our own beliefs, possibly even a determination that our own level of expertise is relatively high (e.g. Ellis & Kruglanski, 1992). Whatever we do, we are in the position of making higher order judgments about the credibility of other initial judgments, whether those initial judgments were made by us or by others.

Judgments about the trustworthiness of knowledge are just one among many different types of metacognitive judgments. There is virtually no end to the number of cognitive assessments that could be made about the thoughts, feelings, and beliefs of the self and others. What does she think, why does she think it, when did she start thinking it, what would get her to stop thinking it? Do I know the answer to your question, when and from whom did I hear the answer, would I have remembered it if I had heard it, what will help me to remember it, and can I be confident that my memory will be accurate? Human action and interaction depend in crucial respects upon our general success in these rough metacognitive waters.

Although the research topic of metacognition was launched by developmental and cognitive psychologists (e.g. Flavell, 1979; Metcalfe & Shimamura, 1994; Nelson, 1992; Wellman, 1985), empirical social psychology provides ample evidence that people make use of metacognitive assessments, whether they are aware of those assessments or not. For instance, it has been found that people search the facial expressions and non-verbal behaviors of others in order to figure out how others perceive a given situation, and this helps them to determine how they themselves feel about that situation (Schachter & Singer, 1962). In research on social influence, it is found that people almost always revise their own judgments to make them more similar to the judgments of others (Asch, 1952; Sherif, 1936), especially when people have (even the slightest) reason to question the credibility of their own knowledge (Festinger, 1950). Some social psychologists have argued that we do not know what we think until we know what other people think (Hardin & Higgins, 1996; Turner, 1991). Even when our own thoughts and feelings are relatively clear to us, we still estimate and adjust for the thoughts and feelings of others in order to best follow our own interaction goals (Jones & Thibaut, 1958). All of these cases involve metacognitive judgments, that is, cognitive assessments that are about the cognitions of the self.

The concept of "metacognition" (e.g. Metcalfe & Shimamura, 1994; Nelson, 1992) is useful for understanding the inferences that are drawn about the mental states of others as well as inferences about one's own mental states, and we wish to focus on both momentary (or on-line) judgments about mental states and more enduring or culturally based assumptions about mental states and processes in general. Invoking metacognition in these contexts allows one to incorporate a good deal of social psychological research that has not previously been considered metacognitive in nature.

Psychological issues that arise from attempts to know what we know and to know what others know hook up with enduring philosophical questions about epistemology and subjectivity, and these are the very issues that social and cognitive psychologists seek to address through empirical means. Crucial questions include all of the following:

How do we know what we know?
How do we know what other people know?
Do we have "direct access" to our own thoughts, feelings, and attitudes?
How accurate are our thoughts, feelings, and attitudes?
How accurate are our perceptions of others' thoughts, feelings, and attitudes?
Is it possible to empathize with others?
Are the processes governing self-knowledge fundamentally similar or different from the processes governing knowledge of other persons?

Issues such as these, traditionally reserved for the philosopher's plate (see Rosenthal, 1991), have been brought back to the table in recent years by metacognitive scientists. In what follows, we review social psychological evidence pertaining to metacognitive knowledge, and we offer some preliminary social and cognitive psychological answers to the many questions this topic invites.

The metacognitive assessment of self-knowledge

In many ways, formal research on metacognition began with the "feeling-of-knowing" phenomenon (e.g. Hart, 1965) according to which people can predict the likelihood that they will be able to remember a specific piece of currently non-recallable information. Contemporary research is epitomized by the three phenomena of "ease of learning" estimates, "judgments of learning," and "feelings of knowing" (see Nelson & Narens, 1994). Most of the empirical research on these metacognitive topics has tended to focus respectively on people's expectations about how easy it will be to learn particular types of information, their beliefs about what types of acquired information will be remembered best, and their estimates of whether or not they will be able to recognize non-recalled information (e.g. Dunlosky & Nelson, 1994; Metcalfe, Schwartz, & Joaquim, 1993; Nelson, Dunlosky, Graf, & Narens, 1994). In this body of literature and in the research we review below, it is possible to distinguish among two different types of information that provide the basis for metacognitive judgments: momentary feelings or impressions, and lay or implicit theories that are more enduring. Cognitive psychologists have usually emphasized the former basis for metacognition and have tended not to consider the more lasting bases of metacognitive knowledge, in part because implicit theories are often linked to cultural norms and beliefs that are assumed to fall outside of the province of cognitive psychology.

Feelings as (metacognitive) information

Feelings of familiarity   Work on subjective feelings of familiarity illustrates the significance of metacognitions that are derived from momentary feelings or sensations. It has been found that exposing people repeatedly to the same propositional statements increases the sense of familiarity that people have with those statements, and that familiarity, in turn, increases the likelihood that those statements will be judged to be valid and true (e.g. Hasher, Goldstein, & Toppino, 1977), providing a kind of experimental evidence for the chilling claim of the Nazi propagandist Goebbels that "if you repeat a lie often enough, people will come to believe it." Because the contents of propositional statements may vary considerably, the sense of familiarity or "fluency" may influence any number of different types of judgments. A good deal of research supports the notion that repeated exposure produces increased liking for stimuli (e.g. Zajonc, 1980). Mandler, Nakamura, and Van Zandt (1987) have reported that repeated exposure to stimuli facilitates judgments of "brightness" as well as "darkness," so the effects of familiarity do not seem to be restricted to evaluative judgments. Kruglanski, Freund and Bar-Tal (1996) have demonstrated recently that mere exposure facilitates judgments that stimuli are either "appealing" or "nonappealing," depending upon participants' initial assessment of those stimuli. Kruglanski et al. (1996) found also that the strength of the relation between repeated exposure and subsequent judgments was magnified under conditions of time pressure (which is assumed to increase the tendency to rely on plausible initial impressions) and was attenuated under conditions of high evaluation-apprehension (which is assumed to lower the tendency to rely on initial impressions).

In further explorations of the consequences of the "feeling of familiarity," Jacoby, Kelley, Brown, and Jasechko (1989) instructed participants to read a list of non-famous names. At a subsequent session, those names were mixed with new non-famous names, and participants were asked to make fame judgments. When the second session was very close in time to the first, old non-famous names were less likely to be mistaken for famous ones than the new non-famous names, because participants readily recognized them as members of the previous non-famous-names list. When the second test came after a 24-hour delay, however, the old non-famous names were not recognized. Under those conditions, they were more likely to be mistaken for famous names than were new non-famous names. Banaji and Greenwald (1995) further showed that this "getting famous overnight" effect is sensitive to the influence of social stereotypes; male names but not female names are ascribed fame under conditions of perceived familiarity.

Taken together, these findings suggest that the subjective sense of familiarity may be interpreted in a number of different ways and that it may lead to many possible behavioral outcomes, depending upon the categories or principles that people apply when rendering an interpretation. It may be argued, in fact, that subjective feelings (such as the feeling of familiarity) are meaningless as sources of information until they have been identified in terms of pre-existing categories that are used for drawing inferences (Trope, 1986), just as it has been argued that physiological arousal is undifferentiated until it has been labeled or an attribution has been made (e.g. Apter, 1989; Schachter & Singer, 1962; Marshall & Zimbardo, 1979). Much like the observations of the post-Kuhnian scientist (e.g. Hanson, 1968), our naive perceptions are "theory-laden" rather than given directly. For example, a momentary sensation may be identified as subjective "confidence" which in turn may prompt the metacognitive inference of "knowing the material" or "being able to do well on an impending exam," but only in the presence of situational cues that may be interpreted in terms of prior notions as to how being confident "feels" as well as an implicit theory about the relation between self-confidence and knowledge (cf. Ellis & Kruglanski, 1992).

Feelings of uncertainty An important implication of the notion that momentary feelings need to be rendered meaningful in terms of a pre-existing theory is that occasionally, competing alternative theories may be activated and alter the interpretation of the data. In this connection, studies conducted by Clore and Parrott (1994) examined the effects of hypnotically induced feelings of uncertainty on stimulus ratings. In particular, some of their participants were led to believe that they should feel uncertain and that they should attribute the uncertainty to the hypnotic experience, while others were made to feel uncertain but were given no attribution for it. Subsequently, participants were asked to read and rate how well they understood a poem. It was hypothesized and found that feelings of uncertainty influenced ratings of poem comprehension only in the absence of an external attribution for the uncertainty. Thus, people may make the metacognitive assumption that feelings of uncertainty may be attributed to qualities of the stimulus, unless they have some other explanation for feeling uncertain (Clore, 1992).

Feelings of happiness   In experiments by Schwarz and Clore (1983), people were asked to rate their overall happiness on a day that was either sunny or rainy. Not too surprisingly, people reported greater happiness on sunny days than on rainy days. Apparently, participants in this study interpreted their momentary moods as deriving from their overall happiness, oblivious to the possibility that the mood might have resulted from a more transient cause such as weather. Indeed, asking people about the weather beforehand was found to eliminate the effect of weather on judgments of well-being. Like other feelings or sensations, then, momentary mood may be regarded as a datum, the meaning of which may be explicated through a variety of implicit theories, such as a metacognitive theory about the relationship between mood (or weather) and global satisfaction. Schwarz and Clore (1983, 1988) conclude that people use "feelings as information," but the meaning of that information is not always clear in the absence of categories for interpretation.

An excessive emphasis on the role of subjective feelings and sensations in self-knowledge could lead one to the conclusion, perhaps prematurely, that knowledge about the self is very different in kind from knowledge about other people, insofar as information about others may not be perceived directly. Taken to its philosophical extreme, this position is known as "solipsism," and it has been critiqued extensively by Wittgenstein (1980) in his arguments against "private language" and his grounding of psychological ascription in social and cultural practices (see Jost, 1995). Our social psychological approach to metacognition similarly leads us to the conclusion that inferences about self-knowledge and other-knowledge may not be so different. If momentary feelings or sensations are conceived of as informationally impoverished in the absence of a folk theory about how such sensations are to be interpreted, then processes of accumulating knowledge about the self may be very similar to processes whereby other people's knowledge is divined. As Bem (1972) concluded, processes of self-perception may not differ qualitatively from processes of other-perception. In all cases, general theories about how to draw valid metacognitive inferences must be applied. Because most metacognitive research to date has emphasized momentary feelings or sensations and much less attention has been paid to the role of pre-existing categories and theories, we turn now to a review of social psychological research on metacognitive beliefs and assumptions that people hold in general about topics as varied as memory, learning, intelligence, and attitude formation.

Theories as metacognitive knowledge

Theories about memorability That situationally given "data" are interpreted in terms of participants' extant theories or conceptions is especially clear in recent research by Strack and his colleagues on the subject of reconstructive memory (Strack & Bless, 1994; Strack & Förster, 1995). In particular, people hold intuitive theories about what sorts of things they are likely to remember and what sorts of things they are likely to forget, and these notions play an important role in confidence judgments about whether or not a stimulus has appeared previously. For instance, students may be more certain about the fact that their professor was not wearing a sombrero during the last class period than about the fact that their professor was not wearing a pair of glasses (Strack & Bless, 1994). This is because people make important metacognitive judgments about whether they would have remembered a particular occurrence, even when they do not remember the actual occurrence (Gentner & Collins, 1981). Strack and Bless (1994) have demonstrated further that people possess very subtle assumptions that numerically distinctive categories will be remembered better than numerically non-distinctive categories. As a result, people are more confident in their decision that a given event did not occur when that type of event would have been infrequent than when it would have been a frequent occurrence. Other work indicates that people are also more confident in their memories when the previously exposed set of items was small rather than large (Strack & Förster, 1995).

Theories about personal stability and change The interpretative element in reconstructive memory is explored further in research by Michael Ross and his colleagues (e.g. Ross, 1989; Ross & Conway, 1986). Specifically, it is proposed that in attempting to remember one's past attitudes, feelings, or abilities, one often begins with present attitudes or mental states and makes adjustments to those on the basis of implicit theories about personal stability and change. Because people generally believe that factors such as intelligence and political party affiliation are stable entities, they tend to overestimate the extent to which their present capacities and affiliations are the same as those they possessed in years gone by (Ross, 1989). On the other hand, because people believe that courses in study skills are effective in producing improvements, they tend to underestimate the studying abilities they possessed prior to taking such a course (Ross & Conway, 1986).

Theories about aging and memory One of the major contributions that metacognitive social psychology can make is to show how these interpretive theories are derived from cultural beliefs such as stereotypes about different

social groups. Work by Levy and Langer (1994), for instance, ⟨⟩
that there are culturally specific beliefs about the inevitability
loss in old age and that these beliefs affect not only expectati⟨⟩
actual performance of elderly people. This research demon⟨⟩
among American hearing individuals, who presumably subsc⟨⟩
stereotype that elderly people have poor memories, there is in fac⟨⟩
in memory with age. However, in two cultural groups that reject such
stereotypes about the elderly (Chinese people and American deaf people),
no decline in memory was observed.

Theories about learning and intelligence   Some of the strongest evidence
pertaining to the social psychology of metacognition comes from a research
program conducted by Dweck and her colleagues (e.g. Dweck, 1991;
Dweck, Hong, & Chiu, 1993; Elliott & Dweck, 1988). In a series of experimental and classroom studies, it has been found that children subscribe to
different assumptions about intelligence and learning and that these
assumptions have important implications for actual intellectual performance. In particular, some children subscribe to "entity theories" of intelligence, according to which people either do or do not have aptitude for
particular intellectual tasks. These children tend to be preoccupied with test
scores and performance goals, and any failures in achievement produce
feelings of helplessness and self-deprecation. Other children subscribe to
"incremental theories" of intelligence, according to which people are
thought to be capable of increasing their aptitude in particular domains.
These children are more interested in learning goals, and in the long run they
tend to achieve intellectual goals more successfully than do entity theorists
and to respond better to temporary setbacks in achievement (Dweck, 1991).
Elliott and Dweck (1988) induced a particular metacognitive orientation by
priming either performance factors (stressing evaluation) or learning factors
(stressing the value of the task itself). This manipulation caused profound
effects on subsequent learning by altering motivational goals. Specifically,
students in the performance goal condition avoided opportunities to learn
new information when there was a risk of making errors or becoming
confused. In addition, self-perceptions of low ability in this group was
associated with negative affect, self-blaming attributional styles, and
deterioration of effort and performance.

Theories about assimilation and contrast   A series of experimental studies
by Wegener and Petty (1995) demonstrated that people hold intuitive
theories about attitudinal processes of assimilation and contrast in social
judgment. For instance, people anticipated that thinking about the weather
in Hawaii or the cultural life of Paris would lead one to perceive the city of
Indianapolis in less favorable terms, thereby indicating an intuitive
understanding of contrast effects. At the same time, people believed that
seeing a group of very attractive models associated with a particular commercial product would lead one to view that product in more favorable

terms, indicating a grasp also of assimilation effects. Thus, people's assumptions about the construction of social attitudes possess considerable sophistication and flexibility, as well as a relatively high degree of accuracy. Wegener and Petty (1995) found that instructing participants not to let contextual features influence their judgments of particular targets had the effect of inducing attempts to correct for the hypothesized biases. When people expected assimilation effects, the correction instructions led them to adjust their judgments away from the context, but when they expected contrast effects the correction instructions led them to adjust their judgments toward the context. Idiographic methods were used to demonstrate that the magnitude of correction is directly related to the extent of bias that people perceive. Although the authors do not discuss their effects in terms of metacognition, this evidence is clearly supportive of the notion that people hold folk theories concerning social cognition and that these theories have important consequences for actual social cognition. Under some circumstances at least, possessing a theory about the direction and magnitude of social or cognitive bias may allow one to adjust one's own thinking accordingly.

Theories about epistemic authority   Work by Ellis and Kruglanski (1992) demonstrates that people make metacognitive judgments about their own levels of "epistemic authority" (or cognitive expertise) in specific domains. These judgments determine the extent to which people are capable of learning from different kinds of instruction, presumably because they feel that they are either capable or incapable of following the instruction. Students who consider themselves to be relatively expert in the domain of mathematics benefited more from first-hand experiential learning (as opposed to demonstrative teaching) than did students who considered themselves to be relatively inexpert, even after controlling statistically for actual differences in mathematical expertise. The authors conclude that: "Only individuals who trust their ability to impose meaning on the 'experience' – that is, people with sufficient self-ascribed epistemic authority, may be capable of learning from repeated exposure, and of developing confidence that they understand what the situation is all about" (p. 370). Thus, metacognitive beliefs about the credibility and reliability of one's own knowledge have important ramifications for actual learning and performance.

Theories about stigmatized groups and intellectual performance   Examining the cognitive consequences of gender stereotypes, Spencer and Steele (1992) reported that women perform more poorly than men on mathematical tests, but only when they hold stereotypic beliefs about female inferiority with regard to mathematical ability. In fact, merely providing participants with information that males and females perform equally well on a given test has been found to eliminate gender differences on that test. Research by Steele and Aronson (1995) demonstrates that African Americans are vulnerable to racial stereotypes about verbal ability and that consequently they perform more poorly than European Americans under conditions that allow for the stereotype to be used. When the test is described as non-diagnostic of verbal ability, then racial differences disappear. Although the effects of social stereotypes on self-conceptions and cognitive performance have not previously been recognized as metacognitive in nature, evidence from studies by Levy and Langer (1994), Spencer and Steele (1992), and Steele and Aronson (1995) seems to demonstrate that cultural stereotypes influence the metacognitive assumptions that people make about their own cognitive capacities, and these assumptions have strong influences on actual cognitive performances.

Two types of metacognitions: fleeting feelings and enduring theories

In sum, it appears that the assessment of self-knowledge is derived from whatever specific information is perceived as relevant to the task at hand or to the general processes by which knowledge is achieved. Such information may consist of subjective feelings and experiences as well as cultural theories and category-based information about people in certain social groups. Subjective feelings are interpreted in terms of prior cognitive notions that may be momentarily activated in the individual's memory. Such notions may include long-standing beliefs as to how knowledge states are represented in momentary sensations (e.g. that a sense of fluency or familiarity indicates the validity of a hypothesis one was entertaining) or naive theories about the workings of memory (e.g. that one may have better memory for unusual or infrequent events). Metacognitive theories engender expectations about cognitive performance, and these expectations are capable of impacting actual judgments, memories, and intellectual performances through social psychological processes of "expectancy confirmation" or the "self-fulfilling prophecy" (Jones, 1990).

Questions of accuracy in self-knowledge

Social metacognitive phenomena of the type we have been reviewing have an obvious bearing on the accuracy of people's self-perceptions and judgments. To the extent that people's attributions about their momentary states, such as causal explanations pertaining to their mood, are false, any inferences based upon those attributions, such as judgments of global life-satisfaction, are likely to be inaccurate. If, however, correct attributions are made, then the inferences derived from those attributions have a greater likelihood of being accurate.

The interpretation of momentary "givens" in terms of prior metacognitive theories often occurs outside of awareness. This is important because even inchoate senses may be imbued with a strong aura of "epistemic authority" (Ellis & Kruglanski, 1992). In other words, people often accept their own perceptual experiences as unquestionably true. Even in Bem's (1972) self-perception theory, one's behavior is given weight as evidence for one's attitudes only when subjective cues pertaining to one's attitudes, feelings, and experiences are considered to be vague, ambiguous, or otherwise uninterpretable. Nevertheless, "feelings," "sensations," and "experiences" are heavily influenced by interpretive and inferential processes based upon potentially malleable lay theories, and so the metacognitive inferences drawn on the basis of those feelings may often lack veridicality, despite the directness of the subjective experience (Schwarz & Clore, 1983, 1988). In philosophy, this relates to the age-old problem of self-deception (e.g. Martin, 1985).

The question may arise as to when or how often correct attributions are made. On this subject, Jacoby and Kelley (1987) argue that "unconscious memories" such as inchoate feelings of "fluency" may often give rise to false judgments, such as incorrect ascriptions of fame, distorted perceptions of the difficulty of anagrams, and false estimates of levels of background noise. The authors further assert that: "To escape the pervasive effects of unconscious memory, one must consciously remember the past experience, understand its influence in the present task, and possess a good theory to serve as an alternative basis for behavior" (p. 314). The question is whether the "good" or "correct" theory will be accessible at the time of judgment and whether it will be recognized as a more valid interpretation of the subjective state than a possible incorrect interpretation. As Jacoby and Kelley (1987, p. 314) note, such conditions may seldom be met, and for this reason subjective experiences or unconscious memories may often give rise to faulty judgments (see also Banaji & Greenwald, 1995).

The dynamics of self-knowledge

The metacognitive processes whereby momentary feelings or sensations are identified and inferences are drawn from these identifications are highly dynamic. Social psychological research indicates that the extent, directionality, and duration of metacognitive inferences should be affected by the individual's motivation and cognitive capacity. When cognitive capacity or processing motivation are low, metacognitive processes are likely to be limited and early interpretations are likely to be anchored or "fixated" upon. However, when information processing capacity and motivation are high, a number of metacognitive interpretations may be entertained. This multiplicity of conceptions may occasionally produce confusion and undermine the individual's sense of secure knowledge. Thus, recent research suggests that conditions such as time pressure or environmental noise tend to limit a person's cognitive capacity and motivation and consequently reduce the number of interpretative hypotheses that he or she considers, increasing at the same time his or her subjective sense of judgmental confidence. By contrast, conditions that increase a person's capacity or processing motivation not only increase the number of hypotheses generated, but they concomitantly reduce his or her confidence (see Kruglanski & Webster, 1996 for a review). These dynamic features of the process whereby self-knowledge is attained have received little attention in contemporary metacognitive research thus far, and their specific examination must await future work. In circumstances where the knower considers multiple hypotheses and draws on multiple conceptions, it may be of interest to ask how those different sources of information are weighted or integrated in forming the ultimate judgment. This issue has received some attention in research on the estimation of other people's knowledge, considered next.

The metacognitive assessment of others' knowledge

Divining other people's knowledge is essential to functional social interaction. It is a primary basis of interpersonal communication (Clark, 1985; Fussell & Krauss, 1990; Hardin & Higgins, 1996), and it plays a pivotal role in social influence (anticipating what kinds of evidence others may find persuasive), provision of social support (understanding the other person's needs) or group decision making and task performance (deciding whose expertise in a given domain is worthy of following). But how does one go about assessing another persons' knowledge? Research has identified several informational sources that people may use for that purpose. First, people may use their own knowledge or opinions as a basis for making projections about the knowledge of others. Second, people may use "actuarial" knowledge or statistical information about what people in general think or what a specific group of people think about a given topic. Third, people may attend to a given person's individualized reactions to a stimulus. All three of these informational sources have figured in social psychological research on metacognitive assessments of other people's minds.

The metacognitive use of attitudinal projection

A major way in which people determine the attitudes and beliefs of others is by determining their own attitudes and beliefs and making adjustments to these default estimates. In a study of the metacognitive assessments that people make about the extent of other people's general knowledge, Nickerson, Baddeley, and Freeman (1987) directly investigated how estimates of other people's knowledge are influenced by what one knows oneself. Participants in their study answered general knowledge questions, the norms for which were provided by Nelson and Narens (1980). The results supported the notions that people are more likely to impute a piece of knowledge to others if they possess this knowledge themselves than if they do not, and people are likely to overestimate the commonality of their own knowledge. People's estimates of others' knowledge were related to their own confidence ratings, and these relations held whether people gave correct or incorrect responses to the general knowledge questions. Although they do not provide specific data in support of this explanation, Nickerson et al. (1987, p. 257) speculated that "We use our own knowledge as the basis for a default model of what other people know . . . . We then use any awareness that our own knowledge is unusual in specific ways to modify our model of what the typical other person knows."

In many ways, the work by Nickerson et al. (1987) reflects the meta-cognitive incorporation of the social psychological problem of "false consensus" (e.g. Ross, Greene, & House, 1977). In a wide variety of domains, it appears that people exaggerate the commonality of their own attitudes, feelings, and behaviors, probably for a multitude of cognitive and motivational reasons (e.g. Krueger & Clement, 1994; Marks & Miller, 1987). An "egocentric bias" has also been identified by Fussell and Krauss (1991), who found that people's estimates of others' abilities to recognize New York City landmarks were biased in the direction of self-knowledge. A number of research programs, then, suggest that people follow a general metacognitive principle which says, in effect, that it is possible to infer the cognitions of others on the basis of cognitions of the self.

Future research would do well to explore the generality of egocentric biases in the estimation of others' knowledge and to identify potential boundary conditions on their occurrence. For instance, metacognitive projection should be less likely when a person considers himself or herself to be relatively uninformed in a given domain (e.g. Ellis & Kruglanski, 1992). Conversely, it is also possible that projection will occur less when a person considers himself or herself to be uniquely well informed in a given area, because such an advanced level of knowledge may not be seen as representative of others in general. In circumstances such as these, the individual might downplay down his or her own knowledge and focus more on the behaviors of the target individual or on actuarial information about the target individual's category membership.

In determining whether or not to extrapolate from one's own beliefs to the beliefs of others, one presumably considers the overall similarity between oneself and the target other. For instance, an adult may be more likely to be biased in the direction of his or her own knowledge when estimating the likely knowledge of other adults then when estimating the likely knowledge of children. Furthermore, whether the information about others' similarity to oneself will be taken into account may depend on the perceiver's momentary cognitive capacity or motivational state.

In a recent study relevant to these concerns, Richter and Kruglanski (1997) found that individuals high in the need for cognitive closure (Kruglanski & Webster, 1996) tended to encode their communications to others in more idiosyncratic terms, thus apparently exhibiting a stronger egocentric bias than did individuals low on the need for cognitive closure. As a consequence, communications encoded by individuals high in the need for closure were less successfully decoded by their recipients than communications encoded by persons low in cognitive closure, presumably because the former group was unwilling to expend the cognitive effort it might take to consider how the other's perspective might differ from their own. In a similar vein, Webster, Kruglanski & Pattison (1997) found that individuals under high need for closure (whether assessed with the use of a personality instrument or manipulated situationally through the induction of mental fatigue) were less capable of empathizing with dissimilar others than were individuals under low need for closure.

Other motivations, in addition to the need for closure, might also complicate the relation between a person's own knowledge and the perceived knowledge of others. Brewer (1991), for example, theorized that people may be both motivated to be similar to others, hence regard themselves as "normal" as it were, and also unique and outstanding, hence different from others in certain respects. Each of these two incompatible goals may become more salient than the other, depending upon the circumstances. When they are motivated to see themselves as essentially similar to others, people probably overestimate the commonality of their own knowledge to a much stronger degree than when they are motivated to express distinctiveness. Rather than feeling similar to people in general, one might be motivated to feel similar only to particular others, such as the members of a significant social group (e.g. Turner, 1991), as well as dissimilar from particular others, such as members of an antagonistic outgroup. Thus, one might overestimate the degree to which one's political attitudes are common to fellow members of one's political party, and underestimate the degree to which they are shared by the opposition.

Although it is plausible under some circumstances, the assumption that, in estimating other people's knowledge, self-knowledge invariably serves as the "anchor" from which further adjustments are made may also need to be re-examined. Recent theorizing about the anchoring and adjustment process suggests that what serves as the anchor is often a matter of category accessibility (Strack & Hannover, 1996). Accordingly, it is possible to imagine situations in which the initial anchor is something other than one's own knowledge on a given topic. Other potential anchors include statistical base rate information as well as individuating information about the target person, especially if either of these types of information is contextually activated and rendered accessible in a given situation. In short, the extent to which people project their own epistemic attitudes onto others may depend on a variety of motivational and information-processing factors.

The metacognitive use of statistical information

Rather than using self-knowledge as a standard from which other people's beliefs are inferred, perceivers sometimes make use of statistical or "base rate" information (e.g. Borgida & Brekke, 1981). If one holds the categorical expectation, for instance, that most women favor abortion rights, then a person is more likely to predict that an individual woman possesses attitudes that are favorable toward abortion rights. Thus, base rate information could be an important source of knowledge about the thoughts, attitudes, and beliefs of other people.

Several kinds of research suggest that people generally underutilize category-based, actuarial information in the face of even the slightest amount of individuating information (Kahneman & Tversky, 1973). Nevertheless, it has been found that base rate information is taken into account by lay perceivers when it is perceived as specifically relevant to the judgment being rendered (Borgida & Brekke, 1981), when the diagnosticity of the individuating information is diminished in some way (Ginosar & Trope, 1980), or when the categorical information is congruent with the perceiver's information-processing goal or task orientation (Kulik & Taylor, 1981; Trope & Ginosar, 1988). Furthermore, research on social stereotypes demonstrates that category-based information is utilized when it is readily accessible in memory (Kruglanski & Freund, 1983; Jamieson & Zanna, 1989), when the perceiver is highly motivated to achieve cognitive closure (Kruglanski & Webster, 1996), or when the perceiver possesses an especially low degree of accuracy motivation (Fiske & Neuberg, 1990). Under these diverse sets of circumstances, it should be expected that people will rely on actuarial information to draw inferences about the mental states of others.

The metacognitive use of individuating information

Research indicates that, all things being equal, people prefer to use whatever personal or individuating information may be at their disposal when making social judgments about another person (e.g. Kahneman & Tversky, 1973). Thus, dispositional factors tend to carry more weight than situational factors when it comes to social perception (e.g. Jones, 1990). Major branches of social psychology are devoted to studying the processes whereby social perceivers infer the attitudes, thoughts, and feelings of target persons on the basis of behaviors performed by the latter (e.g. Heider, 1958; Jones, Kanouse, Kelley, Nisbett, Valins, & Weiner, 1971). This is a voluminous literature indeed, and we have no intention of summarizing it here. Suffice it to say that the processes whereby people draw (metacognitive) conclusions about the mental states of others has long been a central concern of social psychologists, and this work has an obvious bearing on philosophical and psychological questions pertaining to empathy, intentionality, and potential differences between first person and third person knowledge.

A recent dissertation in this research tradition sheds some light on the intuitive theories that people use for drawing one type of inference about the mental states of another person, namely whether that other person is behaving with intentionality or not (Malle, 1995). This work reveals that people use five major criteria for attributing intentionality to others: (a) the desire for a particular outcome; (b) the belief that a given behavior will lead to the desired outcome; (c) a resulting intention to perform that behavior; (d) the skill or ability to perform the behavior; and (e) awareness of having performed that behavior. Thus, attributions of intentionality involve several different types of metacognitive judgments about the mental states of others, and these judgments seem to be structured hierarchically, such that belief and desire are considered to be necessary for inferring that a person possesses an intention. Only when skill and awareness are added to this intention, however, do people tend to conclude that a particular action was performed intentionally. Obviously, the study of attributions that people make about the intentional states of others requires the integration of several sub-areas of psychology, including social psychological work on attribution, cognitive psychological approaches to the topic of metacognition, and developmental theories of mind and intentionality.

To summarize our review of metacognitive assessments that are made about the thoughts, feelings, and attitudes of other people, we have identified three general types of information on which people rely. In seeking to understand the extent and nature of others' knowledge, people draw on self-knowledge, category-based or actuarial information, and individuating information about the target person. Which of these types of information will be weighted most heavily will depend upon a variety of factors, including relative accessibility in memory, judgments of similarity between oneself and the target person, information-processing capacity, and goal-specific motivations linked to the specific situation.

Comparisons between knowledge about the self and knowledge about others

We have argued that the general social and cognitive processes that drive one's sense of self-knowledge are fundamentally similar to the processes of deriving a sense of other people's knowledge. In both cases, one searches for information that is relevant to the determination of knowledge, and this information may include others' descriptions of their subjective mental states, information about social category membership, as well as implicit assumptions and lay theories that provide norms for how to interpret that information in the context of ascribing knowledge. Furthermore, in cases of self- and other-knowledge, the extent and directionality of information processing in light of implicit assumptions and lay theories may be importantly determined by the momentary cognitive capacity available to the individual, as well as by his or her momentarily activated goals and motivations. Given the putative similarity in process, the major difference between the imputation of own and others' knowledge has to do with informational input. By definition, one cannot "feel," "sense," or directly "experience" the subjective events that are occurring for another person. Without lapsing into solipsism (Wittgenstein, 1980), it is possible to ask, from the standpoint of experimental psychology, whether "access" to subjective information confers an accuracy advantage to knowledge imputed to the self as compared with other people. In other words, are people's estimates of their own thoughts and feelings more accurate than their estimates of the thoughts and feelings of relevant others?

Vesonder and Voss (1985) compared the accuracy of students' predictions concerning their own ability to learn a series of paired associates and other persons' abilities to learn the same paired associates. It was found that predictive accuracy did not differ for judgments of self and other, provided that the judgments of the other's abilities took place after an initial observation period in which the other person was seen attempting to learn the items in question. For items that were successfully recalled during the initial observation period, both actors and observers gave optimistic and generally correct predictions, more so than a control group of participants who did not have information about initial performance. Furthermore, for items that were not recalled successfully in the initial session, even the control group of observers showed significantly above chance accuracy, and they did not significantly differ from the other two groups in the accuracy of their predictions. Under some circumstances, then, metacognitive assessments of other persons' knowledge may be just as accurate as metacognitive assessments of self-knowledge.

Jameson, Nelson, Leonesio, and Narens (1993) investigated the differences between these targets (making self-predictions), observers (making other-predictions after exposure to initial performance), and judges (making other-predictions without exposure to initial performance) in the "feeling-of-knowing" paradigm using knowledge of general information items. Results were that targets predicted more accurately than the observers, who were in turn more accurate than the judges. These differences in accuracy were interpreted as indicating that "cues in the target's observable behavior can enhance accuracy beyond what can be attained using only information that is not specifically related to the target and . . . the target also benefits from information about aspects of his own knowledge that is not available to an observer" (Jameson et al., 1993, p. 334). The findings also replicated those of Vesonder and Voss (1985, Experiment 2), according to which people (judges) without prior knowledge about a target person can predict the latter's performance with accuracy levels above chance, based presumably on a combination of base rate or actuarial estimates and the judges' own knowledge estimates.

Both Vesonder and Voss (1985) and Jameson et al. (1993) interpret their results in terms of self-perception on the parts of the targets (e.g. Bem, 1972). People seem to have remembered and interpreted their own prior performance in the same way that external observers did. In other words, people made the same metacognitive use of the initial performance information, whether that information was self-relevant or not. The predictions of self and other performance were related to three cues derived from prior performance: (a) type of recall failure representing errors of omission versus commission; (b) the latency of omission errors; and (c) their plausibility. Specifically, it was found that commission errors typically led people to make inflated estimates of recall, more so than omission errors, even though commission errors were not more valid predictors of recall than omission errors. With regard to the latency of omission errors, it was found that the more time targets took to respond, the more likely people (both actors and observers) were to predict the occurrence of correct future recall. Estimates of recall were also positively related to the perceived plausibility of the commission errors. Taken as a whole, these findings provide some answers to questions about whether certain types of information, such as direct sensations or other subjective cues available to the self, enjoy an advantage in accuracy over other types of information.

Comparing the predictions of naive judges in the experiments by Vesonder and Voss (1985) and Jameson et al. (1993), it appears that, at least when people do not differ much in terms of prior knowledge, neither subjective sensations nor behavioral observations seem to be superior to general actuarial estimates. It is especially important to point out that even direct sensations may be misleading or misinterpreted. In the Jameson et al. (1993) work, both targets and observers tended to rely (inappropriately) on invalid cues, such as whether a given error was one of commission or omission. As recent work amply demonstrates (e.g. Jacoby et al., 1989; Schwarz & Clore, 1983, 1988), subjective feelings, sensations, and direct experiences are often misinterpreted and give rise to erroneous metacognitive inferences. In short, no single type of information seems to be more accurate overall than other types of information (Kruglanski, 1989; Richter & Kruglanski, 1997). Although people may have "privileged" access to some types of information that are unavailable to observers, this does not ensure that their perceptions of self-knowledge are more accurate than others' perceptions of their knowledge.

Conclusions

In this chapter we have used the methods of social and cognitive psychology to address philosophical and psychological questions about how people come up with metacognitive assessments about their own and others' knowledge of the world. Both classes of metacognitive judgments seem indispensable to human social functioning, and so they are engaged in pervasively and routinely. Although the imputation of self and others' knowledge may seem vastly different from some perspectives, they seem to be mediated by similar general processes in which information (perceived to be) relevant to knowledge imputation is considered and weighted. The extent of such consideration and its consequences is determined by, among other things, motivation, cognitive capacity, and cultural beliefs. The imputation of knowledge to oneself and other persons may indeed differ in terms of the informational sources available for these purposes. In particular, subjective "feelings," "sensations," and so-called "inner experiences" are relevant and accessible only with regard to one's own assessment of knowledge. Because subjective events of this type can be subject to misidentification (or misattribution), however, they do not necessarily confer an accuracy advantage to the assessment of self-knowledge as compared with the assessment of others' knowledge. Ultimately, the accuracy of such metacognitions may depend (in part) upon the accuracy of "folk theories" (Greenwood, 1991) that are used as means of organizing and interpreting the everyday data generated by mental life.

Acknowledgments

Funding for this project was supported by NIMH Grant R01–MH32205 and a Research Scientist Award (K05–MH1075) to Thomas O. Nelson and by NIMH Grant R01–MH52578, NSF Grant SBR–9417422, and a Research Scientist Award (K05–MH01213) to Arie W. Kruglanski. Preparation of the manuscript was assisted by Valerie M. Codd and Maya Gershony.

References

Apter, M.J. (1989). *Reversal theory: Motivation, emotion and personality*. New York: Routledge.

Asch, S.E. (1952). *Social psychology*. Englewood Cliffs, NJ: Prentice-Hall.

Banaji, M.R. & Greenwald, A.G. (1995). Implicit gender stereotyping in judgments of fame. *Journal of Personality and Social Psychology, 68*, 181–198.

Bem, D.J. (1972). Self-perception theory. In L. Berkowitz (Ed.), *Advances in experimental social psychology* (Vol. 6, pp. 1–62). New York: Academic Press.

Borgida, E. & Brekke, N. (1981). The base rate fallacy in attribution and prediction. In J.H. Harvey, W. Ickes, & R.E. Kidd (Eds), *New directions in attribution research* (pp. 63–95). Hillsdale, NJ: Erlbaum.

Brewer, M.B. (1991). The social self: On being the same and different at the same time. *Personality and Social Psychology Bulletin, 17*, 475–482.

Clark, H.H. (1985). Language use and language users. In G. Lindzey & E. Aronson (Eds), *The handbook of social psychology* (Vol. 2, pp. 179–232). New York: Random House.

Clore, G.L. (1992). Cognitive phenomenology: Feelings and the construction of judgment. In L.L. Martin and A. Tesser (Eds), *The construction of social judgments* (pp. 133–163). Hillsdale, NJ: Erlbaum.

Clore, G.L. & Parrott, W.G. (1994). Cognitive feelings and metacognitive judgments. *European Journal of Social Psychology, 24*, 101–115.

Dunlosky, J. & Nelson, O.T. (1994). Does the sensitivity of judgments of learning (JOLs) to the effects of various study activities depend on when the JOLs occur? *Journal of Memory and Language, 33*, 545–565.

Dweck, C.S. (1991). Self-theories and goals: Their role in motivation, personality and development. *Nebraska Symposium on Motivation, 38*, 199–235.

Dweck, C., Hong, Y., & Chiu, C. (1993). Implicit theories: Individual differences in the likelihood and meaning of dispositional inference. *Personality and Social Psychology Bulletin, 19*, 644–656.

Elliott, E.S. & Dweck, C. (1988). Goals: An approach to motivation and achievement. *Journal of Personality and Social Psychology, 54*, 5–12.

Ellis, S. & Kruglanski, A.W. (1992). Self as an epistemic authority: Effects of experiential and instructional learning. *Social Cognition, 10*, 357–375.

Festinger, L. (1950). Informal social communication. *Psychological Review, 57*, 271–282.

Fiske, T.F. & Neuberg, L.S. (1990). A continuum of impression formation, from category based to individuating process: Influences of information and motivation of attention and interpretation. *Advances in Experimental Social Psychology, 23*, 1–74.

Flavell, J.H. (1979). Metacognition and cognitive monitoring: A new area of psychological inquiry. *American Psychologist, 34*, 906–911.

Fussell, S.R. & Krauss, M.K. (1990). The effects of intended audience on message production and comprehension: Reference in a common ground framework. *Journal of Experimental Social Psychology, 25*, 203–219.

Fussell, S.R. & Krauss, R.M. (1991). Accuracy and bias in estimates of others' knowledge. *European Journal of Social Psychology, 21*, 445–454.

Gentner, D. & Collins, A. (1981). Studies of inference from lack of knowledge. *Memory and Cognition, 9*, 434–443.

Ginosar, Z. & Trope, Y. (1980). The effects of base rates and individuating information on judgements about another person. *Journal of Experimental Social Psychology, 16*, 228–242.

Greenwood, J.D. (Ed.) (1991). *The future of folk psychology: Intentionality and cognitive science.* New York: Cambridge University Press.

Hanson, N.R. (1968). *Patterns of discovery.* Cambridge: Cambridge University Press.

Hardin, C. & Higgins, E.T. (1996). Shared reality: How social verification makes the subjective objective. In R.M. Sorrentino & E.T. Higgins (Eds), *Handbook of motivation and cognition: Foundation of social behavior* (pp. 28–84). New York: Guilford.

Hart, J. (1965). Memory and the feeling-of-knowing experience. *Journal of Educational Psychology, 56*, 208–216.

Hasher, L., Goldstein, D., & Toppino, T. (1977). Frequency and the conference of referential validity. *Journal of Verbal Learning and Verbal Behavior, 16*, 107–112.

Heider, F. (1958). *The psychology of interpersonal relations.* New York: John Wiley.

Jacoby, L.L. & Kelley, C.M. (1987). Unconscious influences of memory for a prior event. *Personality and Social Psychology Bulletin, 13*, 314–336.

Jacoby, L.L., Kelley, C., Brown, J., & Jasechko, J. (1989). Becoming famous overnight: Limits on the ability to avoid unconscious influences of the past. *Journal of Personality and Social Psychology, 56*, 326–338.

Jameson, A., Nelson, T.O., Leonesio, R.J., & Narens, L. (1993). The feeling of another person's knowing. *Journal of Memory and Language, 32*, 320–335.

Jamieson, D.W. & Zanna, M.P. (1989). Need for structure in attitude formation and expression. In A. Pratkanis, S. Breckler, & A.G. Greenwald (Eds), *Attitude structure and function.* Hillsdale, NJ: Erlbaum.

Jones, E.E. (1990). *Interpersonal perception.* New York: W.H. Freeman.

Jones, E.E., Kanouse, D.E., Kelley, H.H., Nisbett, R.E., Valins, S., & Weiner, B. (Eds) (1971). *Attribution: Perceiving the causes of behavior.* Morristown, NJ: General Learning Press.

Jones, E.E. & Thibaut, J.W. (1958). Interaction goals as bases of inference in interpersonal perception. In R. Tagiuri & L. Petrullo (Eds), *Person perception and interpersonal behavior* (pp. 151–178). Stanford, CA: Stanford University Press.

Jost, J.T. (1995). Toward a Wittgensteinian social psychology of human development. *Theory & Psychology, 5*, 5–25.

Kahneman, D. & Tversky, A. (1973). On the psychology of prediction. *Psychological Review, 80*, 237–51.

Krueger, J. & Clement, R.W. (1994). The truly false consensus effect: An ineradicable and egocentric bias in social perception. *Journal of Personality and Social Psychology, 67*, 596–610.

Kruglanski, A.W. (1989). The psychology of being "right": The problem of accuracy in social perception and cognition. *Psychological Bulletin, 106*, 395–409.

Kruglanski, A.W. & Freund, T. (1983). Bias and error in human judgment. *European Journal of Social Psychology, 13*, 1–44.

Kruglanski, A.W., Fruend, T., & Bar-Tal, D. (1996). Motivational effects in the mere-exposure paradigm. *European Journal of Social Psychology, 26*, 479–499.

Kruglanski, A.W. & Webster, D.M. (1996). Motivated closing of the mind: "seizing" and "freezing". *Psychological Review, 103*, 263–283.

Kulik, J.A. & Taylor, S.E. (1981). Self-monitoring and the use of consensus information. *Journal of Personality, 49*, 75–84.

Levy, B. & Langer, E. (1994). Aging free from negative stereotypes: Successful memory in China and among the American deaf. *Journal of Personality and Social Psychology, 66*, 989–997.

Malle, B.F. (1995). *Intentionality and explanation: A study in the folk theory of behavior*. PhD thesis, Stanford University.

Mandler, G., Nakamura, Y., & Van Zandt, B.J. (1987). Nonspecific effects of exposure to stimuli that cannot be recognized. *Journal of Experimental Psychology: Learning, Memory, and Cognition, 9*, 544–555.

Marks, G. & Miller, N. (1987). Ten years of research on the false consensus effect: An empirical and theoretical review. *Psychological Bulletin, 102*, 72–90.

Marshall, G.D. & Zimbardo, P.G. (1979). Affective consequences of inadequately explained physiological arousal. *Journal of Personality and Social Psychology, 59*, 281–290.

Martin, M.W. (Ed.) (1985). *Self-deception and self-understanding*. Lawrence: University Press of Kansas.

Metcalfe, J., Schwartz, B.L., & Joaquim, S.G. (1993). The cue-familiarity heuristic in metacognition. *Journal of Experimental Psychology, 19*, 851–861.

Metcalfe, J. & Shimamura, A.P. (Eds) (1994). *Metacognition*. Cambridge, MA: MIT Press.

Nelson, T.O. (1992). *Metacognition: Core readings*. Boston: Allyn & Bacon.

Nelson, T.O., Dunlosky, J., Graf, A., & Narens, L. (1994). Utilization of metacognitive judgements in the allocation of study during multitrial learning. *Psychological Science, 5*, 207–213.

Nelson, T.O., & Narens, L. (1980). Norms of 300 general-information questions: Accuracy of recall, latency of recall, and feeling-of-knowing ratings. *Journal of Verbal Learning and Verbal Behavior, 19*, 338–368.

Nelson, T.O. & Narens, L. (1994). Why investigate metacognition? In J. Metcalfe & A.P. Shimamura (Eds), *Metacognition: Knowing about knowing* (pp. 1–25). Cambridge, MA: MIT Press.

Nickerson, R.S., Baddeley, A., & Freeman, B. (1987). Are people's estimates of what other people know influenced by what they themselves know? *Acta Psychologica, 64*, 245–259.

Richter, L. & Kruglanski, A.W. (1997). "Motivated search for common ground: Need for closure effects on "audience design" in interpersonal communication". Unpublished manuscript, University of Maryland.

Rosenthal, D.M. (Ed.) (1991). *The nature of mind*. New York: Oxford University Press.

Ross, M. (1989). Relation of implicit theories to the construction of personal histories. *Psychological Review, 2*, 341–357.

Ross, M. & Conway, M. (1986). Remembering one's own past: The construction of personal histories. In R.M. Sorrentino & E.T. Higgins (Eds), *Handbook of motivation and cognition* (pp. 122–144). New York: Guilford Press.

Ross, L., Greene, D., & House, P. (1977). The "false consensus effect": An egocentric bias in social perception and attribution processes. *Journal of Experimental Social Psychology, 13*, 279–301.

Schachter, S. & Singer, J.E. (1962). Cognitive, social and physiological determinants of emotional state. *Psychological Review, 69*, 379–399.

Schwarz, N. & Clore, G.L. (1983). Mood, misattribution, and judgments of well-being: Informative and directive functions of affective states. *Journal of Personality and Social Psychology, 45*, 513–523.

Schwarz, N. & Clore, G.L. (1988). How do I feel about it? Informational function of affective states. In K. Fiedler & J.P. Forgas (Eds), *Affect, cognition, and social behavior* (pp. 44–62). Toronto: Hogrefe International.

Sherif, M. (1936). *The psychology of social norms*. New York: Harper & Brothers.

Spencer, S.J. & Steele, C.M. (1992). The effect of stereotype vulnerability on women's math performance. Paper presented at the 100th Annual Convention of the American Psychological Association, Washington, DC.

Steele, S.J. & Aronson, J. (1995). Stereotype threat and the intellectual test performance of African Americans. *Journal of Personality and Social Psychology, 69,* 797–811.

Strack, F. & Bless, H. (1994). Memory for nonoccurrences: Metacognitive and presuppositional strategies. *Journal of Memory and Language, 33,* 203–217.

Strack, F. & Förster, J. (1995). Reporting recollective experiences: Direct access to memory systems? *Psychological Science, 6,* 352–358.

Strack, F. & Hannover, B. (1996). Awareness of influence as a precondition for implementing correctional goals. In P.M. Gollwitzer & J.A. Bargh (Eds), *The psychology of action: Linking motivation and cognition to behavior* (pp. 579–596). New York: Guilford Press.

Trope, Y. (1986). Identification and inferential processes in dispositional attribution. *Psychological Review, 93,* 239–257.

Trope, Y. & Ginosar, Z. (1988). On the use of statistical and non-statistical knowledge: A problem-solving approach. In D. Bar-Tal and A.W. Kruglanski (Eds), *The social psychology of knowledge* (pp. 209–230). Cambridge: Cambridge University Press.

Turner, J.C. (1991). *Social influence.* Milton Keynes: Open University Press.

Vesonder, G.T. & Voss, J.F. (1985). On the ability to predict one's own responses while learning. *Journal of Memory and Language, 24,* 363–376.

Webster, D.M., Kruglanski, A.W., & Pattison, D.A. (1997). Motivated language use in intergroup contexts: Need for closure effects on the linguistic intergroup bias. *Journal of Personality and Social Psychology, 72,* 1122–1131.

Wegener, D.T. and Petty, R.E. (1995). Flexible correction processes in social judgement: The role of naive theories in corrections for perceived bias. *Journal of Personality and Social Psychology, 68,* 36–51.

Wellman, H.M. (1985). The origins of metacognition. In D.L. Forrest-Pressley, G.E. Mackinnon, & T.G. Waller (Eds), *Metacognition, cognition, and human performance* (pp. 1–31). New York: Academic Press.

Wittgenstein, L. (1980). *Remarks on the philosophy of psychology (Vols. I and II).* Chicago: University of Chicago Press.

Zajonc, R.B. (1980). Feeling and thinking: Preferences need no inferences. *American Psychologist, 39,* 151–175.

6

Social Influence on Memory

Herbert Bless and Fritz Strack

In textbooks of social psychology, the concept of social influence is often defined as an effort on the part of one person to change behaviors or attitudes of others (e.g. Baron & Byrne, 1994).[1] This definition, however, includes at least two meanings. On the one hand, social influence may describe the massive effects of pressure towards conformity and obedience; on the other hand, it may refer to the more subtle techniques involved in changing behaviors and attitudes (for overviews, see for example Cialdini, 1992; Eagly & Chaiken, 1993; Turner, 1991). Independent of both the various forms of social influence and of the investigated domains, research has primarily focused on individuals' attitudes, values, beliefs, and behaviors. Such influences, however, have rarely been studied in their effect on memory (for exceptions see e.g. Swann, Giuliano, & Wegner, 1982; Wegner, Erber, & Raymond, 1991).

Of course, individuals' recollections may not always be reliable. That is, people may fail to remember an event although it actually occurred, and they may falsely remember the occurrence of an event. Causes for such distortions have been primarily found in the dynamics of encoding and retrieval (e.g. Baddeley, 1990; Roediger & Craik, 1989; Wingfield & Byrnes, 1981). However, it also seems possible that these phenomena may be caused by social influence, i.e. that through the impact of others, the recollection of previous experiences is distorted. In the present chapter, we focus primarily on this latter aspect and discuss whether due to social influence, individuals may remember or misremember the occurrence of an event. In addition, we suggest a conceptualization of social influences in the domain of memory.

From a social psychological perspective, it seems reasonable to assume that the influence others may exert on memory resembles their influence on behaviors, attitudes, and judgments. Such a social psychological perspective involves a conceptualization of memory which emphasizes the constructive aspect of recall and recognition and recognizes that judgments and inferences play an important role. Such a perspective was first advocated by Frederick Bartlett (1932) whose seminal book *Remembering* had the subtitle *A study in experimental and social psychology*. If we assume that these judgments are molded by social influences, it follows that the same is true for memory.

Research in social psychology suggests that social influence may operate in various forms (see Deutsch & Gerard, 1955). First, others may exert a motivational influence on individuals to comply with the majority due to conformity pressure. This form of social influence applies predominantly to judgments, attitudes, and behaviors that are publicly expressed (Asch, 1952). At least initially, private convictions are less likely to be affected. Second, social influence may take the form of informational influence, particularly when individuals feel uncertain about their own attitudes, values, or behaviors (Sherif, 1935). To achieve confidence in the absence of objective standards, individuals may then rely on information that is explicitly or implicitly provided by others (Festinger, 1954),[2] and this may become apparent both in individuals' public and private convictions.

Assuming that social influences on memory do not hinge on public expression, our conceptualization is primarily based on the informational variant of social influence. In the remainder of this chapter, we first link the informational type of social influence and its basic principles to the mechanisms of memory and suggest that individuals are most susceptible to social influence when they feel uncertain about their memories. We then discuss various variables that may increase or decrease individuals' confidence in the presence or absence of their recollections.

Antecedents of social influence: a general framework

In accordance with the general notion of Festinger's social comparison theory (1954), we assume that individuals are particularly susceptible to social influence if they are not confident in their own judgments of the situation. In order to reduce their uncertainty, individuals will rely on information that is, intentionally or unintentionally, subtly or obviously, provided by others. Shifting these considerations from attitudes, beliefs, or behaviors to memory, the belief that an event has occurred can be treated like an attitude that a person may hold. Social influence on memory should then be most likely to occur when individuals lack confidence in their memorial beliefs.

How can individuals not be confident about their memory? If they have to decide if an event has occurred, individuals' uncertainty may result from the fact that the mere absence of a memory trace is by itself not always diagnostic. Imagine, for example, a person being asked whether yesterday she saw a blue Volkswagen parked in front of her house. This situation parallels experimental settings in which participants working on a recognition test have to decide if a specific stimulus has been previously presented, or not. Let us assume that the individual does not have a recollective experience of a blue Volkswagen, or, in the laboratory setting, that the participant does not find a memory trace for the stimulus in question. This absence of a memory trace may either reflect that the stimulus has not been presented, or alternatively, that the stimulus has been presented but its presentation cannot be remembered. Given this deficient diagnosticity of the absence of a memory trace, additional inferences become necessary. These inferences may either increase or decrease individuals' confidence that the absence of a memory trace does, in fact, imply the non-occurrence of the event. Applying Festinger's (1954) theorizing to memory, we generally assume that when people are not confident that the absence of a memory trace implies the absence of a stimulus, they tend to rely on other people to determine whether or not the stimulus had been presented.

Similar considerations can be applied to the presence of a memory trace which may either imply that event has actually occurred or, alternatively, that the memory trace is due to influences independent of the event. In particular, individuals may confuse the source of their memory trace, and falsely attribute the memory trace to the occurrence of the event rather than to post-event information (e.g. Loftus, Miller, & Burns, 1978; Loftus & Hoffman, 1989), imagining the event (e.g. Anderson, 1984; Johnson & Raye, 1981), or other types of source confusions (for a systematic treatment of this issue, see Johnson & Hasher, 1987). Although the present chapter focuses on the ambivalence of the absence rather than on the presence of a memory trace, we believe the same principles to operate in both situations. If individuals are aware of alternative sources for their recollection, they may be more or less confident that their recollection of an event implies its occurrence. Individuals' uncertainty again opens up the field for social influence. Specifically, we assume that the less confident individuals are that the presence of a recollection experience implies that the stimulus had actually been presented, the more individuals will be susceptible to social influence (Johnson, Hashtroudi, & Lindsay, 1993).

It seems important to point out that applying our considerations to the presence of a recollective experience necessarily requires the possibility of a source confusion. Note that in a standard recognition paradigm source confusion is often rather unlikely. We therefore refrain from relating our assumptions about the presence of a recollective experience to those situations.

Interpreting the absence of a memory trace

So far, we have argued that memory is susceptible to social influence if individuals are not confident that the absence of a recollection experience implies the non-occurrence of an event, and if individuals are not confident where the presence of a recollection experience comes from. Thus, it is essential to identify variables that increase or decrease individuals' confidence in their memory experiences, and to test whether social influence on memory is a function of these variables.

In this section, we discuss a number of potential mediators of social influence on memory, distinguishing between features of the stimulus in question, encoding conditions, retrieval conditions, person attributes, and the impact of individuals' subjective theories about memory processes.

These different aspects share the general notion that individuals can apply their metacognitive knowledge (e.g. Brewer & Treyens, 1981) to determine the implication of a missing recollective experience. On the one hand, metacognitive knowledge may imply that an event should be remembered. In this case, individuals should be rather confident that the lack of a recollective experience provides a sound basis to infer the non-occurrence of the event. On the other hand, metacognitive knowledge may imply that an event may not be remembered. In this case, individuals should feel less confident about the implications of the lack of a recollective experience. Under such circumstances, respondents will either guess or engage in an available alternative inferential strategy. One alternative strategy is to rely on information provided by others, and we hypothesize that individuals' uncertainty should make them more susceptible to social influence.

Metacognitions about memorability: A safeguard against social influence?

Whether or not the lack of a recollective experience is sufficient to infer the non-occurrence of an event may often depend on whether the event is perceptually or categorically distinct. As first demonstrated by Von Restorff (1933), individuals are more likely to recall items that are distinct from other items in a learning list rather than non-distinct items (for other examples see Detterman & Ellis, 1972). If individuals are aware that such "salient" items are more likely to elicit a recollective experience than non-salient items, the salience of an event should influence their confidence regarding whether or not the absence of a recollective experience implies non-occurrence.

Specifically, if the item is held to be highly memorable, individuals should be very confident that the absence of a recollective experience implies non-occurrence. In this case, individuals are unlikely to rely on information provided by others, and should therefore be minimally susceptible to social influence. Individuals face a different situation, however, if they cannot remember an event and have no reason to believe that the event in question is particularly memorable. In this case, they remain uncertain whether the absence of a recollective experience is due to the non-occurrence of the event or due to a failure of remembering the event. We assume that under these circumstances, individuals will engage in an alternative inferential strategy. Because one such strategy could be the reliance on information provided by others, individuals in this situation should be more susceptible to social influence.

Strack and Bless (1994) investigated these considerations by employing a recognition paradigm in which the salience of the items and different degrees of social influence were manipulated. Specifically, participants were presented with 35 black-and-white slides depicting different objects that were photographed in a similar fashion. To manipulate low versus high salience within participants, we presented 30 photographs of tools (e.g. a hammer, a screwdriver, silverware, or kitchen utensils), and, dispersed among these tools, four photographs of non-tools, each of which belonged to a unique category (e.g. a bouquet of flowers, a shoe, a book). It was assumed that the four non-tools would be salient in contrast to the remaining objects (see Taylor & Fiske, 1978; Von Restorff, 1933). All slides were presented long enough to be easily recognized (*c.* 1.04 seconds).

After a short break, participants were provided with a booklet containing a recognition task. Specifically, participants were asked whether or not they had seen a specific object on the slides that had previously been projected. Participants responded with respect to four different types of objects: (1) "salient" distractor items (i.e. non-tools not previously projected); (2) "non-salient" distractors (i.e. tools not previously projected); (3) "salient" targets (i.e. non-tools previously projected); and (4) "non-salient" targets (i.e. tools previously projected).

To manipulate social influence we used an experimental paradigm introduced by E. Loftus (1975), in which participants are provided with information by others by subtly introduced presuppositions. Building on previous research, we assumed that questions with a definite article (e.g. "Did you see the hammer?") implicitly presupposed that this item had, in fact, been presented. In contrast, no presupposition is implied if the same question is asked with the indefinite article (e.g. "Did you see a hammer?"). This manipulation typically resulted in more affirmative responses when the definite article was employed, even if the target had not been presented (for an overview see Loftus, 1979). According to these considerations, for some participants the wording of the question employed the definite article, while for the remaining participants the wording of the question employed the indefinite article. We assumed that the differential impact of the definite versus the indefinite article on participants' recognition judgments would reflect the degree of social influence operating in a recognition situation. Note that this argument implies that the impact of the linguistic form is not due to differential memory distortions (e.g. Loftus & Hoffman, 1989). In line with other theorizing (Dodd & Bradshaw, 1980; Smith & Ellsworth, 1987), the argument implies that more complex inferences are involved that may, for example, be determined by characteristics of the communicator (e.g. his or her credibility or expertise).

The results of this study (Strack & Bless, 1994, Experiment 1) revealed that the recognition of targets was almost perfect under all conditions. Whether the item was salient or not, whether the definite or the indefinite article was used, far more than 90% of the old stimuli were correctly recognized. Thus, social influence in form of a presupposition had little impact on targets independent of their salience.

More important with respect to the lack of a recollective experience, however, are the results obtained for the distractor items. As these items had not been presented, participants were unlikely to have a recollective experience for their presentation. As can be seen in Figure 6.1, for non-salient distractors, the use of the definite article led to a significantly higher

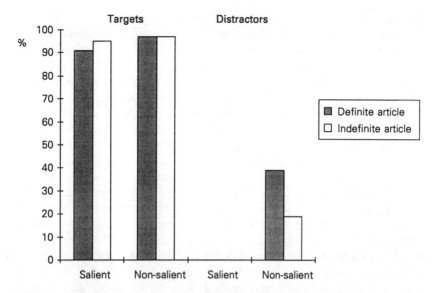

Figure 6.1 *Recognition (percentage of "Yes" responses) for targets and distractors as a function of item salience and presupposition (data from Strack & Bless, 1994, Experiment 1)*

proportion of "yes" responses (38.5%) than the use of the indefinite article (18%), whereas the type of article had no effect for salient distractors. There were absolutely no false alarms for salient distractors.

In sum, these findings suggest that individuals' recognition responses were subject to social influence, and that this influence was mediated by individuals' confidence in the implications of their recollective experiences. In accordance with our assumptions, the impact of the presupposition conveyed by the linguistic cue affected the recognition of non-salient but not of salient items. Given the high subjective memorability of salient items, participants could presumably be very confident that the absence of a recollective experience for these items implied non-occurrence. As a consequence of their confidence, they refrained from applying alternative inference strategies that implied the reliance on information linguistically provided by others. In contrast, given the low subjective memorability of non-salient items, participants were presumably less confident that the absence of a recollective experience for these items implied actual non-occurrence. As a consequence of this uncertainty, participants were more likely to apply alternative inference strategies, and relied on information linguistically provided by others.

Metacognitions on suboptimal encoding conditions: A catalyst for social influence?

While some metacognitions may increase individuals' confidence that their lack of a recollective experience implies non-occurrence, others may decrease this confidence by making alternative explanations for the absence of a memory trace more accessible. One very obvious explanation may, for example, hold that the stimulus in question did not receive sufficient elaboration during encoding (e.g. Craik & Lockhart, 1972). Individuals should therefore be less confident in their (lack of) recollective experiences if they perceive the encoding situations as suboptimal. The decreased confidence should in turn increase the susceptibility to social influence.

To test this hypothesis, we employed the paradigm described above and created conditions under which participants did not have enough time to elaborate on some of the presented items (Strack & Bless, 1994, Experiment 2). For this purpose, 10 tools that were not included in the recognition set were exposed either for only 0.04 seconds in the sub-threshold condition, followed by immediate masking (making recognition virtually impossible) or for 2.04 seconds in the super-threshold condition (making it virtually impossible not to recognize them). The obtained results supported our hypotheses that perceiving the encoding conditions as suboptimal increased individuals' susceptibility to social influence. As can be seen in Figure 6.2a, the recognition of targets was again almost perfect under all conditions. Regardless of whether the item was salient or not, whether the definite or the indefinite article was used or whether some other stimuli were presented suboptimally, far more than 90% of the old stimuli were correctly recognized. Again these results suggest that when participants had a clear recollection of the presentation of the stimulus, they were not susceptible to social influence.

More important with respect to the lack of a recollective experience, however, are again the results obtained for the distractor items. As can be seen in Figure 6.2b, the use of the definite versus indefinite article had no effect on salient distractors, causing not even one false alarm. For non-salient distractors, in contrast, the use of the definite article led to a significantly higher proportion of "yes" responses (52%) than the use of the indefinite article (21%). As expected, the presuppositional effect of the use of the definite article was strongest in the suboptimal condition (67%). Presenting some items suboptimally presumably reduced participants' confidence that the lack of a recollective experience necessarily implied non-occurrence, because they could attribute this lack to the impoverished presentation. As a consequence, participants were more likely to rely on alternative strategies which made them more susceptible to social influence in form of the presupposition.

These conclusions are additionally supported by an examination of participants' confidence in the correctness of their provided answers. After each recognition response, participants were asked to indicate how confident they were about the correctness of their response. As hypothesized, participants were significantly more confident in rejecting salient than non-salient distractors. Moreover, participants' confidence was lower if the short exposure time suggested the possibility that the trace was weakened. Confidence was not affected by these conditions when the test stimuli were

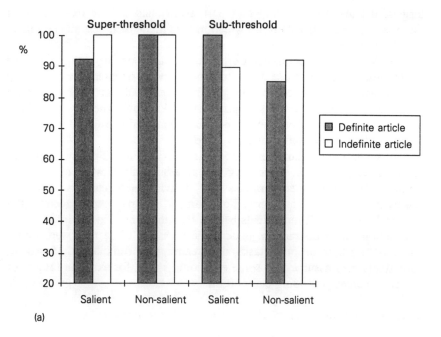

(a)

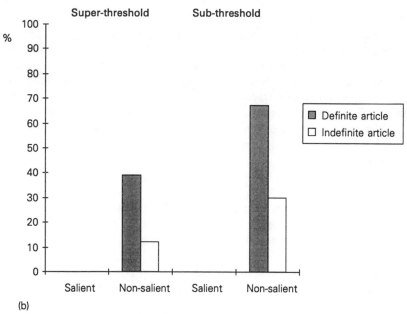

(b)

Figure 6.2   *Recognition for targets and distractors as a function of item salience, presupposition, and perceived encoding conditions (data from Strack & Bless, 1994, Experiment 2)* targets, presumably reflecting that participants had a clear recollection of the presentation of the stimulus, which in turn made them less susceptible to social influence.

Note that these conclusions are primarily based on the results obtained for the distractors. As these distractors were never presented, their encoding was in fact not influenced by the threshold manipulation. The important variable is therefore not a suboptimal encoding but whether individuals perceive the encoding condition to be suboptimal and consider it a potential cause for the absence of a memory trace.

The perception of insufficient elaboration during encoding may, of course, have numerous origins. According to our assumptions, we should obtain similar effects for other variables that individuals perceive as potential causes for suboptimal encoding. For example, we may expect social influence to be stronger if individuals believe that they encoded the information in question under distraction, under time pressure, while they were simultaneously working on other tasks, daydreaming, or ruminating. Moreover, individuals may assume that some emotional states, for example fatigue or anxiety, decrease encoding elaboration.

Metacognitions on suboptimal retrieval encoding conditions

As discussed above, the lack of a recollective experience for an event may either imply its non-occurrence or the prevalence of suboptimal encoding conditions. Suboptimal encoding is, however, not the only alternative to non-occurrence. Individuals may similarly attribute the lack of a recollective experience to suboptimal retrieval conditions. For example, when responding under time pressure, individuals may infer that they would have found an appropriate memory trace had they had the chance to engage in a more extended search. If such a metacognitive insight decreases individuals' confidence that the absence of a memory trace implies non-occurrence, we would expect that these individuals would also be more susceptible to social influence.

Moreover, one might speculate that variables like distraction or anxiety may operate in a similar manner. The relevance of anxiety becomes obvious with respect to students' test anxiety. In the test situation, students may often not remember a specific fact from the learning list, for example from a social psychology textbook. However despite their current lack of recollection, they often claim to know the answer, and that under normal conditions with less anxiety they would have recalled it. Obviously, these considerations must remain speculative and more knowledge bearing on these aspects must be generated.

Individual differences in memory and social influence

Individuals may attribute the lack of a recollective experience not only to situational factors, such as encoding or retrieval conditions, but also to dispositional factors. Obviously, people who believe themselves to have a bad memory should be less confident that the absence of a memory trace implies non-occurrence than people who believe themselves to have an excellent memory. As a consequence of their reduced confidence, these individuals should be more likely to rely on alternative inferential strategies, for example on subtle cues in their environment provided by others. Individuals may chronically assume themselves to have a bad memory, or they may be temporarily less confident in their recollective experiences due to recent failures. As a result, their susceptibility to social influence may be more or less stable across time and situation.

In a related vein, individuals may assume that their memory performance is generally bad, or that they have a bad memory for specific domains. With respect to the latter, individuals may, for example, believe that they can hardly remember names, but that they are good at remembering faces, or vice versa. This perceived domain specificity may make experts and non-experts differentially prone to social influence. For example, experts may assume that they can recall more information from their area of expertise than non-experts. As a consequence, they should be confident that the lack of a recollective experience implies non-occurrence, while non-experts should be more likely to rely on alternative strategies. As a consequence, non-experts should be more susceptible to social influence.[3]

Subjective theories accentuating and minimizing social influence: Anything goes?

In general we assume that individuals' awareness of causes for the lack of their recollective experience, other than the non-occurrence of the stimulus, facilitates social influence. In the examples discussed so far, individuals' assumptions about the operation of memory were generally correct: That is, memory performance is, in fact, better for salient items (Von Restorff, 1933) and it is usually impaired when the information is not processed in depth due to distraction, time pressure, sub-threshold presentation, or individuals' inappropriate levels of arousal (Craik & Lockhart, 1972; for overviews see Baddeley, 1990).

One may easily add numerous variables that have been demonstrated to affect memory performance, such as self-reference (Klein & Kihlstrom, 1986; Rogers, Kuiper, & Kirker, 1977), mood congruity (Bower, 1981), etc. For the present theorizing, however, it is not important whether or not individuals' assumptions about memory processes match actual effects. Individuals only have to believe that their memory is affected by a specific variable. If so, its presence may increase or decrease individuals' confidence in inferring non-occurrence as a function of the subjective theory they hold about this variable. Such theories may be brought to the recognition situation or they may be experimentally induced. In a recent experiment (Foerster & Strack, in press), participants were led to believe that listening to music exerted either a facilitating or an inhibiting effect on their recollection. As a consequence, distractors that belonged to a category of items which were learned while listening to music were more likely to be rejected if participants had been led to believe that music would improve their recollection than by participants who were led to believe that music had a detrimental effect on their memory.

Multiple metacognitions

According to our discussion, numerous variables may influence individuals' attribution of a lack of recollective experience and, as a consequence, individuals' susceptibility to social influence. As a result, more than one influence may operate in a given situation. In this case, the effect of one specific variable depends on its contribution relative to that of other variables. For example, in our study (Strack & Bless, 1994, Experiment 2), salient items were unaffected by the threshold manipulation. In other words, the effect of presenting an item below recognition was overridden by the salience of the item in question. Note, however, that according to our conceptualization, the salience of an item does not necessarily always override other influences. Specifically, we assume that social influence may work also for salient or even highly dramatic events if individuals hold a plausible theory regarding why they do not have a recollective experience for these events. For example, individuals may assume that certain memories are suppressed because these memories are so dramatic. If individuals hold a subjectively plausible theory, social influence may also affect memory of salient and dramatic events.

This latter aspect has received considerable attention in the context of sexual abuse of children that individuals report long after its occurrence. It has been argued that in some cases, the alleged memories of the dramatic events were actively "implanted" by therapists who themselves claim to have recovered the occurrence of a traumatic event in the patient's past (for a discussion see Loftus, 1993). Of course, our approach does not allow an evaluation of the accuracy of these memories. However, in general we believe that memory even of dramatic events may be subject to social influence, and that providing individuals with a plausible theory concerning why they did not have a recollective experience for a long time constitutes a necessary but not a sufficient antecedent of a potential "implantation."

General confidence and self-esteem

All variables discussed so far influencing individuals' reliance on their recollective experiences have been directly linked to memory processes. In addition, we may speculate on general conditions that increase individuals' confidence in their own attitudes, beliefs, behaviors, or recollective experiences, and consequently decrease the susceptibility to social influence. In our view, individuals' self-esteem could constitute a prime candidate for such a general impact. Particularly, we speculate that individuals with chronically or temporarily low self-esteem should be less likely to rely on their own subjective experiences and instead rely on subtle cues in the environment. In contrast, individuals with chronically or temporarily high self-esteem should be more confident in their own subjective experiences. As a consequence, individuals with low self-esteem are expected to be more susceptible to social influence.[4]

Self-esteem may also result from perceiving differential status between questioner and respondent. If so, different aspects of social power may indirectly influence individuals' susceptibility to social influence. Specifically, we may speculate that respondents' confidence in their own recollective experiences decreases as the social status of questioners increases. With respect to interactions between children and adults, we may assume that the younger children are, the less confidence they have in their recollective experiences – presumably reflecting the "expertise" and status of the adult person asking questions. Not surprisingly then, children's suggestibility decreases with their age (for an overview, see Ceci & Bruck, 1993).

Social influence at work

So far, our discussion has focused on various conditions affecting individuals' confidence that their lack of recollections implies non-occurrence. We argued that a reduction in this confidence increases individuals' reliance on information provided by others. After having speculated about the antecedents of social influence on memory, we shall address different aspects of how information is provided. In general we assume that under the specified conditions, any information that individuals perceive as relevant may have the potential to affect individuals' memory judgments. In the reported studies, we emphasized the impact of presuppositions conveyed by subtle linguistic cues when using the definite versus indefinite article.

Presuppositions are, of course, not restricted to the use of the article, but may come in various forms. For example, the question "what make was the car parked in front of the house?" presupposes that there was, in fact, a car at the designated location. Although not being able to recall the make, and although not having a recollective experience for any car, individuals may infer that they saw the car – but simply do not remember. Similarly, a patient being asked by the doctor when a specific symptom ceased to bother her may infer that she did experience this symptom but fails to recall the experience.

Interestingly, one variable may often convey the presupposition and at the same time decrease individuals' confidence in their memory. This dual function becomes evident for example if the same question is asked a second time, after the individual has initially responded that the event in question did not occur. Asking the same question twice may imply that the questioner is not satisfied with individuals' attributing their lack of a recollective experience to the non-occurrence of the event. As a consequence, individuals' confidence in their initial attribution could be diminished. At the same time, restating the same question implicitly presupposes that the event has occurred – otherwise the questioner would have no reason to do so. Support for these considerations is available with respect to the suggestibility of children's testimonies. According to evidence reported by Poole and White (1991) and Moston (1987), children changed their first answer when the interviewer asked the same question a second time (for a related finding in the context of survey responding, see Loftus, Klinger, Smith, & Fiedler, 1990).

To be sure, presuppositions may not always be effective, and individuals' reliance on the information from others is by no means an irresistible automatic mechanism, even if their judgmental confidence is undermined. In particular, if the implied presupposition is questionable, it is unlikely to have a direct effect. For example, Dodd and Bradshaw (1980) found that if a questioner was perceived to be interested in influencing the respondent (e.g. a lawyer in a courtroom), the use of the definite versus the indefinite article had no differential impact on participants' responses. Similarly, Smith and Ellsworth (1987) found that the differential use of the definite versus indefinite article affected witnesses' recall accuracy only if the questioner was assumed to be knowledgeable – and not if he was assumed to be entirely naive – about the events the participants witnessed.

This evidence suggests that if the value of information provided by others is discounted, individuals refrain from using this information and may prefer an alternative inferential strategy if it is applicable. It can be assumed that the more obvious a questioner's self-interest in presupposing some information, the more likely it is that respondents will refrain from using it. Given the present perspective, one may, however, distinguish two aspects. First, the presupposition may be introduced rather obviously. Second, a rather obvious attempt may be made to undermine individuals' confidence in their memory experiences (or the lack of them). We believe that these two aspects may be independent of each other, and that social influence on memory may be particularly sucessful if individuals' confidence in their memory experiences is dramatically undermined while presuppositions are rather subtly introduced.

Interpreting the presence of a memory trace

The present chapter has focused primarily on social influence on memory when individuals lack a recollective experience. We assume that individuals' memory is susceptible to social influence not only in the absence but also in the presence of a memory trace. This is particularly the case if, unlike in the standard recognition paradigm, there exist different sources for a recollective experience (for an overview see Johnson, Hashtroudi, & Lindsay, 1993). For example, a recollective experience may not only be caused by the actual occurrence of the event but by subsequent information (Loftus, 1975), or by merely imagining the event (Johnson & Raye, 1981). If individuals are aware of these alternatives, they may be hesitant to use the presence of a recollective experience to infer that the event occurred under the specified condition. Then, the same principle discussed for the absence of a memory trace may apply for the presence of a memory trace: The less confident individuals are that their recollection implies a specified occurrence, the more they ought to rely on information by others.

We again assume that numerous variables may decrease or increase individuals' reliance on their recollective experience. For example, individuals should be more confident if the event is distinct, and they should therefore be less susceptible to social influence. In contrast, individuals should be less confident, if they hold a subjective theory of how their recollection could be elicited by a similar event, by having only thought of the event, or by having received second-hand information about the event.

The clear presence and the clear absence of a recollective experience are not the only possible experiences. In many cases, individuals may experience something falling in between. For example, despite the lack of a clear recollective experience for the stimulus in question individuals may experience a feeling of familiarity (Jacoby & Dallas, 1981), or have a vague feeling that they know the answer (Koriat, 1995; Koriat, Ben-Zur, & Nussbaum, 1990). In these cases, individuals may not only feel less confident about the implications of their recollection, but about their recollective experience itself, presumably making them even more susceptible to social influence.

Outlook

We have outlined some general considerations about the conditions under which social influence may affect individuals' memory. Specifically, we argued that in many situations, individuals are not confident that the absence of a recollective experience for an event implies the non-occurrence of this event. This reduced confidence about inferences drawn from the lack of a recollective experience conceptually parallels individuals' uncertainty about their attitudes, beliefs, or behaviors. While research has provided substantial evidence that uncertainty in one's own beliefs makes individuals more susceptible to social influence, little empirical or theoretical research is available about the reduced confidence in one's recollective experiences. Adopting previous theorizing from the domain of attitudes and behaviors, the present approach holds that if individuals feel uncertain about the implications of their recollective experiences they are more likely to rely on information provided by others. We identified a number of variables that may increase or decrease individuals' confidence which in turn mediates social influence. For some of these variables we presented evidence supporting our hypothesis, while we could only speculate about the potential impact of other mediators.

Although we could only provide first evidence, for various reasons we believe that the present approach could provide a fruitful framework. First, it directs attention to a widely neglected research area. Second, by applying available research on social influence to attitudes, we were able to derive a number of new and testable hypotheses. Third, and perhaps most importantly, the present conceptualization emphasizes the role of inferences in the domain of memory, which has so far received insufficient attention (for a more extensive discussion see Strack & Bless, 1994).

Acknowledgments

The presented research was supported by grants from the Deutsche Forschungsgemeinschaft (Bl 286/5 to H. Bless, and Str 264/11–1 to Fritz Strack). Address correspondence to Herbert Bless, FB-I, Psychologie, Universität Trier, D-54286 Trier, Germany, e-mail: Bless@uni-trier.de, or to Fritz Strack, Lehrstuhl für Psychologie II, Universität Würzburg, Roentgenring 10, D-97070 Würzburg, Germany, e-mail: strack@psychologie.uni-wuerzburg.de.

Notes

1. Given Schacter and Singer's (1962) work on emotion, it seems legitimate to add emotions to this list, although emotions are hardly found in the "social influence" chapters in social psychology textbooks.

2. Of course, social influence may come in various mixtures of these two ideal forms. Moreover, the presence of others may also influence the level of arousal, and in turn affect performance (Zajonc, 1965). This social facilitation may be considered as an additional variant of social influence.

3. Note that this impact may be overridden by the fact that for non-expert, an item in question may be rather salient.

4. Note that on the surface this assumption differs somewhat from McGuire's (1968) notion of a curvilinear relation between self-esteem and persuasibility.

References

Anderson, R.E. (1984). Did I do it or did I only imagine doing it? *Journal of Experimental Psychology: General, 113*, 594–613.

Asch, S. (1952). *Social psychology*. New York: Prentice-Hall.

Baddeley, A.D. (1990). *Human memory: Theory and practice*. Boston: Allyn & Bacon.

Baron, R.B. & Byrne, D. (1994). *Social psychology. Understanding human interaction* (7th ed.). Boston: Allyn & Bacon.

Bartlett, F.C. (1932). *Remembering: A study in experimental and social psychology*. Cambridge: Cambridge University Press.

Bower, G.H. (1981). Mood and memory. *American Psychologist, 36*, 129–148.

Brewer, W.F. & Treyens, J.C. (1981). Role of schemata in memory for places. *Cognitive Psychology, 13*, 207–230.

Ceci, S.J. & Bruck, M. (1993). Suggestibility of the child witness: A historical review and synthesis. *Psychological Bulletin, 113*, 403–439.

Cialdini, R.B. (1992). *Influence. Science and practice* (3rd ed.) HarperCollins College.

Craik, F.I.M. & Lockhart, R.S. (1972). Levels of processing: A framework for memory research. *Journal of Verbal Learning and Verbal Behavior, 11*, 671–684.

Dettermann, D.K. & Ellis, N.R. (1972). Determinants of induced amnesia in short-term memory. *Journal of Experimental Psychology, 95*, 308–316.

Deutsch, M. & Gerard, H.B. (1955). A study of normative and informational social influence upon individual judgment. *Journal of Abnormal and Social Psychology, 51*, 629–636.

Dodd, D.H. & Bradshaw, J.M. (1980). Leading questions and memory: Pragmatic constraints. *Journal of Verbal Learning and Verbal Behavior, 19*, 695–704.

Eagly, A.H. & Chaiken, S. (1993). *The psychology of attitudes.* Fort Worth: Harcourt Brace Jovanovich.

Festinger, L. (1954). A theory of social comparison processes. *Human Relations, 7*, 117–140.

Foerster, J. & Strack, F. (in press). Subjective theories about encoding may influence recognition. Judgmental regulation in human memory. *Social Cognition.*

Jacoby, L.L. & Dallas, M. (1981). On the relationship between autobiographical memory and perceptional learning. *Journal of Experimental Psychology: General, 110*, 306–340.

Johnson, M.K. & Hasher, L. (1987). Human learning and memory. *Annual Review of Psychology, 38*, 631–686.

Johnson, M.K., Hastroudi, S., & Lindsay, D.S. (1993). Source Monitoring. *Psychological Bulletin, 114*, 3–28.

Johnson, M.K. & Raye, C.L. (1981). Reality monitoring. *Psychological Review, 88*, 67–85.

Klein, S.B. & Kihlstrom, J.F. (1986). Elaboration, organisation and the self-reference effect in memory. *Journal of Experimental Psychology: General, 115*, 26–38.

Koriat, A. (1995). Memory's knowledge of its own knowledge: The accessibility account of the feeling of knowing. In J. Metcalfe & A.P. Shimamura (Eds), *Metacognition. Knowing about knowing.* Cambridge, MA: MIT Press.

Koriat, A., Ben-Zur, H., & Nussbaum, A. (1990). Encoding information for future action: Memory for to-be-performed tasks versus memory for to-be-recalled tasks. *Memory and Cognition, 18*, 568–578.

Loftus, E.F. (1975). Leading questions and the eyewitness report. *Cognitive Psychology, 7*, 560–572.

Loftus, E.F. (1979). *Eyewitness testimony.* Cambridge, MA: Harvard University Press.

Loftus, E.F. (1993). The reality of repressed memories. *American Psychologist*, 518–537.

Loftus, E.F. & Hoffman, H.G. (1989). Misinformation and memory: The creation of new memories. *Journal of Experimental Psychology: General, 118*, 100–104.

Loftus, E.F., Klinger, M.R., Smith, K.D., & Fiedler, J. (1990). A tale of two questions: Benefits of asking more than one question. *Public Opinion Quarterly, 54*, 330–345.

Loftus, E.F., Miller, D.G., & Burns, H.J. (1978). Semantic integration of verbal information into a visual memory. *Journal of Experimental Psychology: Human Learning and Memory, 4*, 19–31.

McGuire, W.J. (1968). Personality and attitude change: An information-processing theory. In A.G. Greenwald, T.C. Brock, & T.M. Ostrom (Eds), *Psychological foundations of attitudes* (pp. 171–196). San Diego, CA: Academic Press.

Moston, S. (1987). The suggestibility of children in interview studies. *Child language, 7*, 67–78.

Poole, D.A. & White, L.T. (1991). Effects of question repetition and retention interval on the eyewitness testimony of children and adults. *Developmental Psychology, 27*, 975–986.

Roediger, H.L., III & Craik, F.I.M. (Eds) (1989). *Varieties of memory and consciousness: Essays in honour of Endel Tulvin.* Hillsdale, NJ: Erlbaum.

Rogers, T.B., Kuiper, N.A., & Kirker, W.S. (1977). Self-reference and the encoding of personal information. *Journal of Personality and Social Psychology, 35*, 677–688.

Schachter, S. & Singer, J.E. (1962). Cognitive, social and physiological determinants of emotional state. *Psychological Review, 69*, 379–399.

Sherif, M. (1935). A study of some social factors in perception. *Archives of Psychology, 2*, 187.

Smith, V.L. & Ellsworth, P.C. (1987). The social psychology of eyewitness accuracy: Misleading questions and communicator expertise. *Journal of Applied Psychology, 72*, 294–300.

Strack, F. & Bless, H. (1994). Memory for non-occurrences: Metacognitive and presuppositional strategies. *Journal of Memory and Language, 33*, 203–217.

Swann, W.B., Giuliano, T., & Wegner, D.M. (1982). Where leading questions can lead: The power of conjecture in social interaction. *Journal of Personality and Social Psychology, 42,* 1025–1035.

Taylor, S.E. & Fiske, S.T. (1978). Salience, attention, and attribution: Top-of-the-head phenomena. In L. Berkowitz (Ed.), *Advances in experimental social psychology* (Vol. 11, pp. 249–288). New York: Academic Press.

Turner, J.C. (1991). *Social influence.* Buckingham: Open University Press; Pacific Grove, CA: Brooks/Cole.

Von Restorff, H. (1933). Über die Wirkung von Bereichsbildungen im Spurenfeld. *Psychologische Forschung, 18,* 299–342.

Wegner, D., Erber, R., & Raymond, P. (1991). Transactive memory in close relationships. *Journal of Personality and Social Psychology, 61,* 923–929.

Wingfield, A. & Byrnes, D.L. (1981). *The psychology of human memory.* New York: Academic Press.

Zajonc, R.B. (1965). Social facilitation. *Science, 149,* 269–274.

7

Beliefs, Confidence and the Widows Ademoski: On Knowing What We Know about Others

William B. Swann Jr and Michael J. Gill

For Irene Ademoski, the shock of learning that her husband of ten years had been found strangled in the trunk of his car was bad enough. Worse yet, the news station had not only failed to contact her prior to broadcasting the grim story, they had even gotten the family's address wrong. When she called the station to complain, the startled manager insisted that he *had* confirmed the address – with a woman who had identified herself as John Ademoski's wife. Mutual accusations ensued, but when the dust finally settled it became clear that the real villain was the deceased: For seven years, John Ademoski had led two parallel lives, one with his first wife and the two children he had sired with her, the other with his second wife and *their* children. Neither wife suspected anything, despite the fact that each of them slept with John for many years, raised his children, and shared numerous life experiences with him.

Most of us find it easy to empathize with the surprise and consternation of the Ademoski widows, for we all have a powerful intuition that we know our relationship partners. In fact, when it comes to lovers, this feeling of mutual understanding and "knowing" is so powerful that we have invented phrases like "soul mate" and "other half" to describe relationships characterized by it.

Despite the pervasive *feeling* that we come to know one another better as relationships progress from casual to intimate, there is little evidence to suggest that this feeling is based on true gains in accuracy. For example, longitudinal studies have shown that if accuracy increases over time at all, after the initial phases of the relationship such gains are minimal (for a review, see Kenny, 1994). Furthermore, evidence from cross-sectional studies that seemingly indicate that acquaintanceship fosters accuracy (e.g. Colvin & Funder, 1991; Funder & Colvin, 1988) may in reality reflect a tendency for people to break off relationships in which inaccuracy reigns; if so, although people in older relationships may enjoy *relatively* high levels of accuracy, their perceptions may be no more accurate than they were when their relationships began. Alternatively, the inherent non-diagnosticity of the small amounts of information available in new relationships may push accuracy *below* levels expected among unacquainted persons (Kenny, 1994); if accuracy later improves to the (quite modest) levels common among unacquainted persons, it may lead to the mistaken impression that accuracy has improved to substantial levels.

The lack of clear evidence that people's perceptions grow increasingly accurate as relationships progress is so surprising because such gains in accuracy seem self-evident to most of us. This state of affairs is also troubling, for insofar as people are blissfully unaware of the accuracy of their impressions, they may grow bullish about beliefs that ought to be treated with a grain of salt. Two studies, for example, indicate that as clinicians acquire information about clients, they believe that their impressions become progressively more accurate *even when* there is no such improvement (Oskamp, 1965; Ryback, 1967). Of course, this evidence does not establish that *everyday person perceivers* will display a similar dissociation between the confidence and accuracy of their impressions. If, for example, clinicians indicate growing confidence in their impressions over time because they sense that perceptions of their expertise are on the line, then everyday person perceivers should display no such shift because they do not feel that they are under scrutiny.

This chapter is devoted to articulating the nature and generality of such dissociations between confidence and accuracy in person perception. To this end, we have developed a conceptual model that articulates one process that may give rise to such dissociations. The concept of *representational richness* lies at the heart of this model.

Confidence, accuracy and representational richness: Investigation 1

We suggest that as people integrate information about their relationship partners into coherent impressions, their representations of those persons become "richer." One way to increase representational richness is by adding novel information. The longer we are acquainted with people, for example, the more information we gather about them and the richer our representations of them become. Representational richness will also increase as our impressions become better integrated and more coherent. As we become more deeply involved with someone, we may carefully organize and integrate what we know about them even though individual elements may be incongruous with one another (e.g. Murray & Holmes, 1993).[1] Whatever the source of increments in representational richness may be, richness will foster accessibility (Bower, 1970; Klein & Loftus, 1991; Sherman & Klein, 1994; Smith, Adams, & Schorr, 1978) and accessibility will, in turn, promote confidence (Koriat, 1993; Kelley & Lindsay, 1993; Nelson & Narens, 1990).

Although representational richness should make people more confident of their perceptions, it will not necessarily contribute to the accuracy of their perceptions. The reason is that *any* information may increase representational richness but only information that is truly diagnostic will foster accuracy (Funder, 1995). Moreover, there is ample evidence that people use non-diagnostic information as a basis for forming impressions of others. For example, people are inclined to infer dispositions from behaviors that are, in reality, constrained by situational factors (e.g. Jones, 1979; Jones & Harris, 1967; Ross, Amabile, & Steinmetz, 1977; Snyder & Jones, 1974), attribute characteristics based on dubious "implicit theories" of personality (Dion, Berscheid, & Walster, 1972; Schneider, 1973), and fail to revise their initial opinions of others even when the evidence suggests they should (Ross, Lepper, & Hubbard, 1975). This tendency to make inferences from *non-diagnostic information* (e.g. category membership, situationally pro-duced behavior, implicit theories of personality), in conjunction with a tendency to use such information as a basis for increasing confidence, could result in people being highly confident of beliefs that are inaccurate and misleading.

To test this conceptualization of confidence and accuracy, we have conducted a series of field and laboratory studies. The first study was an investigation of 57 heterosexual couples aged from 17 to 41 (Swann & Gill, 1997). Participants had been dating from three weeks to just over six years, with an average of one and one-half years.

We arbitrarily designated one member of each couple the perceiver and the other member the target. The task of targets was to rate themselves on a series of four questionnaires, including the Sexual History Questionnaire (SHQ; which includes 10 open-ended questions concerning the respon-dents' past sexual behavior), the Self-Liking/Competence Scale (SLC; a measure of global self-esteem), the Self-Attributes Questionnaire (SAQ; a measure of self-perceived intelligence, social competence, artistic/musical ability, athleticism, and physical attractiveness), and the Activity Preferences Questionnaire (APQ; a measure of enjoyment of 37 leisure activities). While targets rated themselves, perceivers guessed how targets would rate themselves and indicated their confidence that their guesses were correct. Perceivers also estimated how many "hits" they had made (i.e. the number of items on which they had exactly predicted their partner's response).

We tapped representational richness in two ways. First, we measured time in the relationship as a proxy for amount of information. Second, we measured involvement in the relationship as a proxy for motivation to integrate information.

To determine the accuracy of perceivers' knowledge of their partners, we computed separate intraclass correlations (Shrout & Fleiss, 1979) *within each target/perceiver pair* across the items of the SHQ, SLC, SAQ, and the APQ. This statistic measures the extent to which perceivers guessed the self-ratings of targets correctly. Our major prediction was that representational richness would increase confidence but not necessarily accuracy. Regression analyses confirmed that relationship length and involvement were both associated with confidence but had virtually no relation to the accuracy of perceivers' knowledge of their partners' self-ratings. These data supported the idea that representational richness, as gauged by relationship length and involvement, fostered confidence but not accuracy.

To assess directly the relation between confidence and accuracy, we computed two separate statistics. First, we correlated measures of confidence with measures of accuracy. These correlations were tiny and non-significant for three of the four scales, although accuracy and confidence *were* related on the SLC. Second, we compared the number of times perceivers *thought* that they correctly predicted the target's response with the number of times they *actually* predicted the target's response correctly. We discovered that they consistently overestimated the frequency of accurate predictions. In fact, the magnitude of participants' overestimation was striking: perceivers overestimated their success at predicting their partners' responses by 50% on the SHQ (they predicted 6 hits out of 10 when their actual hit rate was 4), 44% on the SLC (they predicted 13 of 20 hits when the actual rate was 9), 60% on the SAQ (they predicted 8 of 15 hits when the actual rate was 5), and 91% on the APQ (they predicted 21 of 37 hits when the actual rate was 11).

In general, then, there was little evidence of close linkages between confidence and accuracy. In addition, confidence ran high while accuracy remained rather modest.

Accuracy of impressions

Although our primary concern was with the relation between confidence and accuracy, we were also interested in the *magnitude of accuracy* among our couples. Alas, one must be cautious in interpreting the magnitude of any given intraclass correlation. One problem is that intraclass correlation coefficients may represent a mixture of several different components of accuracy (e.g. Cronbach, 1955) that may be derived quite differently. For example, a high intraclass correlation may be based on veridical knowledge of the idiosyncratic qualities of a specific target person, such as when Mary correctly infers that Tom is sexually promiscuous upon observing him leer at women. Alternatively, a high correlation may be based on knowledge of the group to which the target person belongs, such as when Mary infers that Tom is promiscuous based on his membership in a fraternity. We refer loosely to this latter form of accuracy as "stereotype accuracy." To distinguish these two components, we used Corsini's (1956) pseudo-couple technique, which involves devising an index of stereotype accuracy by randomly assigning target persons to opposite-sex perceivers and recomputing all correlations. The resulting estimates of stereotype accuracy were lower than the total accuracy scores based on pairing perceivers with their actual relationship partners. Hence, perceivers' impressions represented a combination of stereotype accuracy and accuracy based on idiosyncratic experiences with the partner.[2]

Although it may be fair to say that most perceivers' impressions were at least somewhat accurate, the range of accuracy scores was quite large, including a low of –0.45 and a high of 0.99. There was no evidence for the existence of a group of "accurate perceivers" who consistently made valid inferences about their partners: those who were accurate on one questionnaire were not more likely to be accurate on the other questionnaires. Furthermore, none of the variables we thought might be associated with accuracy – including gender, target self-disclosure, and age – were in fact associated with accuracy.

An important caveat

Although our findings support the notion that representational richness increases confidence but not accuracy, the cross-sectional design we employed is open to a plausible rival hypothesis. If people who were unconfident of their beliefs tended to leave their relationships early, this "differential attrition" would result in relatively high levels of confidence among couples in older relationships – exactly what we found. From this vantage point, people who remained in their relationships might not have grown more confident over time, it was just that they were quite confident of their beliefs to begin with. To test the viability of this rival hypothesis we (Swann & Gill, 1997) conducted a companion study using a longitudinal design. Furthermore, to determine if the confidence/accuracy dissociation would generalize to a distinct group making different judgments, we had a different sample (college roommates) make judgments on a new dimension (i.e. personality traits).

Confidence and accuracy in roommate relationships: Investigation 2

Forty roommates residing in dormitories at the University of Texas at Austin participated. They ranged in age from 17 to 22, with a mean age of 18. None of the roommates knew one another before cohabiting.

During the first week of the semester, participants rated themselves and attempted to predict the self-ratings of their roommates. Participants thus played the role of both perceiver and target.[3] Most of the questionnaires were slightly shortened versions of those completed by the dating couples in Investigation 1. One exception was that we replaced the SHQ with the SAQ-R, a measure that focused on 10 personality characteristics (sense of humor, extroversion, assertiveness, etc.)

In addition to predicting their roommates' self-ratings, participants reported how confident they were that their predictions were correct. To save time, confidence ratings were made once for each of the four questionnaires rather than for each item within each questionnaire. At the end of each questionnaire, participants also estimated the number of items on which they accurately predicted their roommate's response.

We collected these ratings during the first week of the semester and again six weeks later. During the second session participants also answered four questions about their level of involvement in the relationship with their roommate (how much time they spent doing things with their roommate, how many conversations they had, how often these conversations dealt with relatively private issues, and how much they liked their roommate).

Once again, our accuracy measures comprised separate intraclass correlations computed within each target/perceiver pair across the items of the SAQ, SAQ-R, SLC, and APQ. As in the dating couples study, our major prediction was that confidence would increase as a function of representational richness (as gauged by relationship length and involvement), whereas accuracy would not.

Relation of representational richness to confidence and accuracy

As anticipated, relationship length was associated with confidence on the SAQ, the SAQ-R, and the APQ; there was also a weak trend in the predicted direction on the remaining measure, the SLC. This suggests that participants became increasingly confident that they knew their roommates as their representations became richer.

We also expected – and found – that heightened involvement in the relationship was associated with increased confidence on all four measures. Nevertheless, because perceivers made both the involvement and confidence ratings, we worried that response bias might have created an artifactual relation between involvement and confidence. To get an uncontaminated index of the relation between involvement and confidence, we correlated the confidence of perceivers with the involvement ratings of *targets*. Involvement and confidence were still related, suggesting that involvement in the relationship did indeed contribute to the confidence of perceivers.

Having established that both time and involvement were linked to confidence, we went on to ask if either was related to accuracy. For the most part, time was unrelated to accuracy, although there was a slight tendency for accuracy on the SAQ to improve over time. Similarly, there was virtually no relation between involvement and accuracy on the SAQ-R or the SLC and a slight *negative* relation between involvement and accuracy on the SAQ and the APQ. On the latter two measures, then, involvement was associated with increased confidence but *decreased* accuracy. Why? Perhaps involvement encourages perceivers to attend selectively to positive qualities of their partners (Berscheid, Graziano, Monson, & Dermer, 1976) and thus develop representations based on biased samples of information. Consistent with this idea, we found that relationship involvement correlated with the positivity of perceivers' ratings of their roommates.

Our evidence that relationship length and involvement fostered confidence but not accuracy suggests that confidence and accuracy are independent. To evaluate this possibility more directly, we calculated correlations between measures of confidence and accuracy collected both early and late in the semester. Confidence and accuracy were unrelated on the SAQ, the SAQ-R, and the APQ; confidence was associated with higher accuracy on the SLC late but not early in the semester. This replicates the pattern of correlations we found among dating couples, demonstrating once again that people are sensitive to the accuracy of their knowledge of their partners' self-esteem but little else.

As a further index of the relation between confidence and accuracy, we compared the number of times perceivers *thought* that they correctly predicted the target's response with the number of times they *actually* correctly predicted the target's response. These analyses suggested that overconfidence was even higher than it was among dating couples: perceivers overestimated their success at predicting their roommates' responses by 144% on the SAQ, 200% on the SAQ-R, 50% on the SLC, and 100% on the APQ.

Taken together, the results of our studies of dating couples and roommates provide converging evidence that relationship length and involvement foster confidence. Furthermore, the link between time and confidence does not seem to reflect artifactual processes such as a tendency for people who are unconfident to end their relationships. Finally, the fact that relationship length and involvement were associated with increases in confidence but had little impact on accuracy supports our suggestion that confidence grows out of processes that are unrelated to accuracy.

Accuracy of perceivers' impressions

As in the study of dating couples, accuracy among roommates was moderate. Average accuracy on each of our four questionnaires ranged from 0.31 to 0.45 early in the semester and from 0.27 to 0.53 later. Although some people were quite accurate ($r = 0.99$), accuracy on a given questionnaire was unrelated to accuracy on the other questionnaires, thus undermining the idea that there were "accurate perceivers" who were consistently good at inferring their roommates' characteristics. Interestingly, the magnitude of accuracy displayed by roommates often approached the accuracy levels among our dating couples – despite the fact that couples were acquainted for an average of one and one-half years!

We performed analyses of stereotype accuracy paralleling those performed on the responses of dating couples. Total accuracy exceeded stereotype accuracy on every measure except the SLC, suggesting that there was some element of true accuracy in roommates' perceptions of one another.

Impact of amount and integration of information on confidence and accuracy: Investigation 3

As provocative as the results of the foregoing studies may be, they left several issues unresolved. Because we used proxies for representational richness (i.e. relationship length and involvement), we can only infer that richness would influence confidence if manipulated more directly. To remedy this shortcoming, in the next study we (Gill, Swann, & Silvera, 1997) independently manipulated the amount of information received by participants as well as the manner in which they integrated information about a target person.

To manipulate amount of information, we simply varied how much information people received about targets. To manipulate information integration, we told some participants which judgments they would be making about the target. Presumably, knowing which judgments they will be required to make encourages people to integrate information they receive in judgment-relevant ways (Ostrom, Lingle, Pryor, & Geva, 1980). For example, if Joan is asked to "form an impression of the target person's suitability for graduate school," whereas Katherine is asked only to "form an impression of the target person," Joan will be more likely to form an integrated, coherent representation of the target's suitability for graduate school than Katherine. We propose that such coherent, integrated representations will foster greater confidence in judging the target's suitability for graduate school.[4]

To test these ideas, we told participants that they would be watching a videotape in which the target (an opposite-sex stranger) described him or herself. After watching the videotape, participants attempted to predict the target's responses to a sexual history questionnaire as well as a self-concept questionnaire and indicated how confident they were of their predictions.

Participants in the low-information condition listened to the target answer a few background questions only (e.g. hometown, major, career plans); those in the high-information condition listened to this background information and then heard the target describe how he/she would respond to some hypothetical situations (e.g. criticism from a significant other, an invitation to engage in an illegal prank), and reveal his/her attitudes on certain topics (e.g. welfare; the value of "home"). We selected this additional information because it seemed to provide ample fodder for personality inferences about the target.

Participants in the guided-integration condition learned that they would be asked to indicate their impression of the target person's sexual history as well as the target's self-perceived intelligence, social skill, athleticism, artistic ability, and attractiveness. Participants in the unguided-integration condition read only that they would be asked to indicate their impression of the target person.

We expected that: (a) the combination of guided integration and relatively large amounts of information would be especially likely to foster confidence and (b) accuracy would not follow the same pattern of confidence. Planned contrasts supported both of the predictions. On both the SHQ and SAQ, planned contrasts revealed that people in the high-information/guided-integration condition were more confident than the remaining three conditions combined. Accuracy did not differ by condition.

Analyzing our data using a 2 (amount of information: low, high) $\times 2$ (integration: unguided, guided) ANOVA sheds further light on the nature of our confidence effects. When we analyzed SAQ confidence, an interaction between amount of information and nature of integration emerged.

Whereas participants in the guided-integration condition became much more confident when they received high as compared to low information, this difference was smaller in the unguided-integration condition. Apparently, participants in the high-information, guided-integration condition used the additional information they received (i.e. the 15 items) to enrich their representations of the target person's self-concept, whereas participants in the unguided-integration condition enriched their representations of some other aspect of the target. Re-examination of participants' confidence in their sex-history predictions showed a similar, albeit weaker and non-significant, trend.

A full factorial analysis of accuracy corroborated the finding that confidence and accuracy were differentially affected by our manipulation. Examination of the accuracy of sexual-history judgments revealed that participants in the guided-integration condition were slightly *less* accurate than those in the unguided-integration condition. Conceivably, participants in the guided-integration condition based their predictions on what the target said on the videotape (which was non-diagnostic of sexual history), whereas participants in the unguided-integration condition relied on stereotypes and base rates (which may have been somewhat more diagnostic of sexual history). Overall, accuracy on the SHQ was low (average intraclass $r = 0.26$).

Accuracy scores on the SAQ also bore no relation to confidence. Accuracy was moderate (intraclass $r = 0.54$) and was not influenced by the manipulations of amount and integration of information. Somewhat surprisingly, the level of SAQ accuracy among the virtual strangers in this study was quite comparable to that among dating couples who had known one another for an average of one and one-half years.

Gender effects

Males were more confident than females in their ratings of the sexual history of targets. This could be due to a tendency for males to think about sex more than females (Leitenberg & Henning, 1995), and thus to develop relatively rich representations of others' probable or possible sexual histories. This possibility is difficult to evaluate, however, because the sex of perceivers is confounded with the sex of targets, which means that the effect may also be due to a tendency for judgments of female targets to be made more confidently than judgments of male targets. In addition, men's judgments of sexual history were more accurate then women's. This could reflect a tendency for men to be better at inferring targets' sexual histories, or for female targets to be easier to judge than male targets, or for the particular female targets used for this study to be especially easy to judge. The lack of similar gender effects in the study of dating couples favors the third possibility over the first two. In any event, this is one of the few instances in our research in which confidence and accuracy followed in a similar pattern.

In any event, there was no gender effect on confidence ratings on the SAQ, suggesting that men are not uniformly more confident than women in their interpersonal judgments. When we examined the accuracy of judgments on the SAQ we discovered that women were more accurate than men, indicating that the accuracy advantage enjoyed by men on the SHQ was not a general one.

Rival hypotheses

In designing the foregoing study, we realized that our manipulation of amount of information could cause confidence to increase due to *meta-informational cues* – cues that tell someone how informed they are (as compared to cues that contain information relevant to the impression; see Yzerbyt, Schadron, Leyens, & Rocher, 1994, for a discussion of meta-informational cues). From this vantage point, the knowledge that they had received information may have made participants *think* that they ought to be knowledgeable about the target even if they didn't attend to the information, and this belief may have convinced them to indicate relatively high levels of confidence. We included a control condition to address this meta-informational explanation of our data. In this control condition participants received a discounting cue in addition to the manipulation of high information and guided-integration: They were cautioned that the information they would receive might or might not enable them to make accurate judgments of the target. We reasoned that if participants report high levels of confidence merely because meta-informational cues suggest that they should, then this new meta-informational cue should undermine that confidence. In contrast, if participants base their confidence on the richness of their representations of targets, then the discounting cue should not influence confidence (as perceivers will still possess the information). In support of the representational richness explanation we found that the discounting cue had no effect – participants in the discounting-cue condition were just as confident as participants in the identical condition in which no discounting cue was provided. This suggests that meta-informational cues were not responsible for our findings.

We also addressed an ambiguity imposed by our methodology. Whereas in their actual social relationships people attempt to infer what others are *really like*, in our research they sought to infer how participants would answer questionnaires (thus providing a measure of "true" accuracy). To test whether or not our confidence effects would generalize to the types of judgments made in the "real world," we included two additional comparison conditions in which people rated "what the target is really like" rather than "how the target would describe him/herself on questionnaires." In one condition, the procedure was identical to that in the low-information, guided-integration condition; in the other, the procedure was identical to that in the high-information, guided-integration condition. The results paralleled the effects in the original design: The more information participants heard, the more confident they were. Apparently, the tendency for information to foster confidence is not limited to the rather unusual behavior of estimating another person's responses on questionnaires.

The independent contributions of meta-information and representational richness: Investigation 4

Our findings offer converging evidence that information and the manner in which it is integrated can bolster confidence and that this effect is not due to nuances of our methodology or to meta-informational cues. This is not to say, however, that we believe that meta-informational cues play no role in confidence. Rather, we believe that actual information typically contains meta-informational cues (Yzerbyt et al., 1994) and that these cues, in combination with representational richness, exert independent additive effects on confidence. As such, participants receiving meta-informational cues should be more confident than participants who receive no information, and participants receiving *actual* information should be more confident than those who receive only meta-information.

To test these ideas, we (Gill et al., 1997) began by introducing male participants to a study of the impact of "auditory experiences" on impression formation. We told participants that the impressions we form can be affected by things we hear, and that the current study would involve listening to an audiotape and then predicting how a target woman would rate herself on a measure of self-concept and sexual history.

We included three conditions. In the baseline control condition, we told participants that the audiotape contained no information about the target. In the meta-information condition, we told participants that the audiotape contained information about the target when, in reality, it did not. Finally, in the actual-information condition, we correctly informed participants that the audiotape contained information about the target.

The critical manipulation in this study was the nature of the audiotape. Participants in the control condition listened to excerpts from *The prophet* by Kahlil Gibran. Participants in the meta-information condition heard a version of this same tape that was accompanied by quiet, incomprehensible male and female voices in the background. The experimenter encouraged participants to believe that these voices included excerpts from a subliminally presented interview "revealing personality and background information about the target person" and that this information would enter their mind without their awareness (Yzerbyt et al., 1994 have used this procedure effectively in a related context). Finally, participants in the actual-information condition learned that they would hear an interview containing "personality and background information about the target person." They then listened to the target discuss her personality and background. All audiotapes lasted just over three minutes.

Following the audiotapes, participants predicted the target's responses to the Sexual History Questionnaire (SHQ) and the Self-Attributes Questionnaire (SAQ). Participants also indicated how confident they were of each of their predictions. Following completion of these measures, participants completed a thought-listing task as an index of representational richness.

We expected that confidence would be highest among participants in the actual-information condition, as both meta-informational cues and representational richness should contribute to their levels of confidence. Confidence should be somewhat lower in the meta-informational condition and lowest in the no-information control condition. This is exactly what we found. For example, average confidences on the SHQ ratings were 70%, 55%, and 39% for participants in the actual-information, meta-information, and no-information conditions, respectively.

To determine if the meta-informational cue associated with real information was stronger than that associated with subliminal information, we included items asking participants to rate how helpful the auditory experience was in enabling them to form an accurate impression of the target person. Control subjects rated their auditory experience as not at all helpful, whereas participants in both the meta-information and actual information conditions indicated that the tapes were moderately helpful. The fact that participants in the meta-information and informed conditions perceived meta-informational cues as being of equal strength suggests that the difference between these two groups is not due to meta-informational differences between actual and subliminal information. Instead, the information received by participants in the actual-information condition must have produced their confidence.

We measured accuracy by computing intraclass correlations between participants' predictions of the target's questionnaire responses and the target's actual responses. On the SHQ, accuracy did not differ by condition. On the SAQ, meta-information participants were significantly less accurate than controls and informed participants, who did not differ. The fact that accuracy did not vary by condition but confidence did provide further evidence for the dissociation between confidence and accuracy.

As an index of representational richness, we had participants list "everything that comes to your mind when you think about why you rated the female volunteer's sexual history the way you did." We reasoned that participants with relatively rich, and thus accessible, representations should be able to recall more information relevant to their ratings (Bower, 1970; Klein & Loftus, 1991). Participants in the actual-information condition did indeed generate more reasons for their ratings of the target than participants in either of the other two conditions. Indeed, confidence differences between participants in the actual-information and the meta-information conditions disappeared when we covaried this measure of representational richness out of their confidence scores.

The foregoing findings show that representational richness and meta-informational cues make independent contributions to confidence.

Furthermore, the results of our thought-listing measure of representational richness corroborate our claim that relatively rich representations foster confidence.

In combination with the studies described earlier, the results of the foregoing study bolster our conviction that the effects of amount of information are not easily attributable to meta-informational cues. For example, in Investigation 4 actual information had effects on confidence above and beyond the effects of meta-information. And in Investigation 3 actual information made participants more confident even when they were cautioned about its diagnosticity. In the latter case, however, a skeptic could argue that our instructions to form an impression of the target's sexual history and self-concept implicitly suggested to participants that the information we presented to them would enable them to form an accurate impression of these characteristics. To rule out this meta-informational explanation of the results of Investigation 3, we needed a procedure that would cause subjects to integrate information around a particular personality construct without their awareness of doing so.

Unconscious manipulations of information integration: Investigation 5

Research on priming and impression formation (e.g. Bargh & Pietro-monaco, 1982; Higgins, Rholes, & Jones, 1977) suggested a strategy for manipulating the nature of information integration without participants being aware of it. This research suggests that primed personality concepts guide the interpretation of behavior. If so, then priming should cause people to develop relatively rich representations of the target's standing on the primed concept. For example, after being primed with the concept "intelligence," one will (non-consciously) interpret ambiguous behaviors in terms of their relevance to intelligence. As a result, when asked about a target's intelligence, one will have an integrated, coherent judgment available in memory that will be relatively accessible and hence apt to foster confidence.

To test these ideas, a female experimenter escorted participants to a cubicle and explained that they would be participating in two separate experiments. She attributed the somewhat unusual procedure of combining experiments to the fact that each of the two experiments was quite brief – less than 15 minutes – and thus she and another experimenter had agreed to share participants who had signed up for a half-hour of experimental credit.

The experimenter then introduced the first study as "an investigation of the meaning of psychological concepts to non-psychologists." She noted that psychologists are often faulted for defining concepts in overly narrow ways. To determine if this was a problem, she was collecting a sample of definitions from non-psychologists. Later, she planned to identify themes in these definitions and then determine the extent to which psychologists ignored these themes when defining psychological concepts. Participants in the ambition-prime condition received five minutes to define the concept of ambition, whereas participants in the intelligence-prime condition received five minutes to define the concept of intelligence. The experimenter encouraged participants to use examples, to provide multiple definitions, and to keep writing and thinking until they were asked them to stop. After five minutes of writing, the experimenter stopped participants and gave them a bogus debriefing that merely reiterated our cover story.

A second experimenter arrived and escorted participants to a large lab room on a different floor of the psychology building (the different location was designed to maximize the separateness of the "two experiments"). He introduced participants to a study of the accuracy of first impressions in which they would attempt to predict a target person's responses to some personality items after witnessing the target person describe his hypothetical reactions to situations, attitudes, and background. The personality items included artistic ability, ambition, decisiveness, sociability, liberalism, patience, and intelligence. After viewing a videotaped target and completing the personality ratings, participants received a bogus debriefing that reiterated our interest in the "accuracy of first impressions." Next, the experimenter off-handedly presented the participant with an additional questionnaire that asked whether he or she thought that the first experiment had any influence on his or her responses in the second experiment. The few people who answered "yes" were discarded before data analysis, thus ensuring that those whose responses *were* entered into the analysis were not conscious of any relation of the priming manipulation to the impression formation task.

We expected that the priming manipulation would encourage people to integrate information in terms of the primed concept. This should result in a relatively rich representation of the target's standing on that dimension which would, in turn, foster confident ratings on the dimension. Specifically, we predicted that participants in the ambition-prime condition would make more confident ratings of the target's ambition than of the target's intelligence, whereas participants in the intelligence-prime condition would make more confident ratings of the target's intelligence than of the target's ambition.

Just such a pattern of findings emerged. Participants in the ambition-prime condition were more confident in their ratings of the target's ambition than in their ratings of the target's intelligence, whereas participants in the intelligence-prime condition were more confident in their ratings of the target's intelligence than in their ratings of the target's ambition. Furthermore, when we averaged the confidence expressed across all traits other than ambition and intelligence, we found that confidence in the primed concept was greater than this average. Apparently, then, relatively rich representations foster confidence even when people are unaware of the processes that led to such rich representations.

Conclusions and implications

Our data suggest that the confidence of our social perceptions may be unrelated to the accuracy of those perceptions. Whether our participants judged their dating partner, their roommate, or a stranger on a videotape, their feeling that they knew the target person was largely unrelated to the accuracy of their beliefs. We attribute this dissociation to a tendency for people to rely on the richness of their representations when assessing confidence while the diagnosticity of the information on which those judgments are based determines accuracy. In support of this notion, we found that two variables that should theoretically contribute to representational richness – the amount and integration of information underlying beliefs – were indeed related to confidence even when they did not affect accuracy. Moreover, these effects occurred despite a host of variations in the manner in which we operationalized our independent and dependent variables.

Our research also suggests that two distinct forms of information can give rise to confidence. On the one hand, the more actual information we have about someone and the more we integrate that information into a coherent impression, the more confident we become (see Pelham, 1991, for a similar argument). On the other hand, information about information (i.e. meta-information) makes independent contributions to confidence (e.g. Yzerbyt et al., 1994). Disentangling these sources of confidence is often difficult because information about people almost always contains meta-information and meta-information is almost always accompanied by actual information about people. Nevertheless, the two sources of information *can* be disentangled in the laboratory. This means that future researchers should be able to pinpoint the conditions under which confidence grows out of these two distinct sources.

One possible outcome of future research designed to specify the interplay of meta-informational versus informational sources of confidence is that when motivation is low, perceivers base confidence on highly salient, meta-informational cues, but when motivation is higher perceivers base confidence on an analysis of actual information. For example, following a political speech, a disinterested person might confidently characterize a charismatic politician as a "genius" purely on the basis of the charisma conveyed by the politician (a meta-informational cue) whereas a more politically involved person might pay close attention to the politician's arguments and infer intelligence (or lack thereof) from that information. In this sense, there may be parallels between these two sources of confidence and the peripheral versus central routes to persuasion (Petty & Cacioppo, 1986). Just as relatively unmotivated people may be persuaded on the basis of peripheral cues, such as appearance, motivated people tend to travel the central route to persuasion.

When people do acquire actual information, we believe that such information gives rise to confidence by increasing representational richness and accessibility. Either conscious or unconscious mechanisms may mediate the link between representational richness and confidence. The conscious route to confidence presumably involves basing confidence on a consciously generated list of "facts" recruited to support a judgment (e.g. Koriat, Lichtenstein, & Fischoff, 1980), whereas the non-conscious route to confidence involves basing confidence on the accessibility of judgments per se (e.g. Kelley & Lindsay, 1993). In either case, rich representations will produce confidence because they increase the accessibility of "facts" composing a representation (Bower, 1970; Klein & Loftus, 1991), and the accessibility of abstractions (i.e. judgments) gleaned from those facts (Sherman & Klein, 1994). Methodologies are needed that can identify the mechanisms underlying confidence judgments. One possibility is a reaction time methodology that measures the response latency for judgments, the latency for the retrieval of "facts" used to support judgments, and the latency of confidence reports. If judgments and confidence are each reported faster than "facts" are recruited, this suggests that judgments and their associated confidences are not mediated by a conscious review of supporting "facts."

Whether people travel a conscious or non-conscious route to confidence may be determined by motivational factors. For example, in deciding whether a key employee deserves to be terminated, a manager might consciously consider reasons for termination before feeling confident in recommending termination. In contrast, the same manager might feel confident enough to dismiss a custodian based on the ease with which a negative judgment comes to mind. Conceivably, such distinct strategies for gauging confidence grow out of implicit theories which say that consciously reviewing evidence tends to ensure that confidence is well placed (i.e. properly calibrated).

Our evidence of dissociations between confidence and accuracy fits nicely into a growing body of literature suggesting that subjective indicators of knowing are often unreliable indicators of objective knowledge or comprehension (see Jacoby, Bjork, & Kelley, 1994, for a review). For example, people misjudge their comprehension of texts (Glenberg & Epstein, 1985), the correctness of their answers to general knowledge questions (Kelley & Lindsay, 1993), the correctness of recalled letter strings (Koriat, 1993), and the correctness of their eyewitness identifications (Wells & Murray, 1984). Reder and Ritter (1992) have even shown that familiarity with a *question* predicts people's confidence that they know the *answer* better than does familiarity with the answer. Taken as a whole, this literature suggests that what people *think* they know is not always what they *really* know.

A divergence between what we know about others and what we *think* we know may be especially problematic in the age of AIDS. Convinced that they know their partners, many people are relying on this knowledge to keep themselves from becoming infected with the HIV virus:

"When you get to know the person . . . as soon as you begin trusting the person . . . you don't really have to use a condom" . . . . "I knew my partner really well before we had sex, so I didn't have to worry about her sexual history" (Williams et al., 1992, p. 926).

The problem with this strategy of AIDS prevention is that there are good reasons to believe that people may become far more confident of their beliefs than they ought to be. For example, when trying to infer whether or not someone has the HIV virus, people use non-diagnostic cues such as the extent to which people seem familiar (e.g. Swann, Silvera & Proske, 1995). In addition, people seem to be unable to recognize when potential sexual partners are lying to them about their sexual history (Swann et al., 1995). Unable to recognize the non-diagnostic character of the information they receive, people may grow increasingly confident of impressions that are terribly – and tragically – misleading.

And even if overconfidence in their impressions does not lead people to engage in behaviors that place them at risk of premature physical death, it could lead to a type of psychological death. Imagine the profound disorientation and pervasive feelings of betrayal that the Ademoski widows must have suffered when they discovered that their husband had for years maintained a separate wife and family. The psychological turmoil visited upon such victims of deception is especially devastating because they have come to trust their partners so intimately. In these and similar instances, the emotional costs of misplaced confidence may be considerable indeed.

Notes

1. We assume that people form representations of others that are parsed into somewhat separate domains, and that this parsing makes confidence somewhat domain specific. For example, we may have a rich impression of how studious a student is, yet an impoverished representation of his gregariousness. This would result in confident judgments of his studiousness, and a lack of confidence in judgments of his gregariousness. Nevertheless, to the extent that people view domains as related to one another, confidence may carry over from one domain to another.

2. We hasten to add that this technique may underestimate stereotype accuracy because the wide age range of our participants could have led them to entertain different stereotypes (if the stereotypes of 20- vs. 40-year-olds differ and a 20-year-old was randomly paired with a 40-year-old, then our estimate of stereotype accuracy would be artifactually diminished).

3. Interdependency did not affect our analyses, and thus we will not discuss it further.

4. Naturally, people can integrate information subsequent to encoding. However, we feel that such *ex post facto* integration is more effortful than on-line integration and thus would not produce confidence immediately.

References

Bargh, J.A. & Pietromonaco, P. (1982). Automatic information processing and social perception: The influence of trait information presented outside awareness. *Journal of Personality and Social Psychology, 43*, 437–449.

Berscheid, E., Graziano, W., Monson, T., & Dermer, M. (1976). Outcome dependency: Attention, attribution, and attraction. *Journal of Personality and Social Psychology, 34*, 978–989.

Bower, G.H. (1970). Organizational factors in memory. *Cognitive Psychology, 1*, 18–46.

Colvin, C.R. & Funder, D.C. (1991). Predicting personality and behavior: A boundary on the acquaintanceship effect. *Journal of Personality and Social Psychology, 60*, 884–894.

Corsini, R.J. (1956). Understanding and similarity in marriage. *Journal of Abnormal and Social Psychology, 52*, 327–332.

Cronbach, L.J. (1955). Processes affecting scores on "understanding of others" and "assumed similarity." *Psychological Bulletin, 52*, 177–193.

Dion, K.K., Berscheid, E., & Walster, E. (1972). What is beautiful is good. *Journal of Personality and Social Psychology, 24*, 285–290.

Funder, D.C. (1995). On the accuracy of personality judgement: A realistic approach. *Psychological Review, 102*, 652–671.

Funder, D.C. & Colvin, C.R. (1988). Friends and strangers: Acquaintanceship, agreement, and the accuracy of personality judgment. *Journal of Personality and Social Psychology, 55*, 149–158.

Gill, M., Swann, W.B., Jr., & Silvera, D.H. (1997). On the genesis of confidence. Manuscript submitted for publication.

Glenberg, A.M. & Epstein, W. (1985). Calibration of comprehension. *Journal of Experimental Psychology: Learning, Memory, and Cognition, 11*, 702–718.

Higgins, E.T., Rholes, W.S., & Jones, C.R. (1977). Category accessibility and impression formation. *Journal of Experimental Social Psychology, 13*, 141–154.

Jacoby, L.L., Bjork, R.A., & Kelley, C.M. (1994). Illusions of comprehension, competence, and remembering. In D. Druckman & R.A. Bjork (Eds), *Learning, remembering, believing: Enhancing human performance* (pp. 57–80). Washington, DC: National Academy Press.

Jones, E.E. (1979). The rocky road from acts to dispositions. *The American Psychologist, 34*, 107–117.

Jones, E.E. & Harris, V.A. (1967). The attribution of attitudes. *Journal of Experimental Social Psychology, 3*, 1–24.

Kelley, C.M. & Lindsay, D.S. (1993). Remembering mistaken for knowing: Ease of retrieval as a basis for confidence in answers to general knowledge questions. *Journal of Memory and Language, 32*, 1–24.

Kenny, D.A. (1994). *Interpersonal perception: A social relations analysis.* New York: The Guilford Press.

Klein, S.B. & Loftus, J. (1991). Rethinking the role of organization in person memory: An independent trace model. *Journal of Personality and Social Psychology, 59*, 400–410.

Koriat, A. (1993). How do we know that we know? The accessibility model of the feeling of knowing. *Psychological Review, 100*, 609–639.

Koriat, A., Lichtenstein, S., & Fischoff, B. (1980). Reasons for confidence. *Journal of Experimental Psychology: Human Learning and Memory, 6*, 107–118.

Leitenberg, H. & Henning, K. (1995). Sexual fantasy. *Psychological Bulletin, 117*, 469–496.

Murray, S.L. & Holmes, J.G. (1993). Seeing virtues in faults: Negativity and the transformation of interpersonal narratives in close relationships. *Journal of Personality and Social Psychology, 65*, 707–722.

Nelson, T.O. & Narens, L. (1990). Metamemory: A theoretical framework and new findings. In G. Bower (Ed.), *The Psychology of Learning and Motivation* (Vol. 26, pp. 125–173). San Diego, CA: Academic Press.

Oskamp, S. (1965). Overconfidence in case-study judgments. *Journal of Consulting Psychology, 29*, 261–265.

Ostrom, T.M., Lingle, J.H., Pryor, J.B., & Geva, N. (1980). Cognitive organization of person impressions. In R. Hastie, T.M. Ostrom, E.B. Ebbesen, R.S. Wyer, Jr., D. Hamilton, & D.E. Carlston (Eds), *Person memory: The cognitive basis of social perception* (pp. 55–88). Hillsdale, NJ: Erlbaum.

Pelham, B.W. (1991). On confidence and consequence: The certainty and importance of self-knowledge. *Journal of Personality and Social Psychology, 60*, 518–530.

Petty, R.E. & Cacioppo, J.T. (1986). *Communication and persuasion: Central and peripheral routes to persuasion.* New York: Springer-Verlag.

Reder, L.M. & Ritter, F.E. (1992). What determines initial feeling of knowing? Familiarity with question terms, not with the answer. *Journal of Experimental Psychology: Learning, Memory, and Cognition, 18*, 435–451.

Ross, L., Amabile, T.M., & Steinmetz, J.L. (1977). Social roles, social control, and biases in social-perception processes. *Journal of Personality and Social Psychology, 35,* 485–494.

Ross, L., Lepper, M.R., & Hubbard, M. (1975). Perseverance in self-perception and social perception: Biased attribution processes in the debriefing paradigm. *Journal of Personality and Social Psychology, 32,* 880–892.

Ryback, D. (1967). Confidence and accuracy as a function of experience in judgment making in the absence of systematic feedback. *Perceptual and Motor Skills, 24,* 331–334.

Schneider, D.J. (1973). Implicit personality theory: A review. *Psychological Bulletin, 79,* 294–309.

Sherman, J.W. & Klein, S.B. (1994). Development and representation of personality impressions. *Journal of Personality and Social Psychology, 67,* 972–983.

Shrout, P.E. & Fleiss, J.L. (1979). Intraclass correlations: Uses in assessing rater reliability. *Psychological Bulletin, 86,* 420–434.

Smith, E.E., Adams, N.A., & Schorr, D. (1978). Fact retrieval and the paradox of interference. *Cognitive Psychology, 10,* 438–464.

Snyder, M.L. & Jones, E.E. (1974). Attitude attribution when the behavior is constrained. *Journal of Experimental Social Psychology, 10,* 585–600.

Swann, W.B., Jr., Silvera, D.H., & Proske, C.U. (1995). On "knowing your partner": Dangerous illusions in the age of AIDS? *Personal Relationships, 2,* 173–186.

Swann, W.B., Jr. & Gill, M.J. (1997). Confidence and accuracy in person perception: Do we know what we think we know about our relationships partners? *Journal of Personality and Social Psychology, 73,* 747–757.

Wells, G.L. & Murray, S.L. (1984). Eyewitness confidence. In G. Wells & E. Loftus (Eds), *Eyewitness testimony: Psychological perspectives* (pp. 155–170). New York: Cambridge University Press.

Williams, S.S., Kimble, D.L., Covell, N.H., Weiss, L.H., Newton, K.J., Fisher, J.D., & Fisher, W.A. (1992). College students use implicit personality theory instead of safer sex. *Journal of Applied Social Psychology, 22,* 921–933.

Yzerbyt, V.Y., Schadron, G., Leyens, J.P., & Rocher, S. (1994). Social judgeability: The impact of meta-informational cues on the use of stereotypes. *Journal of Personality and Social Psychology, 66,* 48–55.

8

Social Judgeability Concerns in Impression Formation

Vincent Y. Yzerbyt, Benoit Dardenne and
Jacques-Philippe Leyens

Journalist: "You said that this was an emotional verdict. Could you elaborate on that?"
LA District Attorney Gil Garcetti: "Well, it took less than three hours deliberation!"
Broadcast on CNN the day after the acquittal of O.J. Simpson

As the above quotation suggests, a widely shared belief is that sound judgments about people require a substantial amount of time and effort. The general idea is that one should not give too much credit to quick judgments. Of course, because the deliberation about O.J. Simpson will forever remain secret, there is no way to know the information used by the jurors to reach their decision. At first glance, the situation is different when our own judgment is at stake. To the extent that we spend sufficient time and effort, we believe that we are able to assess the validity of our decisions. In other words, we hardly doubt our metacognitive abilities and see ourselves as in the best of positions to appreciate what led us to make a particular judgment. But is the belief that we have access to the sources of our thoughts justified? How do we really know what led us to form a specific impression? And how do we know that our judgment is accurate? In the present chapter, we propose that people often evaluate the validity of their impressions by relying on naive theories about judgment processes.

In the first section, we provide a general overview of the social judgeability model (SJM). We propose that, when people form impressions about others, they check for the trustworthiness of their judgment. This metacognitive exercise aims at bringing the judgment in line with a series of normative standards sedimented in the form of naive theories of judgment. To the extent that current research on person perception embodies a powerful norm concerning social judgment – that perceivers should not make a judgment about a specific target on the sole basis of category-based information – we argue that a similar norm influences people's judgment whenever they evaluate their knowledge about others. However, because perceivers have limited access to the processes underlying a particular impression, a series of irrelevant cues may affect their metacognitive evaluation and create a feeling of confidence. That is, a variety of aspects of the judgmental context are likely to inform perceivers when a particular impression is or is not to be trusted.

In the second section, we test the idea that people are not particularly good at identifying the true sources of their judgment. We provide empirical support showing that perceivers may misinterpret the factors underlying their impression. We show that the subjective availability of individuating information contributes to the expression of (stereotyped) judgments. In the third section, we further examine whether people rely on these rules of judgment for presentational reasons or whether the judgment is truly affected by private beliefs. To this end, we explore the effect of judgeability in a series of settings where social desirability is unlikely to play a role.

In the fourth section, we evaluate the contribution of people's naive theories in the dilution effect. Specifically, we suggest that judgeability effects may contribute to cautious or polarized judgments depending on whether perceivers are more or less aware that their stereotypes influence their ratings. We address alternative accounts of the data in terms of conversational rules. We also detail the unique qualities of the social judgeability model compared to other models of judgment correction.

In the fifth section, we suggest that other well-established findings may be fruitfully examined within the social judgeability framework. We focus on the overattribution bias which corresponds to the fact that people overestimate the causal contribution of dispositional factors and understimate the impact of situational forces. We examine the conditions that may lead perceivers to overlook the situational factors and utter a dispositional judgment. As we show, the mere theoretical adequacy of the judgmental setting can increase observers' feeling of confidence and lead to the expression of a polarized judgment.

In a final section, we suggest that the contribution of naive theories in metacognitive episodes is not restricted to those situations in which perceivers seem to reflect on their judgment after the fact. Instead, implicit rule of judgment construction also exerts an impact on-line and ends up affecting the nature of our judgment in a dramatic way. We provide recent evidence from our laboratory that the mode of information acquisition may also influence impression formation. In other words, whether people actively search for the information or passively receive the data can make a difference at the level of people's subjective confidence.

The social judgeability model

Recent years have witnessed an increased emphasis on the social embeddedness of person perception. Attention has been paid to the pragmatic concerns that could be at work when people are confronted with others (Fiske, 1993; Kunda, 1990). Congruent with this pragmatic trend, the social judgeability model (Leyens, 1993; Leyens, Yzerbyt, & Schadron, 1992,

1994; Schadron & Yzerbyt, 1991; Yzerbyt & Schadron, 1996) tries to improve our understanding of person perception phenomena by taking into account a variety of social factors that influence social judgment.

First, the SJM posits that social judgments are not only constrained by some objective reality supposed to be "out there." Whereas some models of social judgment remain agnostic with regard to the possibility of a true perception of the target people, others tend to make the assumption that a final call can be made. The SJM stresses the inherent flexibility of perception; it acknowledges the fact that people can be appraised in a great variety of ways that are equally "real" (for a related discussion in cognitive psychology, see Medin, 1989; Medin, Goldstone, & Gentner, 1993; Murphy & Medin, 1985). In fact, the degree of adequacy of social perception must be examined in light of the agendas of both the perceivers and the targets (Swann, 1984, 1987).

Because the external reality hardly limits the way people perceive their environment, other concerns need to enter the picture. These additional levels of adequacy, as we call them, limit the possible construals of the target. That is, they are additional ways to impose constraints on people's judgments about others. In addition to the reality level of adequacy, a most important level is the integrity of the personal and social self. The SJM proposes that perceivers make judgments in order to reach desirable conclusions as far as their personal or social identity is concerned (Leyens & Yzerbyt, 1992; Leyens, 1993; Yzerbyt & Castano, 1997; Yzerbyt, Leyens, & Bellour, 1995; see also Kunda, 1990). Clearly, space limitation does not allow us to dwell on this aspect here but a number of theoretical perspectives suggest that social judgments are conditioned by the way they serve the personal (e.g. Swann, 1987) and social (e.g. Tajfel & Turner, 1986) identity.

A third level of adequacy for social judgment and the focus of the present chapter is what we call the normative level. According to the SJM, people like to see their social judgments meet certain socially shared criteria of validity. These criteria can be seen as social norms sanctioning the materials and the processes used to build one's knowledge about others. Interestingly, current models of impression formation give us a hint as to which sources of information should be taken into consideration in order to evaluate others. During the last two decades, researchers have accumulated impressive evidence for the "cognitive miser" view and the idea that categorial information such as stereotypes or schemas ease up the cognitive burden of person perception (for a review, see Fiske & Taylor, 1991). A first stream of evidence comes from research demonstrating an increased reliance on stereotypes when cognitive resources are lacking during impression formation. Researchers have manipulated resource depletion in a number of ways including time allocated to the impression formation task (Kruglanski & Freund, 1983), pace of presentation (Bargh & Thein, 1985; Pratto & Bargh, 1991), task complexity (Bodenhausen & Lichtenstein, 1987), number of target groups (Stangor & Duan, 1991), stimulus set size (Rothbart, Fulero, Jensen, Howard, & Birrel, 1978), distraction by a concurrent task (Gilbert &

Hixon, 1991), arousal during impression formation (Kim & Baron, 1988; Paulhus, Martin, & Murphy, 1992), mood (Bodenhausen, 1993; Hamilton, Stroessner, & Mackie, 1993; Stroessner & Mackie, 1992; Wilder & Shapiro, 1988), and time of day (Bodenhausen, 1990). The message is that perceivers rely on stereotypes to characterize an individual when capacity limitations prevent them from fully examining the available information (Macrae, Hewstone, & Griffiths, 1993). Additional support for the fact that categorial knowledge exerts little pressure on attentional resources comes from priming studies. This line of investigation indicates that the rapidity of processing stereotype-consistent information increases when the stereotype has been activated prior to the presentation of the information (Dovidio, Evans, & Tyler, 1986; Gaertner & McLaughlin, 1983; Macrae, Stangor, & Milne, 1994; Perdue & Gurtman, 1990). More recent work demonstrates the resource-preserving properties of stereotype activation in an even more direct manner. In a series of convincing studies, Macrae, Milne and Bodenhausen (1994) used a dual-task paradigm to show that stereotypes liberate resources that perceivers can then allocate to other activities.

Quite clearly, the two classes of information under consideration in the person perception literature are the specific evidence about the target on the one hand and the prestored knowledge concerning the people belonging to the same category as the target on the other hand. With this distinction in mind, the trend is to adopt a very cautious stand about category-based judgments; they are presented as the default option that is relied upon when cognitive resources are scarce or motivation is lacking. Perceivers are thought to quickly identify the group the target is a member of and to rely on the category-based information even when a consideration of the unique characteristics of the target would be more desirable (for reviews, see Brewer, 1988; Fiske & Neuberg, 1990; Hamilton & Sherman, 1994). In contrast, the ideal impression would be grounded in individuating information. We would like to suggest that the logic of the "official" models embodies and formalizes a widely accepted norm that category-based judgments are less valid than target-based impressions (Yzerbyt & Schadron, 1996). We think that social norms indicate that an impression concerning a specific target should generate a substantial degree of suspicion whenever it is based on category rather than target information. We thus claim that laypeople and person perception researchers share the same social norm. Together with the reality level of adequacy, the integrity and normative levels contribute to shape the inferences perceivers draw about others.

The work developed by Kunda and colleagues (Klein & Kunda, 1992; Kunda, 1990; Kunda, Fong, Sanitioso, & Reber, 1993; Kunda & Sanitioso, 1987) nicely illustrates the way the integrity and the normative levels of adequacy combine with reality to orient judgment. In one study, Klein and Kunda (1992, Experiment 1) showed that, when motivated to hold a particular opinion about a person, people may construct general beliefs justifying their desired view of this person. Participants were induced to view another person as either low or high in ability because he was said to be either their partner or their opponent in a 50-dollar prize game. They were then (allegedly) randomly assigned to the role of questioner in a game and informed that the other person, the answerer, had performed very well on two versus eight questions in a sample quiz. Klein and Kunda's (1992) findings fully support the idea that perceivers do not feel at liberty to believe anything they want about others. Indeed, participants were sensitive to the number of questions answered when they rated the target's ability. They were more impressed by the target's ability and more confident about their evaluation when the target had correctly answered eight rather than two questions. This result demonstrates that participants took the actual evidence into account and were not blindly endorsing their beliefs. However, rather than simply claiming their desired beliefs, participants constructed justifications for them. Compared to those who thought that the target was their partner, participants believing that the other person was their opponent considered that the ability of the target's peers was higher and that luck played a larger role in his successful performance. According to Klein and Kunda (1992, p. 164), "people feel committed to a rational process of belief justification and attempt to rely as best they can on appropriate evidence and rules . . . but their interpretations of the evidence and of the theories they construct are themselves biased by their motives." A critical dimension of social judgment is thus that reality, desired beliefs, and rules of justification combine to shape people's reactions.

In a similar vein, the SJM proposes that perceivers rely on several criteria to evaluate the validity of their judgment. Because the objective level remains largely unconstrained, perceivers are also sensitive to the integrity and normative levels of adequacy in order to express meaningful judgments about others. One key feature affecting the normative level of adequacy, however, is that perceivers are notoriously ill-equipped when it comes to scrutinizing their own cognitive processes (for reviews, see Metcalfe & Shimamura, 1994; Nelson, 1992). In other words, although people are expected to call upon their metacognitive abilities to assess the quality of their knowledge about others, they are not very good at identifying the various ingredients comprising their judgment nor, for that matter, are they good at pinpointing the factors which led them to form a specific impression (Nisbett & Wilson, 1977; Schachter & Singer, 1962). It is our contention that this state of affairs will allow for more diagrammatic information as well as for more formal aspects of the situation to play a role in the metacognitive exercise of evaluating the trustworthiness of judgments. We further unfold this reasoning and provide empirical evidence in the following section.

Impression formation and impression misattribution

Imagine that you interview a candidate for a job as a secretary. Like most people, you may end up asking yourself whether your favorable or unfavorable impression of the person derives from the candidate's intrinsic qualities (a creative mind, a warm personality versus a lack of organization) or from a variety of category-based cues (the candidate is a North African man versus a rather nice-looking female). As we indicated above, current norms of judgment construction indicate that we should expect perceivers to feel comfortable with their impression if it is known to draw upon individuating information. In contrast, people with a similar impression would be very careful if category-based evidence is thought to be the primary basis for their judgment.

There is one difficulty with this reasoning. Indeed, all current perspectives on person perception underline the fact that perceivers are extremely quick at categorizing others on the basis of a minimal amount of information. Categories provide people with a host of information about a specific target. Perceivers are thus likely to know quite a bit about any given person simply because of his or her category membership. The critical question then becomes to determine how exactly people are to interpret the resulting impression. Are perceivers in a position to disentangle the individuating from the category-based pieces of information? The answer seems to be that they are not. In their now classic study, Nisbett and Wilson (1977) suggested that people are quite inefficient at identifying those factors that objectively affected their judgments or behaviors. The message of their provocative review of the literature is that people have little or no direct access to the processes that lead to particular contents of the mind. As a result, naive theories play a major role in people's accounts of why they think what they think or why they do what they do. Building upon this work, we reasoned that social judgment may partly derive from the misattribution of one's stereotypical impression to the available target information.

We (Yzerbyt, Schadron, Leyens, & Rocher, 1994) designed a study in which participants were first provided with category information about a target individual. Half of the participants thought that the target person was a comedian, a profession associated with extroversion, and the remaining participants learned that the target was an archivist, a profession related to introversion. After a minimal presentation of the target via an audiotaped interview, all participants were given a pair of headphones and requested to shadow the voice played in one of the two channels. This dichotic listening task, allegedly used to mimic the cognitive burden of everyday life, was selected because people are unable to monitor the information provided in the unattended channel. At the end of the task, the experimenter informed half of the participants (the "informed" subjects) that they had subliminally received target information via the unattended channel. All subjects were then given a so-called ego-strength scale (ESS) and asked to indicate the target's answers by checking "yes," "no," or "don't know" for each item; most of the items dealt with extroversion and introversion.

According to the SJM, all participants should form an impression about the target on the basis of the category information provided in the first portion of the experiment. Given the normative rules of judgment, we also expected the participants to refrain from judging a specific target on the sole basis of category information. However, to the extent that people are not good at appraising their cognitive processes, the alleged presence of individuating information should allow a misattribution process: the "informed" participants should believe that their impression is grounded on the appropriate kind of evidence. In other words, when perceivers are confronted with diagnostic category information along with illusory target evidence, the resulting impression may be conceived of as one that stems from the individuating information. As a consequence, the final judgment is deemed valid and expressed with some confidence.

In agreement with these predictions, control participants' ratings did not differ as a function of the target's profession. In sharp contrast, the judgments were totally congruent with the stereotypical expectations when the participants thought that they had received individuated information during the shadowing task. This misattribution happened despite the fact that subjects were not able to mention which pieces of information they had received. In a follow-up study (Yzerbyt et al., 1994, Experiment 2), we wanted to evaluate the fact that perceivers needed to believe that they had received target-specific information before they felt entitled to judge. We presented participants with minimal information about a comedian and again told some of them that they had been subliminally confronted with target information. In a third condition, the additional information allegedly concerned the category of comedians as a whole. This third condition provides a stringent test of our hypothesis on several grounds. First, the inclusion of this condition offers a means to check if the instruction about subliminal information simply made the category more salient in the "informed" than in the control condition. It could be that the "informed" participants expressed confident and polarized ratings because they more readily than the control participants activated their categorical knowledge. Second, this condition allows us to examine the conversational impact of the instruction about the presence of subliminal information. Indeed, such an instruction could induce participants to believe that they are expected to judge the target person despite the lack of diagnostic information. In contrast, if they indeed conform to the rule that one should not judge a specific individual on the basis of category information, the participants should clearly refrain from judging the target. As expected, those participants who thought that they had received subliminal information about the category as a whole did not judge the target.

Private beliefs versus impression management

The above studies provide strong empirical support for our hypotheses. Clearly, subjects rely on the rule that one's impression is hardly valid when no individuating information is made available. In sharp contrast, the metacognitive evaluation of their impression leads them to feel comfortable about expressing their views when they think that individuating evidence was made available to them. Importantly, our subjects never received individuating information but were simply led to believe that they had received it. Moreover, they did not feel entitled to judge the target person when they were told that the subliminal information concerned the category the target was a member of. The pattern of data proves encouraging in that it suggests that perceivers asked to judge another person engage in a metacognitive process in which naive theories of judgment of the kind we identified play a role.

The above studies provide convergent evidence that normative rules of judgment are indeed at work when people form impressions about others. In particular, people are reluctant to evaluate another person only on the basis of category information. An important question concerning Yzerbyt et al.'s (1994) findings concerns the extent to which the participants' answers reflect their true impression. The SJM posits that perceivers have internalized a series of widely accepted rules concerning social judgment and that overt responses directly echo the participants' private evaluations. The control condition in which subjects are left uninformed is particularly interesting in this respect. A private belief account holds that these control participants are truly convinced that their impression is ill-founded because it is not based on individuated information. The absence of judgments therefore informs us about the participants' state of knowledge about the target person. An alternative reading of the results might be that control participants do not produce stereotypical answers simply because they are aware that social judgments ought to be grounded on individual information in order to be socially acceptable. In other words, the cautious ratings observed in the control condition could derive from the participants' motivation to appear unprejudiced. The data of the experimental conditions can be interpreted along similar lines. Whereas the private belief perspective stresses the fact that participants only judge the other person because they think it is merited, the impression management account suggests that the stereotypical judgments result from the participants' impression that a judgment is indeed desirable.

To examine the viability of these two alternative interpretations, we again relied on the dichotic listening task paradigm but we introduced one important modification (Yzerbyt, Leyens, & Corneille, in press a). Half of the participants filled in the questionnaire about the target person while being connected to a bogus pipeline apparatus (Jones & Sigall, 1971). This change in procedure allowed us to collect the participants' true impressions about the target. Indeed, research indicates that the bogus pipeline procedure provides one of the best means to eliminate presentational concerns among participants (for a review, see Roese & Jamieson, 1993).

Upon their arrival at the laboratory, all participants were first requested to answer a series of general knowledge questions about their university, allegedly in order to comply with a departmental regulation. This short questionnaire used the same "yes," "no," and "don't know" scale as the

ESS scale and was presented via a computer screen. Unknown to the participants, their answers were directly sent to a remote server. The actual experiment then took place in another laboratory located in a different building. At the end of the dichotic listening task, half of the participants were told that their answers to the ESS scale would be evaluated in light of the information collected by the sophisticated apparatus present in the room. A cover story ensured that participants were totally convinced of the efficacy of the bogus pipeline. Indeed, after the experimenter had connected the participants to the apparatus by way of several electrodes, he presented them with a selection of questions issued from the general knowledge questionnaire answered earlier. The task of the participants was to let the machine guess their true answers. Although the guesses were far from perfect for the first few items, the machine was increasingly correct for the remaining ones and approached a perfect match for the final items. In reality, the machine was reading the participants' answers from the remote server, adding some random noise in the presentation of the initial guesses. All participants, whether they had been confronted with the bogus pipeline or not, were then asked to fill in the ESS scale about the target person.

The private belief interpretation holds that people make a judgment only because it is merited. This means that the difference in social judgment between the informed and uninformed participants should emerge whether or not the participants have been connected to the bogus pipeline apparatus. The impression management view assumes that people do whatever they think is socially acceptable. Because the bogus pipeline forces participants to report their true impression, the difference between informed and uninformed participants observed in the absence of the bogus pipeline should vanish in the presence of the device.

As can be seen in Figure 8.1, our data (Yzerbyt et al., in press a) provide strong support for the private belief interpretation and cannot be accounted for by the presentational view. In line with predictions, the informed participants are more confident and express more stereotypical ratings than the uninformed participants. This pattern emerges whether participants were linked to the bogus pipeline or not. Such a finding shows that, although perceivers are sensitive to a series of naive theories of judgment, their overt answers are much less strategic than may appear at first sight. Interestingly, bogus pipeline perceivers report more stereotypical judgments than the other participants. This additional result indicates that the dichotic listening paradigm is hardly favoring the expression of category-based judgments and further strengthens our social judgeability analysis of earlier findings.

Recent work by Banaji (see Chapter 9 in this volume) bears much resemblance to our demonstration that a variety of cues may lead perceivers to misinterpret the origin of their (stereotyped) impression. In this research, participants are asked to make a judgment of criminality on names that vary in race. Instead of informing some of the participants that subliminal information has been given to them, the experimenter indicates that some of

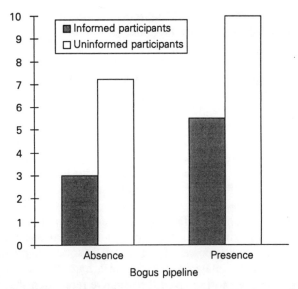

Figure 8.1 *Number of congruent answers (adapted from Yzerbyt et al., in press a, Experiments 1 and 2)*

the names on the list may be familiar because they have appeared in the media as names of criminals. In line with predictions, this simple instruction suffices to produce one and a half more "black" than "white" identifications. More interestingly, participants in the "media" condition are convinced that their evaluation is based on genuine memory of the criminal names. Clearly, the misattribution of the impression to the media coverage leads participants to feel confident about their judgment. As is the case in our own studies, this pattern of findings stresses the difficulty of performing the metacognitive task of evaluating the origin of an impression (see also Greenwald & Banaji, 1995).

Judgeability concerns and the dilution effect

The stereotyping literature is replete with examples of the impact of stereotypic expectations on judgments (Darley & Gross, 1983; Duncan, 1976; Sagar & Schofield, 1980). Other research, however, also reveals that people sometimes disregard category-based information. In a well-known series of studies, Nisbett, Zukier and Lemley (1981) asked their participants to predict the level of electric shock that engineering or music majors would tolerate. Not surprisingly, engineering majors were thought to tolerate more shocks than music majors. This difference vanished, however, when the participants saw a short video excerpt of the target person mentioning name, place of birth and a few other non-diagnostic pieces of information. In other words, the judgments of the target were much less affected by stereotypical knowledge when perceivers received a minimal amount of individuating information. The fact that people are hardly influenced by diagnostic category information has come to be known as the dilution effect. This effect appears when people judge ingroupers as well as outgroupers (Denhaerinck, Leyens, & Yzerbyt, 1989); it is not restricted to judgments but also influences behavior (de Dreu, Yzerbyt, & Leyens, 1995).

Champion among the explanations for the dilution effect is the idea that people face limited intellectual sophistication and rely instead on the representativeness heuristic (Kahneman & Tversky, 1973). Because perceivers have a prototypical representation of the category, provision of trivial information about the target lessens the similarity between this target and the prototypical member of the category. As a result of the reduced similarity, people make less stereotypical judgments (Tversky, 1977). Needless to say, the dilution effect enjoys a more desirable status than other well-established cognitive biases because it stands out as one example of the possibility of escaping the power of stereotypes in social judgments. The fact that perceivers fail to integrate category information when judging individuals may sound reassuring given the negative reputation that stereotypes carry with them. The problem, however, is when this neglect takes place at the expense of the actual informativeness of category-based information.

Given that the dilution effect is a robust phenomenon (Locksley, Borgida, Brekke, & Hepburn, 1980; Locksley, Hepburn, & Ortiz, 1982; Zukier, 1982), it is most intriguing in light of other results in the stereotyping area. For instance, Darley and Gross (1983) found that their participants refrained from judging a target after they had seen a video depicting her in her socio-economic status background. Other subjects expressed stereotypical ratings after they had also seen a second video showing the target person during an intelligence test. What can account for this apparent paradox between a dilution effect, when asked to judge after the first video, and an hypothesis confirmation, when asked to judge after both videos? In our view, social judgeability may prove useful to reconcile these two sets of findings.

A simple analogy between Darley and Gross' (1983) and Nisbett et al.'s (1981) findings may be unwarranted. According to social judgeability theory, the belief that stereotypes unduly influence the impression of a specific individual leads perceivers to withhold their judgment and feel less confident. Conversely, when people believe that individuating information forms the basis of their judgment, they should feel more comfortable at expressing their views. This analysis leads us to distinguish three different situations. The first situation is one in which subjects are requested to produce a judgment about an abstract target person or, more generally, a social group. Quite naturally, stereotypes should emerge because they provide the only relevant information to answer the question. We would argue that Nisbett et al.'s (1981) no-information condition corresponds to such a situation. The second situation happens when perceivers face a specific person and have little or no information to form their judgment. In

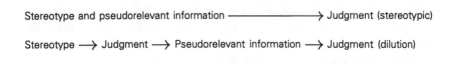

Figure 8.2 *Pseudorelevant information. Design and expected judgment (in parentheses) for the final-judgment-only condition (top) and the two-judgment condition (bottom) (Yzerbyt, Schadron, & Leyens, 1997)*

this case, they should avoid judging along the lines implied by their stereotypes. Indeed, the first video to Darley and Gross' (1983) participants or the short excerpt for Nisbett et al.'s (1981) participants leads perceivers to withhold their judgment. Finally, there is a third situation in which people encounter a real target but receive additional information that looks as if it is relevant. In this case, people should feel entitled to judge and express their impression with some confidence. The two-video condition imagined by Darley and Gross (1983) clearly meets the latter criterion. Not surprisingly, perceivers give stereotypical ratings because they have received no diagnostic information other than a categorical one (Yzerbyt et al., 1994).

The above analysis accounts for a long-standing paradox in the stereotyping literature. Yet, if our a posteriori interpretation is to be taken seriously, it should stand the test of new experimental situations. In a first experiment (Yzerbyt, Schadron, & Leyens, 1997), participants were given pseudorelevant information about a student in business or history and asked to rate his competitiveness and cooperativeness. In line with Hilton and Fein's (1989) distinction, pseudorelevant information is often useful for making trait judgments but irrelevant for the particular judgment at hand. As such, pseudorelevant information should prove most important in providing perceivers with the feeling that they know something about the target person and that their impression is therefore valid. Our key manipulation concerned the presence or absence of a judgment before the participants received the pseudorelevant information (see Figure 8.2). To the extent that an intermediate judgment makes stereotypical knowledge more salient, it should prevent the misattribution of the stereotype-based impression to the pseudorelevant information. In other words, we expected to find diluted ratings in the two-judgment condition and a polarized rating in the final-judgment-only condition because perceivers should be more sensitive to the potential impact of their stereotypical expectations in the former than in the latter condition.

The results fully confirmed our predictions. The judgments in the final-judgment-only condition significantly departed from the scale's midpoint. Moreover, they were not significantly different from a control group in which participants indicated their stereotypic views about the group as a whole. In contrast, the ratings in the two-judgment condition revealed the presence of a dilution effect. In this condition, neither the first nor the second judgment differed significantly from the scale's midpoint. As expected, both were significantly different from the stereotype. In sum, the confrontation with a real target but no individuating information led perceivers to avoid expressing their stereotype in the first judgment; the second judgment remained unchanged in spite of the provision of pseudo-relevant information because participants could not misattribute their stereotype-based impression to the pseudorelevant information.

Our claim that subjects are sensitive to a variety of rules of impression formation leads us to address one potential difficulty. The provision of pseudorelevant information after a first judgment may surreptitiously indicate that subjects ought to stick to their original rating. Fortunately, data from a second experiment (Yzerbyt, Leyens, & Schadron, 1998) do not conform to a conversational interpretation of this kind. In addition to the conversational issue, the other goal of this study was to examine in a more direct manner the conjecture that misattribution facilitates the expression of polarized judgments. To this end, we manipulated the nature of the individuating information.

In a first condition, participants were given category-based information along with pseudorelevant individuating information and asked only a final judgment. We hoped to replicate our earlier findings that people express stereotyped judgments when they think they possess sufficient individuating evidence. Another condition was modeled after our earlier two-judgment situation with one important modification. Indeed, when asked to make a first judgment, these two-judgment participants were given permission to rely on the available category-based information. By doing this, we hoped to bypass standard social judgeability rules and show that the participants were perfectly aware of the relevant stereotype, that is, we expected the first judgment to be stereotypic. We also expected that this modification would have an impact on the second judgment. When given additional pseudo-relevant information about the target, participants should become aware that their stereotype may influence their evaluation. As a result, they should refrain from judging the person. As can be seen in Figure 8.3a, our predictions were totally borne out.

Turning the above conversational interpretation on its head, it is possible to argue that participants first given the permission to use the category and later confronted with the pseudorelevant information may think that pseudorelevant information is entirely worthless but that it was simply provided in order for them to change their stereotypical answer. We see two major problems in this account of our data. For one thing, the assumed lack of relevance of the pseudorelevant information in the two-judgments condition strongly contradicts the evidence accumulated on our pretest subjects and by Hilton and Fein (1989). By definition, pseudorelevant information conveys the feeling that some information has been given about the target. The feeling that a real individual is at stake is thus very likely to emerge when facing that kind of information. For another, and more importantly, the absence of modification of the participants' judgment in

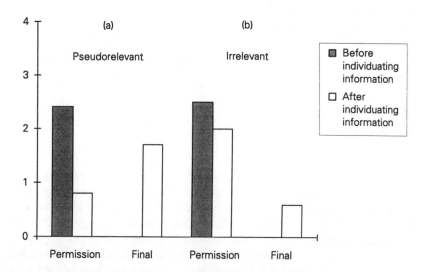

Figure 8.3 *Judgment in the two-judgment and final-judgment only conditions with pseudorelevant and irrelevant information. Scores could range from −4 (not all ambitious) to 4 (very ambitious)*

the two-judgment condition designed by Yzerbyt, Schadron and Leyens (1997) stands in total contradiction to the idea that participants change from a stereotyped to a diluted judgment simply because they think that the experimenter expects them to do so. In conclusion, the fact that participants sometimes did and sometimes did not reproduce their first rating when asked to evaluate the target anew strongly suggests that the lack of impact of the stereotype on the second judgment is the result of people's judgeability concerns.

Our experiment also comprised two additional conditions in which participants received irrelevant rather than pseudorelevant information (see Figure 8.4). According to the social judgeability analysis, participants given category-based and irrelevant individuating information at once should not feel informed about a specific individual. As a consequence, dilution should be found. In sharp contrast, participants asked a first categorical judgment should later remain unaffected by the irrelevant information and keep on expressing polarized ratings. This is because irrelevant information makes explicit that no useful individuating information has been added. Figure 8.3b shows that the predicted pattern was found. These findings reveal the heuristic value of the social judgeability analysis. Not only does the model account for disparate findings in the literature, but a number of new predictions can be tested.

The present findings do not mean that every dilution pattern reported in the literature can be accounted for in social judgeability terms. Different processes can lead to similar results. This is obvious in the case of stereotypic judgments. Clearly, people may end up using their stereotypes because

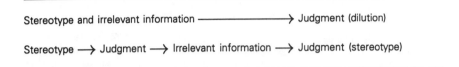

Figure 8.4 *Irrelevant information. Design and expected judgment (in parentheses) for final-judgment-only condition (top) and two-judgment condition (bottom) (Yzerbyt et al., 1998)*

they confirm their hypothesis. Alternatively, perceivers may express stereotypical evaluations because they think that their category-based impression rests on a valid basis, i.e. individuating information. To further complicate matters, several processes can join forces to produce the predicted results. For example, going back to Darley and Gross' (1983) study, both hypothesis confirmation and judgeability rules may have contributed to the formation of impression. We would like to argue that the same situation holds for the dilution effect. In a study by Zukier and Jennings (1984, Experiment 1), participants acted as jurors in a murder trial. Control subjects received diagnostic information indicating guilt, estimated the likelihood that the defendant was guilty, and sentenced him. Other participants received additional non-diagnostic information, i.e. information that was of no help in making the judgment, concerning physical and behavioral characteristics. Whereas in the "typical" condition the defendant was average on a number of dimensions (e.g. "average height and vision"), in the "atypical" condition he was extreme on the same dimensions (e.g. "extremely tall and very good vision"). Only participants confronted with the typical non-diagnostic information diluted their judgments. In line with the classic representativeness interpretation (Tversky, 1977), Zukier and Jennings (1984) argued that typical non-diagnostic information appears inconsistent with an extreme outcome but that atypical non-diagnostic information seems to confirm the likelihood of such an outcome. An alternative interpretation can be formulated within the framework of the social judgeability model. Indeed, a social judgeability analysis suggests that people confronted with atypical information feel better informed about the target and, as a result, express polarized judgments. In contrast, average non-diagnostic information reduces the feeling of being informed and dilution ensues.

Interestingly, there are a number of similarities between the social judgeability model and Martin's (1986) set-reset model (see Martin & Achee, 1992). According to this author, assimilation effects typically observed in priming studies derive from participants' failure to recognize the prior activation of the prime. In other words, to the extent that primes remain in consciousness at the time of judgment, they are used to interpret new information. When participants realize that they have been primed, they seem to "reset" their frame of reference and attempt to partial out the primed information. Admittedly, our participants' reactions in the pseudorelevant conditions (see Figure 8.2) could be interpreted in the context of Martin's (1986) set-reset model. Still, it is less clear how this model could account for the results in the irrelevant conditions (see Figure 8.4). Indeed, participants withheld their judgment when they simultaneously received category and irrelevant information but stuck to their first categorical judgment when the irrelevant information came after the category information. Such a pattern can only be explained by assuming that the participants are sensitive to the very nature of the individuating information, a crucial assumption of the social judgeability model. In the same vein, the ability of the set-reset model to account for our findings can also be questioned on the basis of Yzerbyt, Schadron, and Leyens' (1997) data. Participants in this study received nothing but the category membership before judging a real individual. Because they were not encouraged to rely on their stereotypical knowledge, it is hardly surprising that they conformed to the naive rules of social judgment and diluted their judgments. Contrary to the set-reset model but in line with a social judgeability analysis, participants later provided with pseudorelevant information about the target did not alter their judgment. In conclusion, the social judgeability model seems better able than the set-reset model to handle these various sets of data.

The above results provide convincing evidence that judgeability concerns play a role in the production of dilution effects. However, dilution effects have also been obtained in settings different from the one we used here. For instance, Locksley, Hepburn, and Ortiz (1982) collected beliefs about "night people" and "day people." Three weeks later, one group of participants received only category information about eight individual targets, a second group of participants received both category and non-diagnostic information, and a third group both category and diagnostic information. Dilution occurred when participants received non-diagnostic information despite the fact that the non-diagnostic information very much looked like pseudorelevant information.

A number of recent findings, mostly issued from research on the base rate fallacy, offer a nice way to reconcile Locksley et al.'s (1982) results and our data. Questioning the role of the representativeness heuristic in the production of the base rate fallacy, Gigerenzer (1991) looked at reactions to an uninformative description when participants received no or several other descriptions. He found a striking correlation between the number of descriptions and the mean difference between the answers in the two base rate conditions. More interestingly, Gigerenzer, Hell, and Blank (1988) found that separate analyses on those participants who read several descriptions and encountered the uninformative description first revealed the presence of a strong base rate effect for this description. Along with similar claims about the role of the experimental context on the emergence of the base rate fallacy (Leyens et al., 1994), these findings suggest that the simultaneous presentation of several individuated targets leads participants to differentiate between them. This kind of empirical evidence has obvious implications for

Locksley et al.'s (1982) study. In line with self-categorization theory (Oakes, Haslam, & Turner, 1994), the simultaneous presentation of eight targets who differ only in terms of their category can only make salient the difference between the categories. In contrast, when individuating information is provided, the presentation of eight targets is likely to lead participants to differentiate the targets from one another, resulting in much less discrimination between the two categories (Abele-Brehm, 1996; Gigerenzer, 1991; Leyens et al., 1994).

To sum up, we acknowledge the potential impact of the lack of representativeness of the target in the emergence of dilution effects, but we also suspect that a series of pragmatic and judgeability aspects contributes to produce the specific patterns of data. Clearly, additional research is needed to better understand how various context aspects of the judgmental situation influence the production of social judgments. With this concern in mind, the next section examines the role of naive theories in the emergence of the overattribution bias.

The adequacy of the judgmental context

The overattribution bias (OAB) is one of social psychologists' most cherished patterns of findings (Jones, 1990). Along with the famous Asch paradigm, Milgram's experiments and a few other classic findings, the OAB is a must in any introductory course on social psychology. In addition to being a real winner in the eyes of university teachers, the OAB remains a hotly debated phenomenon in contemporary research circles. Also known as the "fundamental attribution error" (Ross, 1977), the "correspondence bias" (Gilbert & Jones, 1986) or the "observer bias" (Jones & Nisbett, 1972), the OAB corresponds to the fact that observers tend to explain other people's behavior in terms of their intrinsic characteristics and to overlook the impact of situation constraints (Gilbert & Malone, 1995).

The first and perhaps most enlightening experiment illustrating the impact of the overattribution bias is a study by Jones and Harris (1967) in which subjects were asked to read an essay opposing or supporting Castro, the communist Cuban president. In line with Jones and Davis' (1965) correspondent inference theory, subjects who learned that the author had been free to express his own views in the essay simply inferred the presence of corresponding attitudes. In other words, the author who favored Castro was thought to like Castro and the one who opposed Castro in the essay was seen to dislike Castro. More surprisingly, subjects who were told that the author had been forced to advocate the position taken in the essay also inferred the presence of correspondent atttitudes. Although the difference between the favorable and the unfavorable author was less important in the forced-choice than in the free-choice conditions, this pattern is totally at odds with the prediction derived from correspondent inference theory. Indeed, the theory predicts that the absence of choice should logically prevent subjects from making a distinction between the author favoring Castro and the one opposing Castro. Since this seminal study, the OAB has been replicated a great many times and has become a favorite dish on social psychologists' plate (for a review, see Gilbert & Malone, 1995)

From our social judgeability perspective, the attitude attribution paradigm imagined by Jones and Harris (1967) is ideally suited to examine how naive theories affect perceivers' metacognitive work. As we know, participants have every reason to decline the opportunity to judge the target person and, yet, they feel confident enough to make dispositional judgments. What could motivate such a reaction? In our view, the observer's metacognitive work favors the expression of a correspondent judgment partly because the attitude attribution paradigm confronts the observer with a meaningful judgmental setting.

Our analysis builds upon a close inspection of the experimental situation. On the one hand, the whole context stresses a psychological approach to the task (Higgins, 1996; Leyens, Yzerbyt, & Schadron, 1994; Quattrone, 1982; Webster, 1993). Subjects are requested to rely on their interpersonal skills, they are reminded that their role is pretty much like one of a clinician facing a patient, some of the dependent variables involve personality traits, etc. Clearly, thus, the psychological tone of the setting is made very salient. On the other hand, there is little doubt that the attitudinal issues typically used in the attitude attribution paradigm have a strong dispositional tone. In other words, people's position on the issue is probably thought to be dictated by personality factors. Given that subjects see people's views on the specific issue as being determined by their personality and that the judgmental context makes salient the idea that the personality of the author is at stake, there is a strong adequacy between the context and the requested judgment. The question is then: Could such a match play a role in the emergence of the OAB? Could it be that people feel sufficiently entitled to judge because they misinterpret their correspondent inference?

We tested this social judgeability interpretation of Jones and Harris' (1967) well-known attitude attribution paradigm in a series of studies (Leyens, Yzerbyt, & Corneille, 1996). First, we verified that our participants spontaneously accounted for people's opinion about a particular topic, i.e. euthanasia, in terms of their personality whereas they related people's views about an alternative topic, i.e. the closing of the coal mines in the UK, to their social background. We then proceeded to show, and found, that when participants confronted someone who had been forced to write an essay against the legalization of euthanasia, they made a correspondent inference if the context of the study stressed the idea of personality but not if the context emphasized the idea of social background. Conversely, participants overattributed an essay about the closing of coal mines to its author when the context of judgment focused on social background but not when it underlined the idea of personality. For both topics, a control condition stressing neither personality nor social background also failed to produce the classic fundamental attribution error. Clearly, perceivers did not systematically fall prey to the OAB. Instead, they proved to be very sensitive to the theoretical relevance of the target behavior and of their own judgment. Perceivers felt entitled to judge only when the context of their judgment was meaningfully related to the behavior of the target.

The above results are most intriguing in light of current social psychological wisdom. Although many theoretical models address the OAB and all of them display some unique features, it is still possible to distinguish two broad categories of explanation. According to the sequential views, the OAB emerges because perceivers rely on the anchoring-adjustment heuristic (Tversky & Kahneman, 1974). More specifically, sequential views propose that people spontaneously explain an event in terms of the characteristics of the author (the dispositional anchor) and then adjust this first inference by taking into account competing information (the situational adjustment) (Jones, 1979). Presumably, the OAB is the consequence of insufficient adjustment. Strong support for this anchor-adjustment process comes from data showing that motivation reduces the bias (Tetlock, 1985; Webster, 1993; Yost & Weary, 1996). Other studies reveal instead that a shortage of cognitive resources increases the bias (Gilbert, 1989; Gilbert, Pelham, & Krull, 1988; Gilbert & Silvera, 1996). The observation that perceivers may sometimes end up making erroneous situational attributions provided that they start out with a situational anchor offers yet another demonstration of the insufficient adjustment process (Krull, 1993; Quattrone, 1982; Webster, 1993). In sum, the sequential views hold that a better job could be performed if perceivers were to examine the information more closely.

Instead of explaining the OAB by looking at perceivers' cognitive limitations, a second group of explanations celebrates the work people undergo to give meaning to the judgmental setting. These conversational approaches suggest that the OAB paradigm very much urges participants to express a judgment about the author of the essay. Indeed, to the extent that participants are sensitive to the rules of conversation and assume that the experimenter, like them, conforms to these rules (Grice, 1975), they must take the essay to be a valid piece of information and the atttitudinal question to be a legitimate question. In other words, the paradigm entails implicit pressures to rely on the characteristics of the essay to judge the author (Miller & Rorer, 1982; Miller, Schmidt, Meyer, & Collela, 1984; Wright & Wells, 1988). In line with such a conversational analysis, participants do refrain from making an OAB when they receive no information about the author of the essay (Ajzen, Dalto, & Blyth, 1979), when the information that they receive appears completely irrelevant with regard to the author's behavior (Miller & Lawson, 1989), or when they are warned that they may not have the right information to make a judgment (Wright & Wells, 1988).

Both the sequential views and the conversational approaches offer useful insight as to why the OAB may emerge. Interestingly, however, the results presented by one line of research are not easily cast in terms of the alternative framework. For instance, if motivated perceivers are indeed expected to make better sense of the available information than less motivated perceivers, a conversational theorist would probably predict more and not less bias among the former participants. Conversely, the sequential view is ill-equipped to account for the impact of a number of conversational manipulations. More importantly for our purpose, both perspectives are silent as to what would happen when no essay at all is given to the participants. This means that Leyens et al.'s (1996) findings presented above can simply not be accounted for in strict sequential or conversational terms. Only our judgeability analysis of the experimental situation provides a satisfactory explanation of the results. Indeed, whether perceivers did or did not face an adequate judgmental context was clearly a critical factor in the emergence of a correspondent inference.

One interesting way to test the viability of the judgeability interpretation is to show that Leyens et al.'s (1996) participants make a dispositional inference because they rely on the adequacy of the judgmental context as a ready-made indicator of the validity of their inference. Should perceivers be more motivated, they would realize that they received no real information about the target and would refrain from making dispositional inferences. This prediction was tested in a follow-up study (Corneille, Leyens, & Yzerbyt, 1996, Experiment 1). As before, we did not distribute any essay. We told half of the participants that a student had taken part in an experiment in psychology. The remaining participants learned that the experiment concerned sociology. To manipulate the topic, we informed half of the participants that the essay dealt with euthanasia. The other participants were told that the essay was about the closing of mines in the UK. In other words, we activated an adequate context in two of the four conditions. In each condition, half of the participants were made accountable by being told that they would have to explain their answers to the head of research. Earlier work indicates that this kind of accountability instruction is quite successful in motivating the participants to carefully process the information (Tetlock, 1983, 1985). Our prediction was straightforward. On a very general basis, we expected that the adequacy of the judgmental context would lead our subjects to feel entitled to judge the target. This is exactly what we found. More important, the predicted three-way interaction confirmed that the impact of adequacy on the emergence of dispositional inferences was observed only for our non-motivated participants. When made accountable, perceivers did not seem to be happy with the mere adequacy of the context. In contrast, when motivation was low, participants fell prey to the OAB when the essay concerned euthanasia and the study was allegedly conducted in a psychological context. Similarly, low-motivation participants expressed dispositional attributions when the essay dealt with the closing of mines and the experiment was allegedly carried out in the context of research in sociology.

These findings provide a very convincing demonstration of the intrusion of judgeability concerns in the attitude attribution paradigm. As such, they underline the relevance of naive theories of judgment in a wide variety of settings. Interestingly, they do share one important feature with the earlier illustrations of judgeability concerns in stereotyping settings. Indeed, as far as we can tell, these metacognitive inferences very much seem to play a role at the end of the judgmental process. In other words, it is as if perceivers reflect on their impression and its validity right before they are requested to utter their judgment. Is it possible that some sort of metacognitive work takes place along the way rather than at the end of the journey? Could judgeability concerns affect the judgment as the impression is being constructed? In the next section, we present our initial efforts in answering this question.

The many sources of confidence

A paramount feature of the impression formation research examined above is that participants always passively receive rather than search for the information concerning the judgmental target(s). Although such a procedure enables methodological concerns to be met, it fails to provide a full picture of real-life social perception: Perceivers do not only receive information from others, they also invest time and effort to gather new information in order to make up their minds. In our earlier work (Yzerbyt and Leyens, 1991), we explicitly addressed this shortcoming of the impression formation literature. We evaluated the impact of the active selection of the information in a hypothesis confirmation paradigm (Snyder & Swann, 1978). Our participants were asked to request as many pieces of trait information as they saw fit in order to select a series of candidates for a theater role. In perfect agreement with other research on the confirmation bias (Klayman & Ha, 1987) and on the negativity effect (Peeters & Czapinski, 1990), we found that participants requested more information when the traits were positive and confirming rather than negative and disconfirming.

Building on this early empirical demonstration of the role of the active information search in impression formation, Johnston and Macrae (1994) looked at the impact of the mode of information acquisition on stereotype maintenance. These authors provided some of their participants with information concerning a specific target person. Some items of information were consistent with the stereotype, others were inconsistent, still others were neutral. Other participants were allowed to request the specific pieces of information that they wanted. Still others only knew the category membership of the target. The data revealed that, compared to the situation in which all of the evidence was given, the control of the information search led participants to express more stereotypical answers. Because the active search participants did not differ from the category participants, these findings reveal that stereotypes may be more resistant in real-life settings than most laboratory studies seem to indicate.

In our view, these studies are important because they suggest that perceivers may in fact be very sensitive to the mode of acquisition of the information. Specifically, people may have more confidence in the evidence that they themselves gathered than in information they passively received. Unfortunately, two weaknesses in Johnston and Macrae's (1994) demonstration prevent us from drawing firm conclusions regarding our conjecture. First, these authors included no condition in which participants received exactly the same information as the active search participants. Second, the feedback information always confirmed the question asked by the participants, with the consequence that the targets often appeared incoherent. We took care of these problems in a series of experiments (Dardenne & Yzerbyt, 1996).

In a first study (Dardenne & Yzerbyt, 1996, Experiment 1), participants first read a six-trait description of a person. For each trait, a percentage mentioned the proportion of peers attributing that particular trait to the person. Depending on the condition, we created a positive or a negative expectancy. For instance, the positive expectancy participants learned that 64% and 20% of the people thought that the person was spontaneous and envious, respectively. Active search participants then received a list of 12 positive and 12 negative traits and were asked to select six additional traits in order to form an impression. For each trait, the experimenter successively revealed the proportion of people attributing the trait to the person. Importantly, the feedback was always consistent with the initial impression. Passive reception participants were yoked with their active search colleagues in that we simply provided exactly the same information requested by an active search participant to a passive reception participant. Finally, active search and passive reception participants conveyed their impression of the person (likeability) as well as their confidence on a number of dependent measures. Our prediction was that the control of the data collection process would lead participants to make more extreme impressions and to feel more confident. As can be seen in Figure 8.5, the data fully support our hypotheses.

These findings lend credit to the idea that perceivers who control the acquisition of the information express more confident and polarized ratings. They remain silent, however, as far as the underlying process is concerned. One possibility is that polarization takes place at the end of the data collection phase. This "end-product" hypothesis assumes that perceivers in both conditions complete their data collection with a similar impression. Before they convey their impression, they take into account the mode of information acquisition and correct their impression accordingly. Supposedly, a more active control is conducive to better judgments. As a result, perceivers may feel more confident and polarize their judgments. Alternatively, the active search for additional information could have an on-line influence on the impression. According to this hypothesis, perceivers deal with the information in a distinctive manner from early on and may end up with a very different impression. One way to tell apart these two possibilities is to provide information that disconfirms the perceivers' initial hypothesis. Indeed, active and passive perceivers may come up with very different final impressions if the mode of information acquisition exerts its impact from the first piece of information on. On the other hand, if

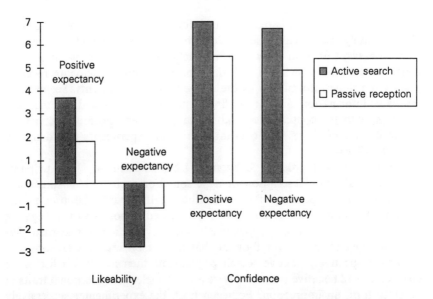

Figure 8.5 *Likeability ratings and level of confidence for active search and passive reception participants (Dardenne and Yzerbyt, 1996, Experiment 1). For likeability ratings, scores range from –9 (very negative) to 9 (very positive); for confidence ratings, scores range from 0 (very low) to 9 (very high)*

perceivers bring in only at the end the fact that they either searched for or received the evidence, active participants should simply be more confident and extreme in their final impressions than passive participants.

In a second study (Dardenne & Yzerbyt, 1996, Experiment 2), we replicated the above experiment except that we provided half of the participants with disconfirming rather than confirming evidence. To the extent that the final impression is very sensitive to the mode of information acquisition (see Figure 8.6), our data clearly support the "on-line" hypothesis. In fact, whereas passive reception ended up with positive impressions, active search always led participants to form negative impressions. This pattern of findings is highly reminiscent of the distinction between the positivity bias and the negativity effect (Peeters & Czapinski, 1990). Apparently, active search perceivers appraise the old and the new information in a more cautious and responsible manner.

In conclusion, the mode of acquisition of the information has a noticeable impact on people's final judgments. Interestingly enough, whereas earlier research indicates that negative information leads to more intense cognitive work (Fiske, 1980; Kahneman & Tversky, 1984), the present data show that a more accountable set of mind leads perceivers to weigh the negative evidence more than the positive evidence. In contrast to a "sufficiency" orientation which favors positive information and confirming evidence, the active search may correspond to a "necessity" orientation in which

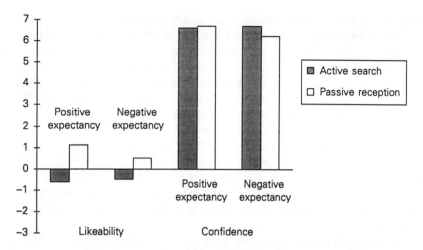

Figure 8.6   *Likeability ratings and level of confidence for active search and passive reception participants (Dardenne and Yzerbyt, 1996, Experiment 2). For likeability ratings, scores range from –9 (very negative) to 9 (very positive); for confidence ratings, scores range from 0 (very low) to 9 (very high)*

perceivers feel highly accountable for their decision. This distinction between the active search and the passive reception of the information shares many characteristics with the well-established impact of mood on impression formation (Bodenhausen, 1993; Fiedler, 1991; Forgas, 1991; see also Mackie & Hamilton, 1993) as well as with many other observations showing the existence of a more conscientious mode of processing the information and a more superficial way of handling the data (Fiske & Taylor, 1991; for a similar argument in the attitude area, see Chaiken, 1987; Petty & Cacioppo, 1986). With regard to stereotyping, the message from our data is not very optimistic. On the one hand, people tend to stick more to their a priori views when they are negative rather than positive. On the other, perceivers are likely to embrace new information more readily when it is derogatory rather than flattering. In short, an egotistic and ethnocentric approach of the world may largely benefit from an active search for information.

Conclusions

The culture we inhabit has its rules of functioning. People carry with them a number of naive theories regarding social judgment. Some conditions are thought to render a judgment valid; others lead to a questionable decision; we may or may not feel entitled to judge. The present chapter examined the impact of two different naive theories. In a first research program, we examined the widely shared assumption that social perceivers are supposed to judge others on the basis of valid individuating judgment. This prescriptive rule, we argued, is largely embodied in current impression formation models. In several experiments, we showed that the mere belief that individuating information has been made available may facilitate the expression of judgments. To the extent that the perceivers' expectations are the only real source of information, people's judgment ends up confirming the stereotypes. Although our findings do not mean that hypothesis confirmation is unlikely to contribute to the maintenance of stereotypes, they stress the fact that implicit rules of judgment can combine with people's limited access to the actual basis of their impression to perpetuate long-standing characterizations of social groups. Our conclusion is further supported by the fact that explicit manipulations of the authentic versus strategic nature of this metacognitive calculus by means of a bogus pipeline failed to support the idea that our participants' answers could be motivated by impression management concerns.

Our work on the dilution effect adds an important aspect to the demonstration of the role of naive theories in social judgment. Instead of informing participants that they had received relevant individuating information, we actually provided all participants with pseudorelevant evidence. Our data suggest that the presence of pseudorelevant information may increase people's reliance on stereotypic knowledge. However, any factor increasing subjects' awareness that category-based information unduly contaminates their individuated judgment will reduce the expression of the stereotype. In other words, social perceivers will refrain from using their stereotypes when rating another person to the extent that they better appreciate the impact of category information. Our findings further show that the neglect of stereotypes in certain judgment situations, i.e. the dilution effect, may have less to do with the heuristic of similarity and comparisons with the prototype than with simple social rules of judgment.

In all these studies, we concentrated our efforts on one particular rule of judgment. Indeed, building upon current impression models, we conjectured that people may be reluctant to base their judgment on stereotypes. Of course, our findings do not mean that perceivers will always guard against category-based judgments. The degree to which the norm is salient in any given situation will be highly related to the kind of social category. People are likely to be less comfortable basing their impression on the social category when the target person is a member of a socially protected group than when ambient norms are less favorable to the group. At the time of this writing, homophobic judgments remain less problematic than impressions based on people's gender. Also, there is no reason to exclude the possibility that perceivers may consider category-based judgments to be quite valid, especially when a group-based interaction appears meaningful (Leyens et al., 1994; Oakes, Haslam, & Turner, 1994; Yzerbyt, Rogier & Fiske, in press b). That is, some people should see no difficulty in relying on group membership in order to judge others. However, the legitimacy of category-based impressions is likely to be sensitive to the specific group at stake and the kind of interaction involved.

More recently, we tested the idea that pseudorelevant information may give perceivers the feeling that they possess a substantial degree of information about the target person in a totally different context. Specifically, our research program turned to the attitude attribution paradigm. Our data suggest that dispositional inferences may often emerge as a consequence of the theoretical match between the kind of judgment requested from the perceiver and the judgmental context. As far as we can see, the data recently collected in our laboratory are hardly accountable in terms of mainstream interpretations of the OAB. Instead, we suspect that perceivers will feel comfortable judging others to the extent that they can come up with a coherent explanation for the observed behavior. Depending on the judgmental context, such a coherent explanation will be more or less easy to construe and observers' confidence in their judgment will be high or low. Clearly, further research is needed to disentangle the role of the various factors at work.

In the last section, we tackled a somewhat different question. Indeed, we built upon earlier work on the active search for information in order to examine the possible impact of naive theories on the confirmation of hypotheses. Our studies reveal that people react very differently to the data when they search rather than receive the information. In our view, on-line metacognitive inferences could explain the difference between the active search and the passive reception. A qualitatively different appraisal of information that one has collected oneself would explain why active search leads the evidence to be processed in a more critical and conscientious way.

In their own way, all the studies examined in the present chapter directly address the normative level of adequacy. As a set, they provide strong evidence in favor of the SJM by showing that naive theories of judgment intrude into the metacognitive assessment of our judgments about others and inform us whether we may or may not trust our impression. There is little doubt that a better awareness of the various ways by which normative standards affect the very fabric of our judgments is one true benefit of the interest in metacognition in social psychology.

Acknowledgments

Most of the studies reported in this chapter were supported by the Belgian National Science Foundation. For their helpful comments on an earlier draft, we are grateful to our colleagues or graduate students Fanny Bellour, Olivier Corneille, Steve Rocher, Anouk Rogier, and Georges Schadron.

References

Abele-Brehm, A. (1996). Assimilation and contrast in social judgment as reflecting pragmatical information use. Paper presented at the XIth general meeting of the European Association of Experimental Social Psychology, Gmunden, Austria, July 13–17, 1996.

Ajzen, I., Dalto, C.A., & Blyth, D.P. (1979). Consistency and bias in the attribution of attitudes. *Journal of Personality and Social Psychology, 37*, 1871–1876.

Bargh, J.A. & Thein, R.D. (1985). Individual construct accessibility, person memory, and the recall-judgment link: The case of information overload. *Journal of Personality and Social Psychology, 49*, 1129–1146.

Bodenhausen, G.V. (1990). Stereotypes as judgmental heuristics: Evidence of circadian variations in discrimination. *Psychological Science, 1*, 319–322.

Bodenhausen, G.V. (1993). Emotions, arousal, and stereotypic judgments: A heuristic model of affect and stereotyping. In D.M. Mackie & D.L. Hamilton (Eds), *Affect, cognition, and stereotyping: Interactive processes in group perception* (pp. 13–37). San Diego, CA: Academic Press.

Bodenhausen, G.V. & Lichtenstein, M. (1987). Social stereotypes and information-processing strategies: The impact of task complexity. *Journal of Personality and Social Psychology, 52*, 871–880.

Brewer, M.B. (1988). A dual process of impression formation. In T.K. Srull & R.S. Wyer (Eds), *Advances in social cognition* (Vol. 1, pp. 1–36). Hillsdale, NJ: Lawrence Erlbaum.

Chaiken, S. (1987). The heuristic model of persuasion. In M.P. Zanna, J.M. Olson, & C.P. Herman (Eds), *Social influence: The Ontario Symposium* (Vol. 5, pp. 3–39). Hillsdale, NJ: Lawrence Erlbaum.

Corneille, O., Leyens, J.-Ph, & Yzerbyt, V. (1996). Dispositional inferences need explanatory coherence: The interplay of accountability and concept applicability in the overattribution bias. Unpublished manuscript. University of Louvain at Louvain-la-Neuve.

Dardenne, B. & Yzerbyt, V.Y. (1996). Implicit theory of judgment construction. Unpublished manuscript. University of Louvain at Louvain-la-Neuve.

Darley, J.M. & Gross, P.H. (1983). A hypothesis-confirming bias in labeling effects. *Journal of Personality and Social Psychology, 44*, 20–33.

de Dreu, C.K.W., Yzerbyt, V.Y., & Leyens, J.-Ph. (1995). Dilution of stereotype-based cooperation in mixed-motive interdependence. *Journal of Experimental Social Psychology, 31*, 575–593.

Denhaerinck, P., Leyens, J.-Ph., & Yzerbyt, V.Y. (1989). The dilution effect and group membership: An instance of the pervasive impact of out-group homogeneity. *European Journal of Social Psychology, 19*, 243–250.

Dovidio, J.F., Evans, N.E., & Tyler, R.B. (1986). Racial stereotypes: The contents of their cognitive representations. *Journal of Experimental Social Psychology, 22*, 22–37.

Duncan, B. (1976). Differential social perception and attribution of intergroup violence: Testing the lower limits of stereotyping Blacks. *Journal of Personality and Social Psychology, 34*, 590–598.

Fiedler, K. (1991). On the task, the measures, and the mood: Research on affect and social cognition. In J.P. Forgas (Ed.), *Emotion and social judgments* (pp. 83–104). Oxford: Pergamon.

Fiske, S.T. (1980). Attention and weight in person perception: The impact of negative and extreme behavior. *Journal of Personality and Social Psychology, 38*, 889–906.

Fiske, S.T. (1993). Social cognition and social perception. *Annual Review of Psychology, 44*, 155–194.

Fiske, S.T. & Neuberg, S.L. (1990). A continuum of impression formation from category based to individuating processes. Influences of information and motivation on attention and interpretation. In M.P. Zanna (Ed.), *Advances in experimental social psychology* (Vol. 23, pp. 1–74). New York: Academic Press.

Fiske, S.T. & Taylor, S.E. (1991). *Social cognition*. New York: McGraw-Hill.

Forgas, J.P. (Ed.) (1991). *Emotion and social judgments*. Oxford: Pergamon.

Gaertner, S.L. & McLaughlin, J.P. (1983). The aversive form of racism. In S.L. Gaertner & J.F. Dovidio (Eds), *Prejudice, discrimination, and racism* (pp. 1–34). Orlando, FL: Academic Press.

Gigerenzer, G. (1991). How to make cognitive illusions disappear: Beyond "heuristics and biases". In W. Stroebe & M. Hewstone (Eds), *European Review of Social Psychology* (Vol. 2, pp. 83–115). Chichester: Wiley.

Gigerenzer, G., Hell, W., & Blank, H. (1988). Presentation and content: The use of base rates as a continuous variable. *Journal of Experimental Psychology: Human Perception and Performance. 14*, 513–525.

Gilbert, D.T. (1989). Thinking lightly about others: Automatic components of the social inference process. In J.S. Uleman & J.A. Bargh (Eds), *Unintended thought: Limits of awareness, intention, and control* (pp. 189–211). New York: Guilford.

Gilbert, D.T. & Hixon, J.G. (1991). The trouble of thinking: Activation and application of stereotypic beliefs. *Journal of Experimental Social Psychology, 60*, 509–517.

Gilbert, D.T. & Jones, E.E. (1986). Perceiver-induced constraint: Interpretations of self-generated reality. *Journal of Personality and Social Psychology, 50*, 269–280.

Gilbert, D.T. & Malone, P.S. (1995). The correspondence bias. *Psychological Bulletin, 117*, 21–38.

Gilbert, D.T., Pelham, B.W., & Krull, D.S. (1988). On cognitive busyness: When person perceivers meet persons perceived. *Journal of Personality and Social Psychology, 54*, 733–740.

Gilbert, D.T. & Silvera, D.H. (1996). Overhelping. *Journal of Personality and Social Psychology, 70*, 678–690.

Greenwald, A.G. & Banaji, M.R. (1995). Implicit social cognition: Attitudes, self-esteem, and stereotypes. *Psychological Review, 102*, 4–27.

Grice, H.P. (1975). Logic and conversation. In P. Cole & J.L. Morgan (Eds), *Syntax and semantics: Speech acts* (Vol. 3, pp. 41–58). Orlando, FL: Academic Press.

Hamilton, D.L. & Sherman, J.W. (1994). Stereotypes. In R.S. Wyer Jr. & T.K. Srull (Eds), *Handbook of social cognition* (Vol 1, pp. 1–68). Hillsdale, NJ: Erlbaum.

Hamilton, D.L., Stroessner, S.J., & Mackie, D.M. (1993). The influence of affect on stereotyping: The case of illusory correlations. In D.M. Mackie & D.L. Hamiton (Eds), *Affect, cognition, and stereotyping: Interactive processes in group perception* (pp. 39–61). San Diego, CA: Academic Press.

Higgins, E.T. (1996). Biases in social cognition: Aboutness as a general principle. In C. McGarty & S.A. Haslam (Eds), *The message of social psychology* (pp. 182–199). Oxford: Blackwell.

Hilton, J.L. & Fein, S. (1989). The role of typical diagnosticity in stereotype-based judgments. *Journal of Personality and Social Psychology, 57*, 201–211.

Johnston, L.C. & Macrae, C.N. (1994). Changing social stereotypes: The case of the information seeker. *European Journal of Social Psychology, 24*, 581–592.

Jones, E.E. (1979). The rocky road from acts to dispositions. *American Psychologist, 34*, 104–117.

Jones, E.E. (1990). *Interpersonal perception*. New York: Freeman.

Jones, E.E. & Davis, K.E. (1965). From acts to disposition: The attribution process in person perception. In L. Berkowitz (Ed.), *Advances in experimental social psychology* (Vol. 2, pp. 219–266). New York: Academic Press.

Jones, E.E. & Harris, V.A. (1967). The attribution af attitudes. *Journal of Experimental Social Psychology, 3*, 1–24.

Jones, E.E. & Nisbett, R. (1972). The actor and the observer: Divergent perceptions of the causes of behavior. In E.E. Jones, D.E. Kanouse, H.H. Kelley, R.E. Nisbett, S. Valins, & B. Weiner (Eds), *Attribution: Perceiving the causes of behavior* (pp. 79–94). Morristown, NJ: General Learning.

Jones, E.E. & Sigall, H. (1971). The bogus pipeline: A new paradigm for measuring affect and attitude. *Psychological Bulletin, 76*, 349–364.

Kahneman, D. & Tversky, A. (1973). On the psychology of prediction. *Psychological Review, 80*, 237–251.

Kahneman, D. & Tversky, A. (1984). Choices, values and frames. *American Psychologist, 39*, 341–350.

Kim, H.S. & Baron, R.S. (1988). Exercise and the illusory correlation: Does arousal heighten stereotypic processing? *Journal of Experimental Social Psychology, 24,* 366–380.

Klayman, J. & Ha, Y. (1987). Confirmation, disconfirmation and information in hypothesis testing. *Psychological Review, 94,* 211–228.

Klein, W.M. & Kunda, Z. (1992). Motivated person perception: Constructing justifications for desired beliefs. *Journal of Experimental Social Psychology, 28,* 145–168.

Kruglanski, A.W. & Freund, T. (1983). The freezing and unfreezing of lay-inferences: Effects of impressional primacy, ethnic stereotyping and numerical anchoring. *Journal of Experimental Social Psychology, 19,* 448–468.

Krull, D.S. (1993). Does the grill change the mill? The effect of the perceiver's inferential goal on the process of social inference. *Personality and Social Psychology Bulletin, 19,* 340–348.

Kunda, Z. (1990). The case of motivated reasoning. *Psychological Bulletin, 108,* 480–498.

Kunda, Z., Fong, G.T., Sanitioso, R., & Reber, E. (1993). Directional questions direct self-conceptions. *Journal of Experimental Social Psychology, 29,* 63–86.

Kunda, Z. & Sanitioso, R. (1987). Motivated changes in the self-concept. *Journal of Experimental Social Psychology, 25,* 272–285.

Leyens, J.-Ph. (1993). Qu'est-ce qu'un bon jugement social? In J.-L. Beauvois, R.-B. Joule, & J.-M. Monteil (Eds), *Perspectives cognitives et conduites sociales IV: Jugements sociaux et changements des attitudes* (pp. 73–81). Neuchâtel, Suisse: Delachaux et Niestlé.

Leyens, J.-Ph. & Yzerbyt, V.Y. (1992). The ingroup overexclusion effect: Impact of valence and confirmation on stereotypical information search. *European Journal of Social Psychology, 22,* 549–569.

Leyens, J.-Ph., Yzerbyt, V.Y., & Corneille, O. (1996). The role of applicability in the emergence of the overattribution bias. *Journal of Personality and Social Psychology, 70,* 219–229.

Leyens, J.-Ph., Yzerbyt, V.Y., & Schadron, G. (1992). The social judgeability approach to stereotypes. In W. Stroebe & M. Hewstone (Eds), *European Review of Social Psychology* (Vol. 3, pp. 91–120). New York: Wiley.

Leyens, J.-Ph., Yzerbyt, V.Y., & Schadron, G. (1994). *Stereotypes and social explanation.* London. Sage.

Locksley, A., Borgida, E., Brekke, N., & Hepburn, C. (1980). Sex stereotypes and social judgment. *Journal of Personality and Social Psychology, 39,* 821–831.

Locksley, A., Hepburn, C., & Ortiz, V. (1982). Social stereotypes and judgments of individuals: An instance of the base-rate fallacy. *Journal of Experimental Social Psychology, 18,* 23–42.

Mackie, D.M. & Hamilton, D.L. (1993). *Affect, cognition, and stereotyping: Interactive processes in group perception* (pp. 39–61). San Diego, CA: Academic Press.

Macrae, C.N., Hewstone, M., & Griffiths, R.J. (1993). Processing load and memory for stereotype-based information. *European Journal of Social Psychology, 23,* 77–87.

Macrae, C.N., Milne, A.B., & Bodenhausen, G.V. (1994). Stereotypes as energy-saving devices: A peek inside the cognitive toolbox. *Journal of Personality and Social Psychology, 66,* 37–47.

Macrae, C.N., Stangor, C., & Milne A.B. (1994). Activating social stereotypes: A functional analysis. *Journal of Experimental and Social Psychology, 30,* 370–389.

Martin, L.L. (1986). Set/reset: The use and disuse of concepts in impression formation. *Journal of Personality and Social Psychology, 51,* 493–504.

Martin, L.L. & Achee, J.W. (1992). Beyond accessibility: The role of processing objectives in judgment. In L.L. Martin & A. Tesser (Eds), *The construction of social judgments* (pp. 195–216). Hillsdale, NJ: Erlbaum.

Medin, D.L. (1989). Concepts and conceptual structure. *American Psychologist, 44,* 1469–1481.

Medin, D.L., Goldstone, R.L., & Gentner, D. (1993). Respects for similarity. *Psychological Review, 100,* 254–278.

Metcalfe, J. & Shimamura, A.P. (1994). *Metacognition.* Cambridge, MA: MIT Press.

Miller, A.G. & Lawson, T. (1989). The effect of an informational option on the fundamental attribution error. *Personality and Social Psychology Bulletin, 15,* 194–204.

Miller, A.G. & Rorer, L.G. (1982). Toward an understanding of the fundamental attribution error: Essay diagnosticity in the attitude attribution paradigm. *Journal of Research in Psychology, 16*, 41–59.

Miller, A.G., Schmidt, D., Meyer, C., & Colella, A. (1984). The perceived value of constrained behavior: Pressures toward biased inference in the attitude attribution paradigm. *Social Psychology Quarterly, 47*, 160–171.

Murphy, G.L. & Medin, D.L. (1985). The role of theories in conceptual coherence. *Psychological Review, 92*, 289–316.

Nelson, T.O. (1992). *Metacognition: core readings* (pp. ix–xi). Boston: Allyn & Bacon.

Nisbett, R.E. & Wilson, T.D. (1977). Telling more than we can know: Verbal reports on mental processes. *Psychological Review, 84*, 231–259.

Nisbett, R.E., Zukier, H., & Lemley, R.E. (1981). The dilution effect: Non-diagnostic information weakens the implications of diagnostic information. *Cognitive Psychology, 13*, 248–277.

Oakes, P.J., Haslam, S.A., & Turner, J.C. (1994). *Stereotypes and social reality*. Oxford: Blackwell.

Paulhus, D.J., Martin, C.L., & Murphy, G.K. (1992). Some effects of arousal on sex stereotyping. *Personality and Social Psychology Bulletin, 18*, 325–330.

Peeters, G. & Czapinski, J. (1990). Positive-negative asymmetry in evaluations: The dictinction between affective and informational negativity effects. In W. Stroebe & M. Hewstone (Eds), *European review of social psychology* (Vol. 1, pp. 33–60). Chichester, UK: Wiley.

Perdue, C.W. & Gurtman, M.B. (1990). Evidence for the automaticity of ageism. *Journal of Experimental Social Psychology, 26*, 199–216.

Petty, R.E. & Cacioppo, J.T. (1986). The elaboration likelihood model of persuasion. In L. Berkowitz (Ed.), *Advances in experimental social psychology* (Vol. 19, pp. 123–205). New York: Academic Press.

Pratto, F. & Bargh, J.A. (1991). Stereotyping based on apparently individuating information: Trait and global components of sex stereotypes under attention overload. *Journal of Experimental Social Psychology, 27*, 26–47.

Quattrone, G.A. (1982). Overattribution and unit formation: When behavior engulfs the person. *Journal of Personality and Social Psychology, 42*, 593–607.

Roese, N.J. & Jamieson, D.W. (1993). Twenty years of bogus pipeline research: A critical review and meta-analysis. *Psychological Bulletin, 114*, 353–375.

Ross, L. (1977). The intuitive psychologists and his shortcomings: Distortions in the attribution process. In L. Berkowitz (Ed.), *Advances in Experimental Social Psychology* (Vol. 10, pp. 173–220). New York: Academic Press.

Rothbart, M., Fulero, S., Jensen, C., Howard, J., & Birrel, P. (1978). From individual to group impressions: Availability heuristics in stereotype formation. *Journal of Experimental Social Psychology, 14*, 237–255.

Sagar, H.A. & Schofield, J.W. (1980). Racial and behavioral cues in black and white children's perceptions of ambiguously aggressive acts. *Journal of Personality and Social Psychology, 39*, 590–598.

Schachter, S. & Singer, J. (1962). Cognitive, social, and physiological determinants of emotional state. *Psychological Review, 69*, 379–399.

Schadron, G. & Yzerbyt, V.Y. (1991). Social judgeability: Another framework for the study of social inference. *Cahiers de Psychologie Cognitive/European Bulletin of Cognitive Psychology, 11*, 229–258.

Snyder, M. & Swann, W.B. (1978). Hypothesis testing processes in social interaction. *Journal of Personality and Social Psychology, 36*, 1202–1212.

Stangor, C. & Duan, C. (1991). Effects of multiple tasks demands upon memory for information about social groups. *Journal of Experimental Social Psychology, 27*, 357–378.

Stroessner, S.J. & Mackie, D.M. (1992). The impact of induced affect on the perception of variability in social groups. *Personality and Social Psychology Bulletin, 18*, 546–554.

Swann, W.B. (1984). Quest for accuracy in person perception: A matter of pragmatics. *Psychological Review, 91*, 457–477.

Swann, W.B. (1987). Identity negotiation: Where two roads meet. *Journal of Personality and Social Psychology, 53*, 1038–1051.

Tajfel, H. & Turner, J.C. (1986). An integrative theory of intergroup relations. In S. Worchel & W.G. Austin (Eds), *Psychology of intergroup relations* (pp. 7–24). Chicago: Nelson-Hall.

Tetlock, P.E. (1983). Accountability and the complexity of thought. *Journal of Personality and Social Psychology, 45*, 74–83.

Tetlock, P.E. (1985). Accountability: A social check on the fundamental attribution error. *Social Psychology Quarterly, 48*, 227–236.

Tversky, A. (1977). Features of similarity. *Psychological Review, 84*, 327–352.

Tversky, A. & Kahneman, D. (1974). Judgment under uncertainty: Heuristics and biases. *Science, 185*, 1123–1131.

Webster, D.M. (1993). Motivated augmentation and reduction of the overattribution bias. *Journal of Personality and Social Psychology, 65*, 261–271.

Wilder, D.A. & Shapiro, P.N. (1988). Role of competition-induced anxiety in limiting the beneficial impact of positive behavior by an out-group member. *Journal of Personality and Social Psychology, 56*, 60–69.

Wright, E.F. & Wells, G.L. (1988). Is the attitude-attribution paradigm suitable for investigating the dispositional bias? *Personality and Social Psychology Bulletin, 14*, 183–190.

Yost, J.H. & Weary, G. (1996). Depression and the correspondent inference bias: Evidence for more effortful cognitive processing. *Personality and Social Psychology Bulletin, 22*, 192–200.

Yzerbyt, V.Y. & Castano, E. (1997). Group identification, group homogeneity and ingroup overexclusion: How difficult is it to be a Walloon? Unpublished manuscript. University of Louvain at Louvain-la-Neuve.

Yzerbyt, V.Y. & Leyens, J.-Ph. (1991). Requesting information to form an impression: The influence of valence and confirmatory status. *Journal of Experimental Social Psychology, 27*, 337–356.

Yzerbyt, V.Y., Leyens, J.-Ph., & Bellour, F. (1995). The ingroup overexclusion effect: Identity concerns in decisions about group membership. *European Journal of Social Psychology, 25*, 1–16.

Yzerbyt, V.Y., Leyens, J.-Ph., & Corneille, O. (in press a). Social judgeability and the bogus pipeline: The role of naive theories of judgment in impression formation. *Social Cognition*.

Yzerbyt, V.Y., Rogier, A., & Fiske, S. (in press b). Subjective essentialism and social attribution: On translating situational constraints into stereotypes. *Personality and Social Psychology Bulletin, 23*, 1312–1322.

Yzerbyt, V.Y., Leyens, J.-Ph., & Schadron, G. (1998). Social judgeability and the dilution of stereotypes: The impact of the nature and sequence of information. *Personality and Social Psychology Bulletin*.

Yzerbyt, V.Y. & Schadron, G. (1996). *Connaître et juger autrui*. Grenoble: Presses Universitaires de Grenoble.

Yzerbyt, V.Y., Schadron, G., & Leyens, J.-Ph. (1997). Social judgeability concerns and the dilution of stereotypes. *Swiss Journal of Psychology, 56*, 95–105.

Yzerbyt, V.Y., Schadron, G., Leyens, J.-Ph., & Rocher, S. (1994). Social judgeability: The impact of meta-informational cues on the use of stereotypes. *Journal of Personality and Social Psychology, 66*, 48–55.

Zukier, H. (1982). The dilution effect: The role of the correlation and the dispersion of predictor variables in the use of non-diagnostic information. *Journal of Personality and Social Psychology, 43*, 1163–1174.

Zukier, H. & Jennings, D.L. (1984). Nondiagnosticity and strategies in prediction. *Social Cognition, 2*, 187–198.

9

The Consciousness of Social Beliefs: A Program of Research on Stereotyping and Prejudice

Mahzarin R. Banaji and Nilanjana Dasgupta

In the mid-1990s, two important volumes on metacognition appeared. A collection of core readings containing classic and contemporary articles (Nelson, 1992) was followed by a volume of recent theoretical and empirical contributions (Metcalfe & Shimamura, 1994). Together they showed the prominence that the study of metacognition has come to occupy in psychology, and are testimony to the unique advances that are possible through an explicit effort to examine self-reflective processes. Through this research, the use of terms such as monitoring, control, feeling of knowing, and consciousness made previously marginalized constructs legitimate targets of scientific analysis. In so doing, the study of metacognition has expanded the realm of research questions that future generations of psychologists will be permitted to ask about cognition.

The present volume is unusual in its inclusion of social psychological perspectives on metacognition, and in this regard stands in contrast even to its two immediate predecessors. The gathering of social psychological perspectives is more than a simple addition to ongoing analyses, for social psychology has historically been engaged in the study of processes that assume self-reflection. Whether it be the study of attitudes, beliefs, or self-related processes, metacognitive processes have been centrally implicated in theory and research. To study an individual's beliefs about a social group, or attitudes toward political events, or assessments of self-worth, fundamentally requires an assumption that such knowledge exists at levels of consciousness to which access is possible. In addition, the seeming disparities between attitudes and action, between intention and behavior, between the proffered and real causes of behavior, have made metacognitive processes of natural interest. The inclusion of social psychology's core concerns in ongoing analyses of metacognition influences the nature of the theoretical questions that are asked and the target domains that are studied.

The joint focus on social and cognitive perspectives highlights an interesting divergence in the manner in which the histories of the two fields have unfolded with regard to the study of mental processes more generally. In cognitive psychology, the understanding is that metacognitive processes have been ignored, and only through explicit argument have they been included in the fray of legitimate questions. The remnants of a displeasure with introspection practiced at the turn of the century and the behaviorist interlude are cited as historical reasons that kept the study of metacognition at bay (Nelson, 1992; Tulving, 1994). In social psychology, where the dominant method routinely required self-reports of mental processes such as feelings, opinions, beliefs, intentions, and values, the output of conscious, self-aware entities reflecting on the contents of their consciousness was hardly questioned. In fact, it is only rarely that the problematic aspects of a social psychology that has been so constructed have been questioned (Greenwald & Banaji, 1995; Nisbett & Wilson, 1977). The meeting point of two fields with differing priorities but many of the same fundamental concerns is bound to be an interesting one.

Our interest focuses on the ways in which characteristic features of consciousness (such as awareness, intentionality, and control) shape beliefs, attitudes, and behavior. For the past several years, we have been engaged in a program of research specifically concerned with beliefs and attitudes toward social groups and their members. Although the target domain may be most easily labeled as the study of stereotyping and prejudice, the core issues concern questions of consciousness. The domain of stereotyping and prejudice has unique features when viewed through the metacognitive lens. The most obvious concern is with how humans make use of knowledge that is known about a category (Many Xs are Y) in judgments of instances (X_1 is Y). This domain also tackles the disparity between knowledge that is inherent in a culture as a whole (Xs are Y) and an individual's own endorsement of that belief (Xs are not Y). To what extent do judgments reflect culturally held beliefs versus ones that are consciously endorsed by the individual? Are individuals able to control and shape their judgments in accordance with their conscious intentions? And finally, in contemporary societies that agree on the negative social consequences of stereotyping and prejudice, this domain offers an opportunity to examine the similarities and differences in the actions of those who hold consciously favorable attitudes from those who hold consciously unfavorable ones. Do such groups also vary in their implicit or unconsciously expressed beliefs?

Although several attempts have been made to offer a classification of the questions regarding consciousness, in this context we will work with one suggested by Johnson-Laird (1983). To answer the question "What should a theory of consciousness explain?" Johnson-Laird proposed a tractable set of problems that a theory of consciousness must solve. Four such problems were generated, with the goal of making the study of consciousness amenable to uniquely psychological (rather than philosophical) inquiry: awareness, control, self-awareness, and intentionality. In this chapter, we use the issues and data generated by the target domain of implicit social beliefs as a relatively unique platform to analyze questions of consciousness. In particular, we study beliefs about social groups (e.g. gender, race) that are spontaneously used by participants, but without awareness of their usage, without control over their expression, and without intention to use them in judgment of others. The issue of self-awareness will not be addressed here, for our data do not speak directly to this aspect of consciousness. If we venture beyond the data themselves, issues of awareness, control, and intentionality also speak to the troubling and largely philosophical discussion to date regarding the responsibility individuals have for their actions, and the legitimacy of individual rewards and punishments for actions that are attributed to conscious agents. These are essential questions that the study of metacognition raises, but they remain muted if analyses remain focused on metacognitive processes in traditional domains (e.g. test performance, puzzle-solving).

The problem of awareness

For many judgments and decisions humans make, there is a perceived cause of the behavior that is assumed by the actor to be the actual cause. Such causes may often be offered in self-reports to explain or justify actions. Decisions and judgments can be assumed to be guided by higher-order beliefs, such as in the hypothetical statement "It is important to judge X fairly." Participants in our experiments on stereotyping and prejudice, with few exceptions, would endorse such a statement, perhaps even agreeing with more elaborate statements of fairness in the treatment of individuals. Yet, as a growing literature in social psychology demonstrates, there is not sufficient reason to assume that decisions fall into line with self-reports of higher-order beliefs, nor that there is reassuring accuracy in prediction of the actual cause of an action. In this regard, the findings we will highlight will bear some resemblance to the theme of other research on metacognition such as the inability to know what is known (Glenberg, Wilkinson, & Epstein, 1982), the shaky basis of confidence judgments (Loftus, Miller, & Burns, 1978; Shaw, 1996; Wilson & LaFleur, 1995), the difficulty with reality monitoring (Johnson & Raye, 1981), and more generally to research on judgments elicited under conditions of uncertainty.

Consider the task for a subject in one of our experiments based on a method used by Larry Jacoby (Jacoby, Kelley, Brown, & Jasechko, 1989) to study the unconscious influence of the past on the present. The subject is exposed to a list of names, famous and non-famous, male and female. Later, the subject is presented with the same names in addition to new (previously unseen) names with the same characteristics. The task is to identify whether each name represents the name of a famous person or not. Faced with this task, Jacoby et al. (1989) correctly predicted the specific error that subjects are poised to make. Unable to separate the source of familiarity of a name (i.e. the familiarity that accrues to a name from prior exposure versus familiarity that accrues from the actual fame of the name), participants are twice as likely to incorrectly judge a familiar (previously seen) non-famous name to be famous than an unfamiliar (previously unseen) non-famous name to be famous. A mistaken belief about the source of familiarity leads to an erroneous attribution of familiarity to fame. The source of the bias stems from the often correct logic "This name feels familiar, therefore it must be famous," that nevertheless fails in this ordinary and commonly occurring context.

Our interest being in social groups, the additional variable of name gender was introduced, and the finding across several experiments bore out the hypothesis that the accurate belief of greater male fame would operate through the more likely assignment of fame to non-famous male than female names (Banaji & Greenwald, 1995). A feeling of familiarity with previously exposed names was assumed to interact with a general belief about greater male fame to produce the faulty attribution on familiarized non-famous male names. In this case the belief is true when applied to the population as a whole (i.e. fame is indeed more strongly associated with males as a group than females as a group), but the application of the belief in the individual cases captured in this experimental analog represents an error. The belief in greater male fame can be quite easily verbalized, but in this context, the application of the belief appears to operate without awareness. We know from questions posed to subjects that they remained quite unaware of the source of influence (i.e. gender) that urged judgment of a familiarized male name to be famous than an equally familiarized female name. Such unawareness produced a particular decision effect, as revealed in signal detection analysis, specifically, in the differential criterion for judging familiarized male versus female names: The subjective threshold or criterion, captured by the statistic β for judging male fame was set significantly lower than that for judging female fame.

Being unaware of the source of influence on one's judgment (in this case, being unable to control the effects of prior exposure and being unaware of the role of gender in influencing judgment) is not an uncommon occurrence. These experiments capture the ways in which our beliefs, operating unconsciously, can lead to benefits such as fame being undeservedly bestowed (or not) on unsuspecting targets (see Banaji, Blair, & Glaser, 1997). Here, the problem of awareness is the problem of a self-reflective being whose bounded rationality also leads to errors of consequence. The same fundamental processes that allow effective categorization and generalization also produce judgments that may be inaccurate and inequitable.

In another series of studies, we temporarily activated abstract knowledge about specific constructs such as *dependence* and *aggressiveness* (Banaji, Hardin, & Rothman, 1993) and in a quite different setting obtained judgments of individuals named Donna and Donald who performed identical actions. Following the large literature on construct accessibility effects (Higgins, 1989), we predicted that previous exposure to abstract knowledge about traits would increase their use in person judgment, but only when the gender of the specific target was stereotypically congruent with the previously activated knowledge. Even more strongly than expected, results showed that previously activated abstract knowledge did not influence person judgment at all when the target did not carry the stereotypic group marker (i.e. when a male target was judged after exposure to dependence-related information and when a female target was judged after exposure to aggression-related information). Targets were judged more harshly only in the condition of jointly occurring knowledge activation and the fit of stereotypic group membership (i.e. when a female target was judged after exposure to dependence-related knowledge and a male target was judged after exposure to aggression-related knowledge).

Rather than a specific feeling of familiarity with a particular item of knowledge as in the previous fame experiments, exposure to abstract statements appears to have changed the threshold of judgment such that passers-by who fit the social category associated with the activation were handed a more extreme negative judgment. Had awareness of the influencing agent existed, the judgment outcome would have surely differed. As other research indicates, metacognitive correction processes are often engaged in the presence of awareness of perceived bias. Awareness of prior activation has been found to alleviate bias and sometimes even reverse its direction (Lombardi, Higgins, & Bargh, 1987; Strack, Schwarz, Bless, Kubler, & Wanke, 1993; Wegener & Petty, in press). These data suggest that the effects obtained in the present studies may have been removed or reversed in the presence of awareness.

In ongoing research (Walsh, Banaji, & Greenwald, 1995), we have used a variant of the gender-fame task to examine errors that may occur under even more striking cognitive circumstances. Subjects are asked to make a judgment on names that also vary in social category – in this case, however, the judgment is one of criminality, and the names vary in race (black, white, Asian). Importantly, a different basis for familiarity is provided that involves no prior exposure to names. Unlike the fame studies where previous familiarity with names was necessary to create uncertainty about the cause of later perceptual fluency, and unlike the trait judgment studies in which trait knowledge was activated in an unrelated context prior to judgment, in these studies we merely suggested that memory for names may exist. Subjects were told that some of the names on the list might be familiar to them because they had appeared in the media as names of criminals. In multiple experiments, we have shown that this instruction alone can produce one and a half times more black than white identifications with the producers of this error being persuaded that their judgment was based on genuine memory for criminal names.

Among the surprising aspects of this research has been the difficulty in removing the race bias in spite of specific instructions to do so, including alerting subjects that racist individuals are more likely to identify black compared with white names. Beliefs about social groups, whether they are descriptors of the group or not, are in obvious error when applied to the individual case in which they are undeserved, as many decades of civil rights legislation remind us. The participants in our experiments are neither racist in the accepted sense, nor are they intentionally inclined to cause harm to the individuals they identified as criminals. In fact, explicit measures of racism and belief in the fairness of the criminal justice system show participants to be egalitarian and even to be progressive moral agents. However, such beliefs are not correlated with the bias observed on the criminal name identification task. Performance on these two tasks are guided by different types of knowledge. These data reveal that the mere suggestion of name familiarity (in the absence of actual familiarity) is sufficient to produce misidentifications with potentially serious consequences.

Together, these experiments reveal that awareness of the source of influence on judgment is not always or easily possible, and that such conditions are ideal to study the unconscious influence of social beliefs and memory on judgment (Greenwald & Banaji, 1995). In the fame studies, it was difficult for participants to undertake the metacognitive exercise of knowing the source of felt familiarity of a name. In the trait judgment studies, the influence of the prior event was even better hidden from awareness, perhaps even leading perceivers to the belief that their judgment reflected properties of the target itself. Finally, in the race-crime studies, knowledge about the link between race and crime at the group level was sufficient to cause individual misidentifications in the absence of any episodic memory basis at all.

Another line of research further informs about the ways in which social judgments may be influenced by metacognitive processes (i.e. subjective willingness to judge others) without perceivers' awareness of the origin of that influence (Leyens, Yzerbyt, & Schadron, 1992; Yzerbyt, Schadron, Leyens, & Rocher, 1994). In this work Yzerbyt and colleagues examined the conditions under which subjective feelings of confidence propel biased judgments of persons in the absence of awareness of the source of subjective confidence. Similar to the race-crime studies described previously, this work also documents the ease with which metacognitive processes such as feelings of confidence or familiarity can be (falsely) induced and erroneously applied to judgments of individuals.

In a series of studies, Yzerbyt et al. exposed subjects to audio information about an individual member of a known social category (e.g. librarian, comedian). A feeling of confidence and subjective readiness to judge was induced in half of the subjects by misinforming them that they had received diagnostic information about the target in a previous dichotic listening task. The mere suggestion that relevant individuating information had been received was shown to evoke more extreme stereotypical judgments of the target librarian or comedian compared with a control condition. In addition, subjects who received the false familiarity suggestion exhibited greater confidence in the accuracy of their judgments despite their inability to recall specific information that had ostensibly been received. The process described by Yzerbyt and colleagues is similar to that of the race-crime studies in which the baseline condition produced incorrect identifications based on a simple suggestion that there might be some memory for names of criminals.

While few published studies have directly investigated the effect of illusory confidence or willingness to judge on stereotyping (with the exception of Yzerbyt et al., 1994), the findings of several other studies may be understood as being consistent with such an interpretation (Banaji, Hardin, & Rothman, 1993; Beckett & Park, 1995; Bodenhausen & Wyer, 1985; Darley & Gross, 1983; Johnson, Whitestone, Jackson, & Gatto, 1995; Landy & Sigall, 1979; Ugwuegbu, 1979). In all these studies, exposure to non-diagnostic information evoked in perceivers a greater willingness to render a stereotypic judgment. In contrast, experimental conditions in which only social category information was available was not sufficient to evoke the same response. As yet, it is unclear what conditions exactly lead to the increased use of social beliefs in the absence of any additional activation (such as in the race-crime case) versus the conditions that require specific if subtle prior activation to produce stereotyping (e.g. Banaji, Hardin, & Rothman, 1993; Yzerbyt, et al. 1994). In summary, data from several studies when interpreted in terms of the illusory confidence framework suggest that metacognitive decisions about the social judgeability of targets, albeit implicit and perhaps necessarily so, produces increased stereotype usage.

The problem of control

Most central to a cognitive and social view of unconscious processes is the notion of control. A growing literature demonstrates that social actors' ability to control and modify their beliefs, judgments, and behavior is constrained by variables such as the awareness of inappropriate influences on judgments and behavior, the availability of cognitive resources to make spontaneous corrections, and the knowledge of suitable strategies to implement such corrections. The greater the degree of conscious deliberation that can be exerted over an action, a thought, or a feeling, the greater is the assumed control over it. The term "automatic" has come to capture most commonly those psychological processes that operate outside conscious control. In a well-established procedure to measure control, the assumption is a simple one – that the speed of response to a stimulus in the context of another is an indicator of the underlying strength of association (e.g. semantic or evaluative) between the pair. Thus, relatively fast responses are assumed to tap thoughts and feelings that are deployed without conscious deliberation. This assumption has served the field well, and the cooperation of microcomputers has significantly speeded up psychology's understanding of automatic processes. The most common measure of control remains response latency (measured in milliseconds), although other measures such as approach and avoidance techniques involving motor tasks may become tractable measures of automaticity in the future (Chen & Bargh, 1996).

In our program of research, the issue of control has been cast in the form of the automaticity of judgments elicited by social group knowledge. Among the most fundamental of social groups is that of gender. Very early, children learn to associate attributes differentially with being female and male (Fagot, 1985; Fagot & Leinbach, 1989; Martin & Little, 1990), and we assume that such learning would be shown to occur even earlier than documented if non-verbal measures of such associations were obtained. In our experiments, we have obtained evidence of people's ability to classify gender-related information from a variety of domains into female–male categories. First names are an obvious choice, but so are other attributes such as traits (e.g. emotional, aggressive), occupations (e.g. secretary, mechanic), kinship terms (e.g. aunt, uncle), and verbal and pictorial representations of objects (e.g. skirt, cigar). Using a task routinely employed to study semantic memory, we have shown that feminine primes reliably facilitate judgments of female names and that masculine primes reliably facilitate judgments of male names (Banaji & Hardin, 1996). In other words, the congruence between the gender of prime and target automatically facilitates and intereferes with the judgment.

Having ascertained that this is the case, we sought to show the robustness of this learning by giving participants information that could assist in circumventing the spontaneous behavior pattern (Blair & Banaji, 1996). We created two conditions varying the stimulus onset asynchrony (SOA), such that prime-target pairs appeared in quick succession (350 milliseconds) or were relatively slower (2000 milliseconds). In each condition, half the participants were told to expect either stereotypic or counterstereotypic pairings. When stereotypic pairings between prime and target were expected (i.e. male prime – male target; female prime – female target), the pattern of data was expected to mimic the previously obtained one in the baseline condition of no instruction. The condition of greater interest in understanding the role of control was one in which instructions prepared subjects to expect counterstereotypic pairings and armed them with a strategy to respond more quickly to such pairings than stereotypical ones.

The assumption is that in the counterstereotypic condition, the judgment should be relatively easy when both sufficient resources (e.g. 2000 milliseconds SOA) and a suitable strategy to counteract biases are available to control spontaneous responses to gender-congruent pairings. In contrast, when sufficient resources are not available (e.g. 350 milliseconds SOA) nor an effective strategy easily identifiable, gender knowledge automatically evoked from words (even those whose primary meaning is not gender relevant, e.g. mechanic or sewing), should not allow control over automatic responses to gender-congruent pairings. Results showed support for these predictions, expressed in the form of a four-way interaction between SOA, strategy prime gender, and target gender. These studies have shown that a higher-order goal can be effective but only under conditions that allow control. It is not our understanding that such conditions are a common occurrence in everyday life.

In a more recently developed task, Greenwald, McGhee, and Schwartz (1998) have used a different interference task to examine a similar issue. The procedure, called the Implicit Association Test (IAT) was devised to

measure strength of attitudes through a comparison of theoretically predicted compatible and incompatible responses. Imagine the following
experimental scenario. You are asked to classify two types of stimuli on a
computer keyboard, using two different keys (A and B) to do so. Let us
assume that the categories to be classified were names of *flowers* (daffodil,
rose) on key A and *insects* (fly, cockroach) on key B. As you might imagine,
the task is an easy one to perform, i.e. producing overall high speed and a
low error rate. Suppose that you were then trained to classify a different set
of two categories, *positive* (cake, baby) or *negative* (devil, vomit) words. As
you might imagine, this task too should be easily performed, again yielding
fast response latencies and a low error rate.

Now, suppose that the task were to become more complex, with the
judgment requiring a decision about either of the two levels of both classification tasks in a joint task, i.e. the stimulus could be an item from any one
of the four categories: Insects, flowers, pleasant words, unpleasant words.
Responses to the items however, still use only two keys: Insect names and
negative words use key A, whereas flower names and positive words use key
B. Now, response time should fall, and error rates should increase. The data
of interest are obtained by comparing the latencies on this joint task with
performance on the alternative joint task, insects and positive words on key
A and flowers and negative words on key B. The first joint task is an
evaluatively compatible one (positive words and flowers versus negative
words and insects), thus classification latencies are expected to be much
faster for this task than the second, evaluatively incompatible task (positive
words and insects versus negative words and flowers). The difference in
latencies in the compatible and incompatible conditions is taken as a
measure of the relative favorability toward flowers compared with insects.

The task is a generic one, with the ability to readily substitute insects and
flowers with other categories as Greenwald et al. (1998) did. They found
that subjects were faster to classify black and white names when black
names were paired via a key to unpleasant words and white names were
paired via a key to pleasant words. They also showed that Korean and
Japanese subjects showed opposite patterns of implicit attitudes indicating
greater ingroup than outgroup liking. The subjective experience when performing the IAT is quite instructive. The compatible condition (black–
negative, white–positive) is palpably easier than the incompatible condition,
even among those who consciously hold no negative evaluation of black
Americans, for the task does not allow control over this implicit negative
attitude. As expected, Greenwald et al. (1998) report a lack of correlation
between explicit (semantic differential) measures of attitude and the implicit
measure of attitude obtained on the IAT. Their data illustrate the failure to
exert conscious control over automatic attitudes despite perceivers' awareness of the presence of prejudice in their spontaneous judgments and their
conscious disavowal of such prejudice.

Taken together, these studies demonstrate most obviously and strongly
the difficulty in curbing the unconscious operation of social beliefs in

judgments. In the automatic gender stereotyping studies, participants were unable to control automatic activation of stereotyping. So also in the IAT studies, the negative attitudes toward social groups were revealed in the inability to control automatically activated preferences.

Higher-level social beliefs (theories about how beliefs ought to operate, how they ought to be controlled or tempered, etc.) can produce control, but only over those expressions that lie more squarely within conscious thought. Such higher-order beliefs, captured on more explicit measures cannot exert control over automatic versions of beliefs toward the same object. Both consciously controlled and relatively automatic beliefs have obvious impact on behavior and influence the shape of interpersonal interaction, but it is unclear at this point how deep and extensive is the contribution of each form of social expression. Our indulgence of implicit processes reflects their relatively dormant status in psychological research and our view that the influence of implicit processes is pervasive and influential.

The problem of intentionality

It is not common for psychologists to dwell on questions of free-will and responsibility for actions. Yet, it is clear that advances in experimental psychology's analyses of unconscious processes must necessarily inform discussions of these matters, traditionally the subject of philosophical, political, and legal debate. We raise some links here, but with great caution, because there is only speculation to offer about these issues that have received little empirical scrutiny. The notion of responsibility for actions is closely tied to the construct of intention, and this, in turn, is closely linked to the constructs of awareness and control that have recently been experimentally studied. If we challenge the long-standing assumption that accurate awareness of the cause of an action or ability to exert conscious control over the action is possible, the notion of intention also becomes suspect. In the data presented earlier in which awareness and control over stereotypes and prejudice are minimal or nonexistent, it is difficult to assume that any conscious intention to misjudge was operative. In other words, conscious intentions cannot be reliable predictors of implicit judgment, feeling, and action.

Those who express no explicit intention to harm, to be prejudiced, or to be unfair in their social judgments may nevertheless cause harm, act prejudicially, and behave in contradiction to their egalitarian beliefs. Such a dissociation between lack of intention to harm on the one hand and discriminatory impact on the other hand has been the topic of much discussion in the law. For the notion of intention, the implications of unconscious processes are deep, although they do not immediately help resolve the questions that arise. We admittedly raise the link between the data we have examined and the legal standing of the notion of intention speculatively. We do so however, in order to imagine the possibility of a future application of scientific evidence about unconscious social judgment for the law.

The notion of intention has been formally recognized in Anglo-American jurisprudence since the time of Edward I (The Statute of Edward, 1325). In general, a prosecutor must be prepared to prove more than the fact that the defendant performed a prohibited act. The assumption in the law is that the act alone is not criminal unless it be accompanied by a specified mental state. The legal maxim, the act is not guilty until the mind is guilty, applies in almost all of criminal law. The doctrine, in its shortened form is referred to as *mens rea*, or the guilty mind, and a similar set of assumptions underlies civil law as well. Yet, legal positions on matters involving intention have been quite inconsistent. At times, employers' hiring practices are judged to be unlawful if they operate to maintain the effect of prior discrimination regardless of their conscious intention to discriminate. A practice was deemed invalid, e.g. Duke Power Co. was held responsible, when it caused disparate impact on a social group (*Griggs v. Duke Power Co.*). Additionally, in *Griggs* the Supreme Court ruled that the burden of proof lay with the employer (the actor/perceiver in our case) to show that its practices were fair and not discriminatory toward members of differing social groups.

Yet, an examination of American legal case history reveals there are far more legal cases on the other side. Not only was *Griggs* itself overturned, in most civil rights cases from the last two decades, the court has held that discriminatory intent must be proven for the act to be considered unlawful. The most striking of these cases is *Washington v. Davis*, involving the use of a test in which white police officers had a success rate that was four times greater than that of black police officers, and the test was not shown to predict on-the-job performance. Here, the court went so far as to say that no intention to harm meant that no injury had even occurred. A tension resides between the notion of discriminatory *intention* versus discriminatory *impact*, i.e. an emphasis on actor intention versus harm to the target. That is the issue on which the court remains inconsistent and divided. And it remains so on ideological grounds rather than as a result of evidence about the extent to which ordinary social agents, both individual and institutional, can produce harm. This is, of course, an old theme in social psychology but one that has acquired new power to inform because of our recent ability now to identify the cognitive and metacognitive mechanisms by which such acts come to be realized (Banaji, Blair, & Glaser, 1997).

The notion of intention, while clearly connected to the concepts of awareness and control (i.e. without awareness and control it is difficult to imagine an intentional act), is also connected to the concept of goals. That is, intentions usually operate in the service of particular goals, and both have been traditionally assumed to be components of conscious thought. However, recent theorizing offered by Bargh and colleagues examines the extent to which goals and motives may be automatically activated (Bargh & Gollwitzer, 1994). These investigators have demonstrated that socio-behavioral goals (such as achievement motivation) can be automatically activated and influence behavior (e.g. produce higher scores on a test). They argue that goals and motives that are consciously versus unconsciously activated can have equivalent impact (Chartrand & Bargh, in press). To return to the point about social judgments that have discriminatory impact, such studies and their accompanying logic indicate that it may be quite difficult to separate the impact of actions that are caused by conscious intention from "auto-motive" ones. Perhaps a shift in our thinking about intention is in order, moving away from current legal and lay definitions of the term (intentional: done deliberately, *American Heritage Dictionary*, 1992). At the very least, the debate would need to include a discussion of how we are to treat the distinction between intentions and goals that are consciously expressed and expressible and those that are not, especially if data about the influence of unconscious intentions continue to accumulate.

Research on implicit social judgment processes, in particular the data on influences that lie outside conscious awareness, control, and intention, can transform the study of metacognition by bringing into its purview processes and issues that would not otherwise have been encountered. This research emphasizes the importance of studying metacognitive processes in the context of the social world in which they operate and have their influence.

Ackowledgments

This work was supported in part by a grant from National Science Foundation (SBR-9422241). We are grateful to R. Bhaskar for comments on a previous draft.

References

Banaji, M.R., Blair, I.V., & Glaser, J. (1997). Environments and unconscious processes. In R.S. Wyer, Jr (Ed.), *Advances in social cognition, 10*. Mahwah, NJ: Lawrence Erlbaum Associates.

Banaji, M.R. & Greenwald, A.G. (1995). Implicit gender stereotyping in judgments of fame. *Journal of Personality and Social Psychology, 68*, 181–198.

Banaji, M.R. & Hardin, C.D. (1996). Automatic stereotyping. *Psychological Science, 7*, 136–141.

Banaji, M.R., Hardin, C.D., & Rothman, A. (1993). Implicit stereotyping in person judgment. *Journal of Personality and Social Psychology, 65*, 272–281.

Bargh, J.A. & Gollwitzer, P.M. (1994). Environmental control of goal-directed action: Automatic and strategic contingencies between situations and behavior. *Nebraska Symposium on Motivation, 41*, 71–124.

Beckett, N.E. & Park, B.M. (1995). Use of category versus individuating information: Making base rates salient. *Personality and Social Psychology Bulletin, 21*, 21–31.

Blair, I.V. & Banaji, M.R. (1996). Automatic and controlled processes in stereotype priming. *Journal of Personality and Social Psychology, 70*, 1142–1163.

Bodenhausen, G.V. & Wyer, R.S. (1985). Effects of stereotypes in decision making and information-processing strategies. *Journal of Personality and Social Psychology, 48*, 267–282.

Chartrand, T.L. & Bargh, J.A. (in press). Automatic activation of impression formation and memorization goals: Nonconscious goal priming reproduces effects of explicit task instructions. *Journal of Personality and Social Psychology.*

Chen, M. & Bargh, J.A. (1996). An automatic effect of (all) attitudes on behavior: Preconscious approach and avoidance responses to liked and disliked stimuli. Unpublished manuscript. New York University.

Darley, J.M. & Gross, P.H. (1983). A hypothesis-confirming bias in labeling effects. *Journal of Personality and Social Psychology, 44,* 20–33.

Glenberg, A.M., Wilkinson, A.C., & Epstein, W. (1982). The illusion of knowing: Failure in the self-assessment of comprehension. *Memory and Cognition, 10,* 597–602.

Greenwald, A.G. & Banaji, M.R. (1995). Implicit social cognition: Attitudes, self-esteem, and stereotypes. *Psychological Review, 102,* 4–27.

Greenwald, A.G., McGhee, D.E. & Schwartz, J.K. (1998). Measuring individual differences in inplicit cognition: The Implicit Association Test. *Journal of Personality and Social Psychology.*

Griggs v. Duke Power Co. (1971). 401 US 424.

Fagot, B.I. (1985). Changes in thinking about early sex role development. *Developmental Review, 5,* 83–98.

Fagot, B.I. & Leinbach, M.D. (1989). The young child's gender schema: Environmental input, internal organization. *Child Development, 60,* 663–672.

Higgins, E.T. (1989). Knowledge accessibility and activation: Subjectivity and suffering from unconscious sources. In J.S. Uleman and J.A. Bargh (Eds), *Unintended thought* (pp. 75–123). New York: Guilford Press.

Jacoby, L.L., Kelley, C.M., Brown, J., & Jasechko, J. (1989). Becoming famous overnight: Limits on the ability to avoid unconscious influences of the past. *Journal of Personality and Social Psychology, 56,* 326–338.

Johnson, M.K. & Raye, C.L. (1981). Reality monitoring. *Psychological Review, 88,* 67–85.

Johnson, J.D., Whitestone, E., Jackson, L.A., & Gatto, L. (1995). Justice is still not colorblind: Differential racial effects of exposure to inadmissible evidence. *Personality and Social Psychology Bulletin, 21,* 893–898.

Johnson-Laird, P.N. (1983). A computational analysis of consciousness. *Cognition and Brain Theory, 6,* 499–508.

Landy, D. & Sigall, H. (1979). Beauty is talent: Task evaluation as a function of the performer's physical attractiveness. *Journal of Personality and Social Psychology, 29,* 299–304.

Leyens, J-P., Yzerbyt, V.Y., & Schadron, G. (1992). Stereotypes and social judgeability. In W. Stroebe & M. Hewstone (Eds), *European Review of Social Psychology* (Vol 3, pp. 91–120). Chichester, England: Wiley.

Loftus, E.F., Miller, D.G., & Burns, H.J. (1978). Semantic integration of verbal information into a visual memory. *Journal of Experimental Psychology: Human Learning and Memory, 4,* 19–31.

Lombardi, W.J., Higgins, E.T., & Bargh, J.A. (1987). The role of consciousness in priming effects on categorization: Assimilation versus contrast as a function of awareness of the priming task. *Personality and Social Psychology Bulletin, 13,* 411–429.

Martin, C.L. & Little, J.K. (1990). The relation of gender understanding to children's sex-typed preferences and gender stereotypes. *Child Development, 61,* 1427–1439.

Metcalfe, J. & Shimamura, A.P. (1994). *Metacognition.* Cambridge, MA: MIT Press.

Nelson, T.O. (1992). Preface. In T.O. Nelson (Ed.), *Metacognition: Core Readings* (pp. ix–xi). Boston: Allyn & Bacon.

Nisbett, R.E. & Wilson, T.D. (1977). Telling more than we can know: Verbal reports on mental processes. *Psychological Review, 84,* 231–259.

Shaw, J.S. (1996). Increases in eyewitness confidence resulting from postevent questioning. *Journal of Experimental Psychology: Applied, 2,* 126–146.

Strack, F., Schwarz, N., Bless, H., Kubler, A., & Wanke, M. (1993). Awareness of the influence as a determinant of assimilation versus contrast. *European Journal of Social Psychology, 23,* 53–62.

Tulving, E. (1994). Foreword. In J. Metcalfe & A.P. Shimamura (Eds), *Metacognition*. (pp vii–x). Cambridge, MA: MIT Press.

Ugwuegbu, D.C.E. (1979). Racial and evidential factors in juror attribution of legal responsibility. *Journal of Experimental Social Psychology, 15,* 133–146.

Washington v. Davis (1976). 426 US 229.

Walsh, W.A., Banaji, M.R., & Greenwald, A.G. (1995). A failure to eliminate race bias in judgments of criminals. Paper presented at the meetings of the American Psychological Society, New York.

Wegener, D.T. & Petty, R.E. (in press). Flexible correction processes in social judgment: The role of naive theories in corrections for perceived bias. *Journal of Personality and Social Psychology.*

Wilson, T.D. & LaFleur, S.J. (1995). Knowing what you'll do: Effects of analyzing reasons on self-prediction. *Journal of Personality and Social Psychology, 68,* 21–35.

Yzerbyt, V.Y., Schadron, G., Leyens, J-P., & Rocher, S. (1994). Social judgeability: The impact of meta-informational cues on the use of stereotypes. *Journal of Personality and Social Psychology, 66,* 48–55.

10

Protecting Our Minds: The Role of Lay Beliefs

Timothy D. Wilson, Daniel T. Gilbert and Thalia P. Wheatley

Imagine that you are watching the news on television one evening. The newscaster says that the next story is about a severe famine in another country, and warns viewers that "the footage is very disturbing; it contains graphic pictures of men, women, and children who died of starvation and whose bodies have decomposed in the tropical sun." What would you do? Would you lean forward to get a closer look at the pictures, or reach for the remote control and change the channel?

Now suppose that you are listening to an interview with a noted politician. The politician starts to argue that the nation's laws on capital punishment should be changed. You are familiar with this politician and know that you disagree with virtually everything he stands for, including his views on capital punishment. What would you do in this case? Would you listen to his speech or change the channel?

In each case, your decision is likely to be based, at least in part, on your theories about how your emotions and beliefs change. In the first scenario, your theory might be that the graphic pictures would have an adverse effect on your mood and thus you should not look at them. There is nothing much you can do about the famine, you might think, so why spoil your mood by looking at graphic pictures of a terrible human tragedy? It is not uncommon to avoid stimuli that we think will elicit negative emotions, such as closing our eyes at gory scenes in the movies or turning off the radio when our ex-lover's favorite song is played. In each of these instances people assume that if they encountered these stimuli (gory pictures, sad songs) they could not help but be affected negatively; thus, it is best to avoid them.

People seem to have different theories about how their beliefs change. You might find a politician's speech annoying and change the channel to avoid the negative affect elicited by Senator Blabbermouth's latest thoughts about capital punishment. Would you be concerned, however, that your beliefs about capital punishment were in jeopardy and would change in some way you could not control? People seem not to fear as much that their beliefs will change in unwanted ways. It would seem strange to hear someone say, "I held my ears during the speech because I didn't want my beliefs to change."

This chapter is concerned with theories about unwanted influences on one's own beliefs and emotions. As noted by Wilson and Brekke (1994), people are often at risk of mental contamination, defined as "the process whereby a person has an unwanted judgment, emotion, or behavior because of mental processing that is unconscious or uncontrollable" (Wilson & Brekke, 1994, p. 117). Wilson and Brekke argued that people's susceptibility to mental contamination is in part a function of the accuracy of lay theories about how the mind operates. The strategies people use to avoid contamination – such as covering their eyes or changing the channel – are largely a function of their theories about how their attitudes, emotions, and beliefs change. Thus, it is important to understand the nature of these theories.

Psychologists in many disciplines have become interested in people's beliefs about their own minds, as reflected by the contributions to this volume. Terms such as metacognition, common-sense psychology, folk psychology, and lay theories are now commonplace. We believe, however, that these terms have come to be used in two different ways that are important to distinguish.

Implicit versus explicit common-sense psychology

The study of lay beliefs can be traced to the beginnings of social psychology as a discipline. Early social psychologists such as Lewin, Heider, and Asch applied Gestalt principles to social perception, arguing that people's phenomenological experience of the world are often better predictors of their behavior than objective reality. Lewin (1943), for example, argued that, "If an individual sits in a room trusting that the ceiling will not come down, should only his 'subjective probability' be taken into account for predicting behavior or should we also consider the 'objective probability' of the ceiling's coming down as determined by engineers? To my mind, only the first has to be taken into account" (p. 308). Similarly, Heider (1958) developed a theory of "naive" or "common-sense" psychology, arguing that an understanding of such a belief system is critical regardless of its accuracy. "If a person believes that the lines in his palm foretell his future," Heider (1958) wrote, "this belief must be taken into account in explaining certain of his expectations and actions" (p. 5). A similar emphasis on people's beliefs about and perceptions of the social world can be found in the work of other seminal psychologists, such as Asch (1952), Bruner and Tagiuri (1954), Ichheiser (1949), Kelly (1955), Newcomb (1947), and Sherif and Sherif (1969).

An interest in lay beliefs and folk psychology continues to this day (Fletcher, 1984; Furnham, 1983, 1988; Kelley, 1992; Kruglanski, 1989; Stich, 1983; Wegner & Vallacher, 1981; Wellman, 1992; Wrightsman, 1992). Interestingly, however, the study of folk psychology has evolved to mean two very different things (Fletcher, 1984; Wegner & Vallacher, 1981). The first meaning, which Wegner and Vallacher (1981) term implicit psychology, refers to the cognitive system that is responsible for our subjective impressions of the world. Ross and Nisbett (1991) refer to this type of processing as the "tools of construal" (p. 12), which include knowledge structures, judgmental heuristics, and the mental procedures by which people form their subjective impressions of the world (for recent reviews see Carlston & Smith, 1996; and Smith, 1998). Consistent with the term "implicit," these processes operate largely outside of awareness, yet they mediate evaluations, judgments, and actions (e.g. Greenwald & Banaji, 1995; Jacoby, Lindsay, & Toth, 1992; Schacter, 1987). It is unlikely, for example, that people can describe the precise way in which they use schemas and exemplars when forming social judgments.

A second meaning of common-sense psychology is people's meta-beliefs about their cognitive processes (Nisbett & Wilson, 1977b; Wegner & Vallacher, 1981), such as people's theories about the causes of their responses and how their memory operates. Wegner and Vallacher (1981) refer to these types of beliefs as explicit common-sense psychology or "*how people think they think* about the social world" (p. 226, emphasis in original). As implied by the term "explicit" this type of lay belief is more conscious than the procedural knowledge that determines our perceptions of the social world.

It is becoming increasingly clear that to predict human behavior we must understand both implicit and explicit beliefs about the world and how these different types of beliefs interact. Attempts to study these processes are increasing in different areas of psychology, such as research on meta-memory and metacognition (e.g. Flavell, 1979; Koriat, 1993; Nelson, 1996). As mentioned, our concern is with people's theories about how they protect their minds from unwanted influences. Some of these theories, we will argue, are quite accurate, and people do a reasonable job of managing some mental states, such as their emotions. These theories are incorrect in some interesting ways, however, which make people susceptible to unwanted influences, particularly on their beliefs.

Lay theories about mental protection

To return to our opening example, do people use effective strategies to protect their emotional states when they encounter upsetting photographs? Do they use effective strategies to protect their beliefs about capital punishment when listening to a distrusted politician? The strategies people might use can be captured in a general model of lay theories about mental protection (see Figure 10.1). The left-hand column depicts people's mental states in various stages of contamination, whereas the right-hand column depicts people's defenses against contamination. This process begins when people believe they are about to encounter a stimulus that can have an unwanted influence on their mental states, such as gory pictures or a speech by a distrusted politician. This sets in motion the protection strategies

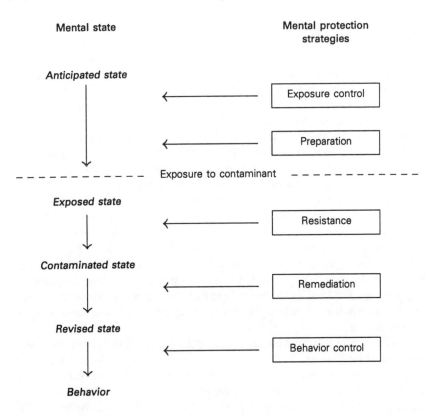

Figure 10.1 *A model of mental protection*

outlined in the right-hand column of Figure 10.1, which can be considered to be a series of defenses against contamination.

The first two lines of defense occur before people are exposed to the stimulus. The first is what Gilbert (1993) termed *exposure control*, which is the decision whether to allow the stimulus to enter our minds. In many ways this is the most effective form of mental protection, because the contaminating stimulus does not enter our minds. As noted by Gilbert (1993) this strategy can be costly, because we shut ourselves off from information that might prove useful or beneficial. Walking around with our eyes shut and ears covered does not foster personal growth or change. Further, exposure control is not always an option. We may not be fore-warned that we are about to encounter a contaminating stimulus and thus do not have the opportunity to prevent ourselves from seeing it.

The second line of defense is *preparation*. If we know that we are about to encounter a contaminating stimulus we can try to prepare ourselves, per-haps by trying to reappraise the meaning of the stimulus in a nonthreat-ening manner ("I bet the pictures won't be of real human bodies; they were staged to make it look real.") Other prophylactic strategies might help as well, such as taking a deep breath and relaxing, telling ourselves that it won't last that long, or admonishing ourselves not to be so squeamish. To the extent that such mental preparations are successful, the impact of the stimulus will be reduced.

All of the other defenses occur after people are exposed to the stimulus. The next defense is *resistance*, which occurs after the stimulus is encoded but before it has changed people's affect or beliefs, resulting in what we call an exposed state. (Whether such a mental state is possible is a question we will address shortly; recall that the model is meant to capture lay beliefs about mental processing and contamination.) Resistance involves any mental operation that attempts to prevent an encoded stimulus from having an adverse effect, similar to an immunological response that kills a virus after it enters the body but before it causes disease.

If resistance fails, people end up in a contaminated state: Their emotions or beliefs are influenced in an unwanted manner. The next line of defense is *remediation*, defined as any mental operation that attempts to undo the damage done by a contaminant. If remediation is at all successful people end up with a revised state, which is the mental state that has changed as a result of remediation. (If remediation is completely successful then the revised state is the same as the original mental state.) If remediation fails or is insufficient to correct the damage, then people's last line of defense is *behavior control*. This is the attempt to prevent one's contaminated state from influencing behavior in an unwanted manner. If our mood has been ruined, for example, we might nonetheless try to act pleasantly when our child or spouse walks into the room.

We assume that the most effective defenses are those that occur earlier rather than later in the sequence. Consider the analogy to physical disease, in which the contaminant is a virus that causes the flu. The most effective way of preventing the flu is to keep the virus out of our bodies, reducing contact with people who are sick (exposure control). If this strategy is unavailable – for example, if we are nurses, physicians, or preschool teachers – we can try to make sure our immune systems are operating effectively before we are exposed, by, for example, getting a flu shot and lots of rest (preparation). Once we know we have been exposed to the virus we can try to neutralize it before it causes the flu, perhaps by avoiding stress or taking Vitamin C (resistance). If we find ourselves with flu symptoms despite these strategies, we can try to help our bodies get rid of the virus as quickly as possible (remediation). If all else fails we can tough it out, trying to ignore our symptoms and get some work done (behavior control).

There seems to be a good correspondence, in the physical realm, between the defenses that are most effective and the defenses people prefer. The earlier the defense the more effective it is and the more people prefer it. A simple thought experiment will illustrate this point: Would you prefer to be exposed to the HIV virus with the hope that your body is able to resist infection, or to avoid exposure to the HIV virus? Clearly, people prefer to keep physical contaminants out of their bodies.

What about in the psychological realm? It is undoubtedly true in this domain, as well, that the earlier the defense, the more likely that contamination will be avoided. However, people's preferences in this domain are not so straightforward or in such good correspondence with the strategies that are most effective. For example, people seem not to have an indiscriminate preference for exposure control. Unlike viruses, psychological contaminants can have good and bad effects and it is not always easy to tell, in advance, whether our psychological states will change for the better or for the worse. A violent scene in a movie, for instance, might trigger disgust and nausea or add significantly to the dramatic impact of the film. Further, if we shut our eyes for the entire film we will miss the love scenes. Unlike viruses, psychological contaminants can have positive as well as negative effects, thus people are more willing to be exposed to them.

We turn now to a discussion of the strategies people prefer to use to prevent mental contamination and how effective these strategies are. Although the model in Figure 10.1 is meant to apply to the protection of both affect and cognition, it is useful to discuss these states separately, because the strategies people prefer differ for these types of mental states.

Protecting affective states

There is a considerable amount of research on the ways in which people attempt to manage their moods and emotions (e.g. Parrott, 1993; Salovey, Hsee, & Mayer, 1993; Wegner & Erber, 1993). Most of this research has focused on people's attempts to alter their current mood to a more desired state (typically a negative to a positive state, though there are circumstances under which people want to change a positive state to a negative one; see Parrott, 1993). In our terms, this research focuses on remediation: People are already "contaminated" in the sense that they are experiencing an undesired emotional state; the strategies they use to change this state to a more desired one are of interest. Several remediation strategies have been examined, such as the attempt to help others as a means of improving one's moods (e.g. Salovey, Mayer, & Rosenhan, 1991; Schaller & Cialdini, 1990) and reducing anger by distracting oneself or reinterpreting the provocation that caused the anger (Tice & Baumeister, 1993; Zillmann, 1993).

There has also been some attention to people's theories about how to arrange their environments in ways that maximize pleasure (e.g. Hsee & Abelson, 1991; Linville & Fischer, 1991; Tice & Baumeister, 1993). Linville and Fischer (1991), for example, found that people preferred to space out a series of negative events rather than experiencing them all at once, presumably so that they had the resources to deal with each event without being overwhelmed. There is very little research, however, on the question of how people protect themselves against the effects of a specific stimulus on their emotions, or on how effective these strategies are. If people know that they are about to encounter a violent scene in a movie, a rejection letter from a journal, or a phone call from an ex-spouse, what do they do? Under what conditions are they able to avoid the unwanted emotional reactions?

Though we know of little research that addresses these questions, we offer the following speculations. First, we suspect that people are reasonably good at regulating their emotions, in that most have a reasonable degree of "emotional intelligence" (Salovey & Mayer, 1990). Although there are undoubtedly individual differences in this skill (e.g. Catanzaro & Mearns, 1990), most people manage their emotions quite well. Sometimes, of course, we cannot avoid unwanted emotional reactions, such as the feelings of anger and depression we experience when an article we have spent years writing is rejected by a prestigious journal. Much of our lives is spent pursuing happiness, though, and most of us learn strategies that work, at least much of the time.

This is not to say that all of people's theories about their affective experiences are correct. One area in which people might be especially inaccurate is in predicting the intensity and duration of their affective reactions to future events. For example, Gilbert, Pinel, Wilson, Blumberg and Wheatley (1997) have found evidence for a durability illusion, whereby people overestimate how long their affective reactions (particularly negative ones) will last. One reason for this is that people underestimate how well they will rationalize future outcomes; they think their affect is dictated almost entirely by the objective nature of external events and fail to recognize that they possess a sophisticated "psychological immune system" that enables them to rationalize and self-regulate their emotional states.

Our concern here is with people's attempts to avoid contaminated emotions in the present. Whereas such attempts will not always succeed, we suspect that there is fairly good calibration between people's theories about the strategies that work and the strategies that are effective. In terms of the specific strategies people use, we suggest that people prefer resistance, preparation, and judicious exposure control. If people take steps in advance to avoid the negative effects of a stimulus (mental preparation) and adopt strategies to neutralize bad effects after exposure (resistance), they have the best of both worlds: They can encode the stimulus and make an informed judgment as to whether to let it influence them. Stimuli with negative effects can be screened and resisted, whereas those with positive effects can be admitted into the mind. This strategy is in principle adaptive; people would avoid the problem of self-censorship inherent in exposure control (e.g. missing information that would have been beneficial) but still avoid the unwanted effects of negative stimuli.

Often, however, people recognize that preparation and resistance are not very effective. Emotional reactions to stimuli are often quick and uncontrollable, even if we have had time to mentally prepare for them. Further, it is difficult to place an emotional stimulus in a mental holding pattern until we have had the opportunity to resist its influence. Thus, we suggest that people frequently use exposure control to manage their emotions – more so, as we will see shortly, than they use exposure control to manage their beliefs.

Protecting beliefs

People are not nearly so adept at managing their beliefs, we suggest, because theories about beliefs are more poorly calibrated than theories about emotion. For example, people seem to think that their beliefs are under more conscious control than their emotions are. People recognize that emotional reactions are difficult to control; everyone has seen athletes and politicians cry during farewell speeches, despite every effort to maintain their composure. Beliefs seem more controllable: We weigh what we know about the topic and decide what position to take. We have never seen a news conference at which a politician has tried desperately to keep his or her beliefs from changing.

And yet, there is considerable evidence that belief formation is less controllable than people think. For example, there is evidence that advertising can shape people's attitudes in powerful ways (e.g. Liebert & Sprafkin, 1988; Lodish et al., 1995; Ryan, 1991) in spite of the fact that most people deny that advertising affects their attitudes (Wilson & Brekke, 1994). Further, people underestimate the extent to which their attitudes have changed, even when this change is substantial (Bem & McConnell, 1970; Goethals & Reckman, 1973; Ross, 1989).

Perhaps the most striking evidence for the lack of controllability of belief comes from Gilbert's (1991, Gilbert, Krull, & Malone, 1990; Gilbert, Tafarodi, & Malone, 1993) research on belief acceptance. Gilbert argues that human belief formation operates like a system advocated by Spinoza. People initially accept as true every proposition they comprehend, and then decide whether to "unbelieve" it or not. Thus, when people read the statement, "Jack is seven feet tall" they initially believe it, at least for a fleeting moment. People can quickly unaccept this statement if they have reason to believe that it is false, but they must have sufficient motivation and capacity to do so.

We do not have the space to review all of the research relevant to Gilbert's Spinozan hypothesis of belief formation (see Gilbert, 1991, 1993). For present purposes we note that this process of automatic acceptance of information is highly counterintuitive. People do not have the phenomenal experience of believing → evaluating → accepting/unaccepting propositions. Instead, people tend to think that belief formation follows a two-step process described by Descartes: First people comprehend a proposition (e.g. "Jack is seven feet tall"), then they freely decide whether to accept it as true (e.g. whether it fits with their belief system). People's theory is that their beliefs are more controllable than they in fact may be.

Because people overestimate the amount of control they have over their beliefs, they might adopt nonoptimal strategies when defending their beliefs.

We consider now people's preferences for each of the mental defense strategies outlined in Figure 10.1, and the effectiveness of these strategies in the realm of belief protection.

Exposure control   We suspect that people are much more likely to use exposure control to protect their affect than to protect their beliefs. People will avoid exposure to information that they think will produce psychological discomfort; for example, Frey (1986) has found that people will avoid information that implies they made a faulty decision and Swann (1990) has found that people will avoid information that contradicts their self-views. The motive to avoid information in these cases appears to be to protect affective states, namely the discomfort that would result from exposure. Do people avoid information because they believe it might change their beliefs in unwanted ways, independently of the effects of this information on their affect? We suspect that such exposure control is rare. We have never heard anyone say, "I think I'll change the channel, otherwise I might start to believe what that joker is saying."

Preparation   If people know in advance that their beliefs are about to be challenged in an undesired way, do they prepare for this challenge successfully? The literature on persuasion and attitude change suggests that some forms of mental preparation are effective. According to the Elaboration Likelihood Model of persuasion (Petty & Cacioppo, 1986), any mental preparation that increases people's ability or motivation to resist a persuasive message can lower the effectiveness of that message. McGuire (1964), for example, increased people's ability to resist a subsequent message by providing them with ammunition in advance, in the form of arguments that might be used and refutations of these arguments.

This work does not fit our concept of preparation very well, however, because it involves giving people information they did not have before (counterarguments). The more relevant question is, if people are forewarned about an attempt to change their attitudes, can they do something on their own to reduce the impact of the persuasion attempt? The answer is yes, as long as people are motivated to maintain their beliefs. If they are – when, for example, the issue is of high personal relevance – they engage in "anticipatory counterarguing," whereby they think of arguments consistent with their position and arguments against contrary positions (e.g. Petty & Cacioppo, 1977). Such anticipatory counterarguing reduces the impact of the subsequent message.

Another kind of forewarning has also been shown to be effective: Informing people that someone is about to change their attitudes but not saying which attitude will be attacked. Under these conditions people cannot generate counterarguments because they do not know what the topic will be. Forewarning of persuasive intent appears to heighten the motivation to generate counterarguments during the message, however, particularly if the topic turns out to be one people care about (Petty &

Cacioppo, 1979). This type of forewarning fits our definitions of remediation better, however, because it works by changing what people do after exposure to the stimulus (the persuasive message). We will return to this topic in a moment.

People seem to recognize the importance of mentally preparing for a persuasive message, as indicated by the fact that they engage in counter-arguing when forewarned. Nonetheless, we suspect that people are a bit too reticent about preparation, assuming that later defenses are just as effective. Consider people's reaction to advertising. Most people would prefer not to let their consumer decisions be overly influenced by advertising; for example, they would not want to buy a car solely because the manufacturer claimed it was of high quality. Which of the mental defenses listed in Figure 10.1 are used to combat the unwanted effects of advertising? We suspect that exposure control is rarely used. True enough, people might change the channel when a commercial comes on because they find it annoying or want to see what is on another channel. The reason for such exposure control, however, appears not to be to prevent their beliefs from changing. People do not say, "Help, where's the remote control – my beliefs about Buicks are about to change!" Instead they change channels more to manage their affect ("Argh, it's that 'ring around the collar' commercial again").

Nor do people use preparation very often, despite the evidence that this strategy can be effective. It takes mental effort to generate counterarguments and people are unlikely to go to this effort before watching every commercial that happens to be shown on television. Even though people often know in advance who the sponsors of a television program are and that the intent of the commercials will be to change their beliefs, they do not mentally prepare for the commercials in advance. They do not spend the first 10 minutes of a program, before the first commercial comes on, rehearsing their arguments for why they prefer Volvos to Buicks.

One reason for the failure to use exposure control and preparation for television commercials may be that people do not care much about their consumer attitudes. These attitudes might be of such low personal relevance that they are not motivated to defend them (Chaiken, 1987; Petty & Cacioppo, 1986). Although this is undoubtedly true in some instances (who wants to go to the trouble of generating counterarguments against Buicks if you have no plans to buy a car?). We suspect there is another reason: People have faith in their ability to resist or remediate attempts to change their beliefs – faith that is, at least to some extent, misplaced.

Resistance   We take a very hard line on people's ability to resist attempts to change their beliefs: They can't. To be able to resist an attack on our beliefs we would have to be able to encode a message without it influencing us, placing it in a kind of mental holding pattern. We would then have to neutralize the message in some way, such as by thinking of counterarguments. As reviewed earlier, however, Gilbert's (1991, 1993) Spinozan theory of belief acceptance holds that people initially believe everything they comprehend. According to this view, people cannot encode something without believing it; thus, mental resistance is impossible.

We suggest that this is one of the most glaring ways in which lay theories are incorrect: A faith in resistance as a means of protecting beliefs. People seem to believe that there is little risk to encountering potentially false information, because they can always weed out the truth from the fiction, discarding those propositions that do not hold up under scrutiny. Gilbert and his colleagues have found in numerous experiments, however, that there is danger involved: If people do not have the motivation or cognitive capacity to "unaccept" information they encode, they cannot help but believe it (Gilbert et al., 1990, 1993). A consequence of this misplaced faith in mental resistance is that people rely less on exposure control and preparation than perhaps they should.

Remediation Gilbert's work demonstrates that remediation is possible when people have sufficient motivation and cognitive capacity. People are able to "unaccept" false information under these conditions, recognizing that what they initially believed is false (e.g. that Jack is not seven feet tall). There are, however, dangers in relying too much on remediation. First, people may not have the requisite capacity to reject falsehoods. Second, in order to engage in the unacceptance process, people must know that their beliefs have changed. As discussed previously, however, people's attitudes can change substantially without their knowing it (e.g. Goethals & Reckman, 1973) If people are unaware that an attitude or belief has changed they will not exert any effort to undo this change.

Behavior control Trying to control one's behavior is probably rare in the realm of beliefs. After all, if people have new beliefs they think are true, there is no reason not to act on these beliefs. There may be times when people hold new beliefs with low confidence and thus decide not to act on them, especially if they are in the presence of people who disagree with these beliefs. Consider a lifelong liberal who listens to a conservative talk-show host and finds herself agreeing with some of the host's right-wing views. At the next Democratic caucus she might decide against announcing that that Rush Limbaugh fellow really knows his stuff. As with remediation, however, there are dangers involved with a reliance on behavior control. In order to use this strategy people have to know that their beliefs have changed, which is not always the case. If they do, they might find it difficult to suppress their beliefs (DePaulo, 1992; Wegner, 1994).

If people truly want to avoid unwanted belief change, they are better off using earlier mental strategies such as exposure control and mental preparation. As we have discussed, however, there are costs involved with these strategies as well. If we use exposure control too much we might well miss information we would prefer to have. Constantly preparing ourselves for potentially unwanted messages would be very time consuming and effortful; if we engaged in preemptory counterarguing for every television commercial we were about to see, we would never enjoy the show. None-theless, people might be better off if they recognized the limits of resistance, remediation, and behavior control and engaged in some judicious exposure control and mental preparation.

Cross-contamination

Our separation of contamination into the affective and belief realms, is admittedly simplistic, because the stimuli that we encounter rarely influence only affect our beliefs. Typically, both types of mental states are influenced. Affect and cognition are intimately related; most theories of attitudes, for example, define attitudes as consisting of both affective and cognitive components (e.g. Breckler, 1984; Crites, Fabrigar, & Petty, 1994). Affect influences belief and belief influences affect, thus it may be misleading to consider changes in one type of mental state alone.

We believe that it has been useful to discuss affective and cognitive contamination separately, to illustrate the different theories people have about how their emotions and beliefs change. We acknowledge, however, that it is rare for beliefs and affect to change in a vacuum. A stimulus such as a persuasive message typically influences both affect and cognition, and people must take this into account when managing their emotions and beliefs.

If people believe that a stimulus will negatively influence both their emotions and feelings, the strategies they should adopt are relatively straightforward: Marshal all available defenses against the unwanted influences. Suppose, for example, that a notorious liar is about to tell you that he or she had an affair with your spouse. You are certain that it is lie; on the date in question you and your spouse were on vacation in another city. Nonetheless, having to hear about the liar's supposed affair might adversely influence both your affect and beliefs. It will be unpleasant to listen to the liar's detailed account of making love to your spouse. Further, even though you know it is a lie, the innuendo might increase your doubts about your spouse's fidelity, especially if you are unable to fully "unaccept" the false information (Gilbert, 1991; Wegner, Wenzlaff, Kerker, & Beattie, 1981). Because people are motivated to avoid both the emotional and cognitive consequences of the liar's account they will defend against it, probably by using exposure control (electing not to listen to it). This example is portrayed at the top of Figure 10.2. We call this *double contamination*, because the stimulus (e.g. the liar's account) has unwanted effects on both affect and cognition.

Sometimes, however, a stimulus can adversely affect one type of mental state but have a desired effect on the other. We term this state of affairs *cross-contamination*, and illustrate it at the middle and bottom of Figure 10.2. These cases are more complicated for people trying to manage their mental states, because the strategies needed to protect one type of state

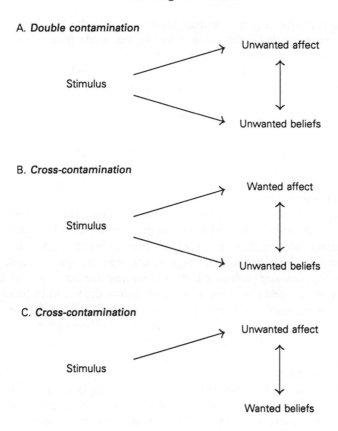

Figure 10.2 *Double contamination and cross-contamination*

might have an adverse effect on the other. The middle part of Figure 10.2 represents the case whereby a stimulus has a desired effect on emotions but an undesired effect on beliefs. People might encounter information that they believe is false or misleading, but which nonetheless has positive emotional consequences, as in the case of a false compliment. Suppose a student said "Professor, you are the best teacher I have ever had." We might very much want to believe the student, due to the professional pride that would result. However, we might doubt the sincerity of the student, particularly when his very next statement is, "Will you write me a letter of recommendation?". We do not want to be duped by his false praise, and yet successfully defending ourselves against it will prevent us from experiencing positive affect.

Another example of this kind of cross-contamination is the halo effect, in which our affect toward a person distorts our views of that person's objective qualities. Suppose, for instance, that our favorite student submits a mediocre term paper. Assuming that we want to maintain our favorable feelings toward the student and grade her paper objectively, we are in a bind: The more we like the student (desired affect) the less objective our grade (undesired belief); the more objective the grade (desired belief) the less positive our feelings (undesired affect).

The second type of cross-contamination is portrayed at the bottom of Figure 10.2: the case whereby a stimulus has a desired effect on beliefs but an undesired effect on emotions. Consider Monica, who suspects that her husband is having an affair. When she confronts her husband she wants to know the truth, and thus uses all of the defenses depicted in Figure 10.1 to make sure that she does not believe false information. She is so successful in her attempt to avoid contaminated beliefs that she sees through his denials, realizing that he is, in fact, having an affair – knowledge that has very negative affective consequences.

One way to resolve the dilemma of cross-contamination is to engage in rampant self-deception, whereby we adopt only those beliefs that create positive affect. We could decide to believe all compliments, that our favorite students always write perfect term papers, and that our spouse would never have an affair. Studies on halo effects, self-serving attributions, and unrealistic optimism suggest that people often do distort the world in these affectively pleasing ways (e.g. Nisbett & Wilson, 1977a; Taylor & Brown, 1988; Weinstein, 1980). However, there are limits to self-deception, and times when people want to avoid contaminated beliefs. Consider moviegoers attending the film *JFK* by Oliver Stone. Having read reviews of the movie, they might be wary that they will be exposed to a portrayal of Kennedy's assassination that is unsupported by the facts. They may also want to be entertained as much as possible. Though they could maximize their enjoyment by believing the movie's portrayal of the conspiracy to murder Kennedy, they might decide that an evening's entertainment is not worth believing such an outlandish theory. By maintaining their skepticism, however, they do not enjoy the movie.

Our earlier discussion of the difficulty of controlling our mental states suggests that people cannot easily choose when and when not to engage in self-deception. It is not as if a moviegoer can say, "I want to enjoy the movie, so after the opening credits I will believe everything I hear." People have some control; as we saw, they can decide whether or not to engage in active counterarguing. Suspending disbelief only works so well, however; the more outlandish the facts we encounter, the more difficult it is to avoid counterarguing. And the opposite is true as well: When we are trying our best not to believe something we might unwittingly accept what we hear, especially when we are under cognitive load.

Earlier, we discussed the difficulties of defending against stimuli that will adversely affect our affect or our beliefs. The present discussion suggests that cases of cross-contamination are even more difficult to manage, because successfully managing one type of mental state (e.g. our beliefs) can have negative consequences on the other type of mental state (e.g. our affect). We are not mental surgeons who can isolate and remove one type of mental state while leaving the other unaltered.

Empirical evidence

Much of our discussion thus far has been speculative. We have relied largely
on metaphors and studies conducted for other purposes; there is not a great
deal of research directly examining the strategies people use to avoid
affective and cognitive contamination. We turn now to recent studies of
ours that have addressed some of these questions.

We have focused on people's attempts to avoid contaminated beliefs,
because as discussed earlier, people's lay theories appear to be especially
incorrect in this domain. As also discussed, however, it is very difficult to
study beliefs in a vacuum separate from affect. Many of the situations we
have studied are better described as cases of double contamination, in which
people believe that a stimulus will influence both their beliefs and affect in
unwanted ways (see Figure 10.2, p. 183).

In our initial work we surveyed people about how their beliefs would be
influenced by various kinds of contaminating information. Wilson, Brekke,
Etling, and Houston (1992), for example, gave participants two scenarios
in which people wanted to form unbiased beliefs. The first was an election
for mayor in which people needed to decide which candidate they preferred. We described a variety of stimuli that might influence their beliefs
about the candidates, four of which we assumed would be invalid, in
participants' eyes: subliminal messages hidden in television programs, the
candidates' pictures on fliers accompanied by no other information,
television commercials that portrayed the candidates in a positive light but
did not discuss their stances on the issues, and a newspaper article that
falsely accused a candidate of stealing campaign funds. The second situation was one in which people imagined that they were the personnel
director of a small company that was hiring new employees. We again
described information that might influence people's beliefs (in this case
about the job applicants), some of which was assumed to be invalid: The
applicants' gender and a letter of recommendation from the applicants'
mothers.

Participants were asked two questions about each stimulus: How much
they would want to be influenced by it and how much they thought they
really would be influenced by it (rated on the same nine-point scales). As
seen in Figure 10.3, most people believed the stimuli were contaminants, in
that their ratings of how much they wanted the stimuli to affect them
(desired influence) were quite low. The mean rating of how much people
wanted their personnel decision to be decided by a candidate's gender, for
example, was 1.74, close to the endpoint of the rating scale (1 = "not at
all").

The middle bars in Figure 10.3 are the average ratings of how much
people thought they really *would* be influenced by each stimulus (actual
influence on self). In every case except one, the mean of these ratings was
significantly higher than people's ratings of desired influence (the exception
was for the letter of recommendation from a job applicant's mother; the

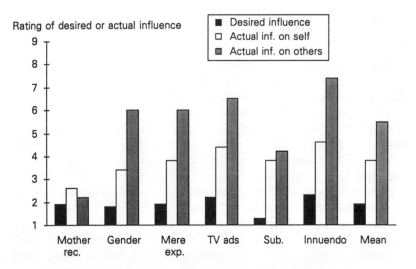

Figure 10.3 *Desired versus actual influences on the self versus others of mental contaminants. The ratings of desired influence are how much people said they would want to be influenced by each type of information, on nine-point scales on which 1 = not at all and 9 = very much. The ratings of actual influence are how much people said that they or someone else really would be influenced by each type of information, on the same nine-point scales.*

difference here was significant at the 0.08 level).[1] Every participant estimated that the actual effect would be greater than the desired effect for at least one stimulus. Thus, with the exception of the letter of recommendation from a candidate's mother, the stimuli were viewed as potential contaminants: Their actual influence was seen as greater than desired.

The question arises as to the strategies people use to defend themselves against these potential contaminants. One clue comes from the responses of additional participants who were asked to estimate how much other people would be influenced by the stimuli. As seen in the right-hand bars in Figure 10.3, the ratings of influence on others were higher than the ratings of influence on oneself, for every stimulus except the letter of recommendation from a candidate's mother and the subliminal messages about a mayoral candidate. With these exceptions, the difference between ratings of influence on others versus oneself was highly significant for all of the stimuli.

The belief that other people would be more influenced by mental contaminants than oneself has been found in a variety of other studies (see Wilson & Brekke, 1994). One reason for this difference, we suggest, is that people believe that they have a greater ability to resist or remediate the effects of a contaminant than other people do. Clearly, they do not believe that the effects of the stimuli are completely avoidable; after all, their ratings of actual influence on the self are greater than their ratings of desired influence. The fact that their ratings of actual influence are lower for themselves than for others, however, suggests that people believe they have the ability to control the unwanted effects of the stimuli to some extent.

What about the two stimuli that are exceptions to this pattern of results, namely the ratings of influence on self versus others for the subliminal messages and a letter of recommendation from a job applicant's mother? These results are not inconsistent with the hypothesis that people believe they can resist or remediate the unwanted effects of mental contaminants. The effects of a stimulus can only be resisted or remediated if people know that they have perceived it, and by definition, a subliminal message is perceived nonconsciously. Thus, it is not surprising that one of the few stimuli people think will influence them as much as others is the one that is by definition uncontrollable. The letter of recommendation from an applicant's mother is in a separate category; it is the only stimulus that people thought would not influence anyone very much. People seemed to feel that there was no need to try to defend against this stimulus because it was relatively powerless to influence them. Presumably we would have found the same pattern of results for any stimulus believed to be ineffectual, such as job applicant's shoe size.

Support for these conclusions comes from another version of the survey we conducted, in which participants (randomly assigned) received the same scenarios about the mayoral election and personnel decision. Instead of estimating how much each stimulus would influence their beliefs, however, we asked these participants a question about how much they would want to receive and use the information. For each stimulus, people chose one of five options: Whether they would want the information to make up their minds (e.g. whether they would want to know the gender of a job candidate in order to decide whether to hire him or her), whether they would want the information even though it would not influence their decision, whether they would not want the information because it might influence their decision in an undesirable way, whether they would not want the information because it would be bothersome or a waste of time, or whether they didn't care whether they had the information or not.

Figure 10.4 displays the percentage of people who chose each option for each stimulus. First, very few people said that they would want the information to make up their minds, confirming our conclusion that these stimuli are viewed as potential contaminants (the percentage of people who chose this option ranged from 13% for the newspaper innuendo to 0% for the subliminal messages and television ads). This response could, of course, mean two things: Either that the stimuli were non-diagnostic and powerless to influence them (like a candidate's shoe size) or that the stimuli were potential contaminants (like a job candidate's gender). Consistent with the data shown in Figure 10.3, people seem to view a letter of recommendation from a job candidate's mother as a non-diagnostic stimulus without power; 79% said either that they didn't care whether they got this information or that they would not want it because it would be a waste of time.

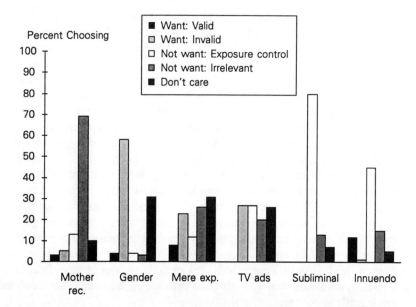

Figure 10.4   *Preferences for how to deal with various mental contaminants. For each stimulus, people chose one of five options: Whether they would want the information to make up their minds (Want: Valid); whether they would want the information even though it would not influence their decision (Want: Invalid); whether they would not want the information because it might influence their decision in an undesirable way (Not want: Exposure control); whether they would not want the information because it would be bothersome or a waste of time (Not want: Irrelevant); or whether they didn't care whether they had the information or not (Don't care). The percentages of people who chose each option are displayed.*

Earlier we saw that each of the other stimuli was viewed as a potential contaminant, in that people rated actual influence as significantly greater than their desired influence. People's responses in the second survey illuminate how people think they can deal with this potential contamination. As discussed earlier, the most effective strategy is exposure control, whereby people prevent the contaminant from ever entering the mental system. This strategy was rarely preferred, however, as indicated by the relatively small percentage of people who said that they would prefer not to receive the information "because it might influence my decision in an undesirable way." For example, only 5% of the people chose this option for the gender of a job candidate.

Once again the exception to this pattern of results was people's ratings of subliminal messages: 79% said that they would prefer not to receive such messages because of their potential undesired influence. This exception, however, seems to prove the rule that people have faith in their ability to resist or remediate the effects of most contaminants. If they cannot consciously perceive a contaminant (a subliminal message) they prefer not to receive it. Most people are willing to be exposed to all of the other stimuli, however, which are consciously perceived. There was some variation in people's choice of the exposure control option; interestingly, many (46%) said they would prefer not to receive the false innuendo about a political candidate, whereas, as just mentioned, only 5% said they would prefer not to know the gender of a job candidate.

We suspect that this difference reflects people's beliefs about the "interest value" of a piece of information. A false news story about a political candidate has little redeeming value; people do not think it is diagnostic (see Figure 10.3, p. 186) and apparently have little curiosity about it (as indicated by how few people said they would want to receive this information; see Figure 10.4). People seem to be quite curious, however, about the gender of a job candidate. As seen in Figure 10.3, most people recognize that this information might influence them more than they want it to. Nonetheless, in our second survey most people said either that they would want to have this information even though it would not influence them or that they didn't care whether they received it. This pattern of results, we suggest, is indicative of people's faith in their ability to resist or remediate unwanted influences: They know that gender can influence them more than they want but are still willing to receive this information, because they think they can take mental steps to prevent too much unwanted influence. True, they recognize that they cannot completely control the unwanted effects of this information, but they believe they can control it more than other people can (see Figure 10.3).

The survey work we have been describing has clear limitations. Perhaps the biggest is that people were rating hypothetical scenarios; they may well use different strategies to avoid contamination when they are faced with a real decision. In our next studies we thus asked people to make real decisions about real stimuli. We tried to find situations which were of some consequence to people, so that they would be motivated to form unbiased beliefs. In the first study, we asked college women to evaluate two brands of condoms and choose one to take home for their personal use (Wilson, Etling, & Houston, 1993). Given the risk of sexually transmitted diseases such as AIDS, the decision of what brand of condom to use is of considerable importance; thus, the women should have been motivated to avoid any unwanted influences on their decision.

We gave participants two sources of information about the quality and reliability of the brands of condoms. One type of information was designed to be quite valid and useful whereas the other was designed to be invalid but potentially contaminating. The valid information was a summary of an actual article in *Consumer Reports* magazine containing information about the quality of the condoms, including data from objective tests of their strength and the preferences of a large survey of readers. The potential contaminant was a summary of reports from two students who discussed their experiences with the condoms. These reports were quite vivid; one woman described an incident where a condom burst while she and her lover

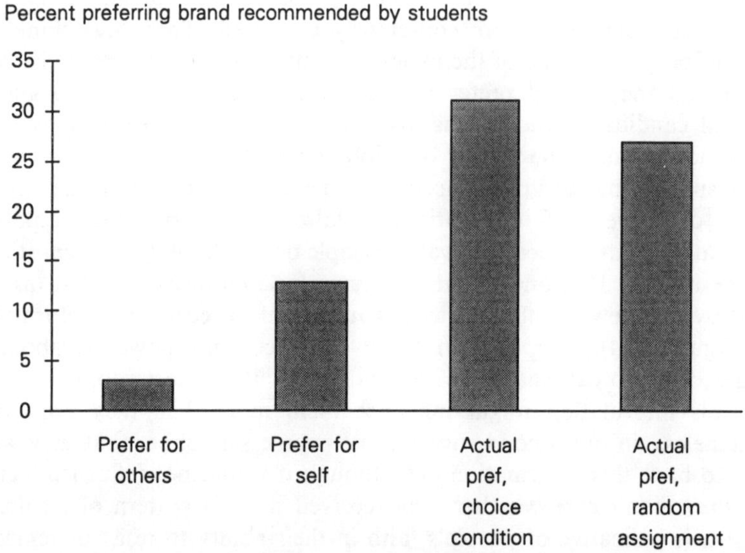

Percent preferring brand recommended by students

Figure 10.5 *Percentage of people desiring influence by student information versus actually choosing condom recommended by the students*

were having sex and the fears of pregnancy and disease that resulted. It just so happened that the brand recommended by *Consumer Reports* was different from the one recommended by the student testimonials; thus, participants had to decide which recommendation was more valid.

To see which type of information participants preferred to use, we first asked women to read the *Consumer Reports* information and the student testimonials and indicate how much they would want either a close friend or they themselves to be influenced by each type of information. As seen on the left-hand side of Figure 10.5, most people viewed the information from *Consumer Reports* as more valid; only 3% said they would want a close friend to choose the brand recommended in the student testimonials and only 13% said that they themselves would want to choose the brand recommended in the student testimonials. Thus, most participants agreed with us that the *Consumer Reports* information was more valid than the student testimonials.

We gave a separate group of participants a description of both types of information and allowed them to choose (privately and anonymously) whether they wanted to see the *Consumer Reports* data, the student testimonials, or both. After examining one or both of these types of information participants indicated which brand of condom they preferred. Which type of information did people choose to see? As we have discussed, one of the best defenses against unwanted influences is exposure control; thus, if people were concerned that the student testimonials would influence them too much, they might elect not to read them. As we have also discussed, however, people often decide not to use exposure control, possibly because of their faith in their ability to resist or remediate unwanted influences. Consistent with this hypothesis, only 12% of the participants elected not to read the student testimonials. Most people (77%) decided to read both types of information, whereas 12% elected to see only the student testimonials.

Was this faith in resistance and remediation well-founded? Not entirely. Of the people who chose to see both types of information, 31% ended up preferring the brand recommended by the students, which was significantly higher than the percentage of people in the other sample who said they would prefer that a close friend or they themselves be influenced by the student information. Thus, using people's own preferences as the standard of which type of information was most valid, a significant proportion of people ended up being overly influenced by invalid information. This comparison, it should be noted, involves a subject self-selection problem: Not everyone chose to see both kinds of information. We also included a condition in which people were randomly assigned to receive both the *Consumer Reports* information and student testimonials. As seen in Figure 10.5, the percentage of people in this condition who preferred the condom recommended by the students was comparable to those who chose to see both kinds of information.

The Wilson et al. (1993) condom study provides some support for the hypothesis that people are generally unwilling to use exposure control to avoid contaminated beliefs. Even though most people believed that the student testimonials were relatively uninformative, most opted to read them, perhaps out of curiosity. There was a danger to this decision, however: Some ended up being more influenced by the testimonials than was desirable. It is not entirely clear from this study, however, whether people's decision to see the student testimonials was based on their faith in their ability to resist or remediate any unwanted influences on their beliefs. Wilson, Houston, and Meyers (in press) recently conducted a study to look more directly at people's faith in resistance and remediation, and the consequences of this faith.

In order to motivate people to avoid unwanted influences on their beliefs, Wilson et al. (in press) selected people who had strong attitudes on a particular issue and told them that they would try to change that attitude. Participants were then allowed to select which kind of information to receive: Subliminal messages or a speech containing persuasive arguments. Wilson et al. hypothesized that people would be more likely to choose to see the speech, believing that they could more easily defend against it. In fact, however, the speech was predicted to change their attitudes more than the subliminal messages.

On the basis of pretesting, we selected participants who felt strongly that marijuana should not be legalized and that this issue was important to them. The purpose of the study, they were told, was to examine the best ways to change people's attitudes on the issue of marijuana legalization, by showing them one of two videotapes that had been prepared "in conjunction with NORML, the National Organization for the Reform of Marijuana Laws, a Washington-based organization dedicated to the legalization of marijuana." Thus, given people's prior attitudes, they should have been quite motivated to avoid changing their attitudes, especially by an organization such as NORML.

We told participants that they could choose which of the two videotapes to see and emphasized that they should choose the one that they thought would be least likely to change their attitudes. On one videotape (the *speech video*), they were told, an individual would present arguments supporting the legalization of marijuana. The other (the *subliminal video*), we said, "is designed to change people's attitudes with subliminal messages, which are perceived by the mind outside of conscious awareness." Participants were told that they would see the same speaker as in the other tape but would not consciously hear what he said. Several subliminal messages were supposedly embedded in this tape, designed to make people more favorable toward the legalization of marijuana. We emphasized that people should choose to see the video they thought would change their attitudes the least.

We in fact had two videos like the ones we described to participants. On the speech video a speaker presented a series of persuasive arguments as to why marijuana should be legalized. These arguments were designed to be as persuasive as possible and included such things as information about the benefits of marijuana for some health problems and the economic advantages of legalization. The subliminal video was identical except that the soundtrack was recorded backward. Thus, participants saw the same male speaker, but his arguments were unintelligible (unless people could decipher the backward speech, which was highly unlikely; Vokey & Read, 1985). It also contained some intermittent flashes and barely audible interjections by another voice that said things such as, "legalize it," to make it seem more "subliminal." After watching the video they had chosen, participants rated their attitude toward the legalization of marijuana. By comparing this to their pretest attitude, we computed an index of attitude change. The amount of attitude change among people who watched the videos was compared to a control group of participants who attended the laboratory session but did not watch either videotape.

The first question of interest is which video people chose to watch. As predicted, most people (69%) chose the speech video; this percentage was significantly different from chance. The second question is which tape actually changed people's attitudes the most. As seen in Figure 10.6, people who watched the speech video changed their attitudes more, in the direction of becoming more favorable toward the legalization of marijuana, than control participants or people who watched the subliminal video. Again, there is a subject self-selection problem with comparing people who chose to see the speech versus the subliminal variables; one group may have been more predisposed to change their attitudes than the other. To address this problem we randomly assigned some participants to see either the speech or subliminal video. As seen in Figure 10.6, similar results were found: People

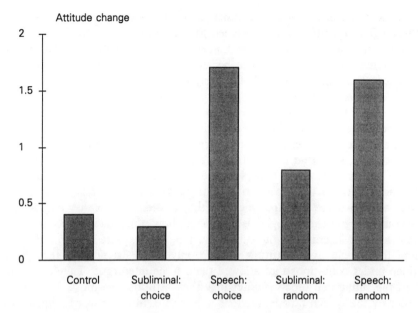

Figure 10.6 *Attitude change toward the legalization of marijuana. The
mean difference in attitude toward the legalization at the study and at a
pretesting session several weeks earlier. The higher the number, the more the
change in the direction of favorability toward legalization.*

who watched the speech video changed their attitudes more than people
who watched the subliminal video.

These results are not particularly surprising to people who are familiar
with the social psychological literature on attitude change. There is ample
evidence that persuasive communications can change attitudes (e.g.
Chaiken, 1987; Petty & Cacioppo, 1986) and that subliminal messages of
the type we used are ineffective (e.g. Vokey & Read, 1985). What is
interesting is that people's theories about the effectiveness of the two kinds
of stimuli do not match these well-known findings. A majority of people
surveyed in national samples reports that they believe that subliminal
messages are effective (e.g. Zanot, Pincus, & Lamp, 1983). Our study
suggests that people believe such messages can be more powerful, and more
difficult to resist, than a set of persuasive arguments. Our study also indicates that these beliefs are wrong, at least for the videotapes in our
experiment. Assuming that people's goal was to avoid changing their
attitude, most of them assigned themselves to precisely the wrong condition.

Why did people think that the speech video would influence them less?
We suggest that people believed they could more easily resist or remediate
its effects. To see if this was the case, we asked participants to indicate how
much several possible reasons for choosing a tape applied to them. The
reason that correlated the highest with choosing the speech video was, "It is
possible that both tapes could have changed my attitudes, but I thought

that the one I chose would be easier to resist, because I could more easily think of arguments that contradicted the message."

We conducted some follow-up studies to test further the idea that people preferred to see the speech video because they thought they could generate counterarguments that would effectively prevent the speech from changing their attitudes. For example, in one study we asked people to estimate how much they thought the speech video would change their attitudes when watched under three different conditions, which varied in the ease with which people could generate counterarguments: (a) when they were tired or preoccupied, such that they heard the arguments but could not think much about them; (b) when they watched the tape "normally and straight through" without being able to stop or pause the tape; and (c) when they were able to pause the tape whenever they desired so that they could think of counterarguments. People also estimated how much their attitudes would change after listening to the subliminal tape. As expected, people thought that they could avoid attitude change only when listening to the speech video under conditions that allowed them to counterargue. They estimated that the subliminal tape would change their attitudes the most, followed in order by the speech tape in versions a, b, and c. In other words, when they could stop and pause the tape and think of counterarguments (version c), they estimated that their attitude would change the least. When it was most difficult to think of counterarguments (version a), they thought that their attitude would change only slightly less than it would in response to the subliminal video.

A critic might argue that people in Wilson et al. (in press) first study might not have been motivated solely to avoid attitude change. It is possible, for example, that people were open-minded on the issue of marijuana legalization and felt that if they were going to change their attitude, they would rather change in response to a set of well-reasoned arguments than in response to subliminal messages. Recall, however, that we instructed people to choose the tape that they thought would be least likely to change their attitudes; further, people felt strongly about this issue and thought it was important, thus they should have been resistant to change.

Nonetheless, some people may have adopted this open-minded approach to the speech video and chose it because they were willing to be influenced by it. To find out, we conducted another study in which participants were given the same descriptions of the two videotapes and asked (1) how much they thought each one would change their attitude toward the legalization of marijuana; and (2) how *willing* they would be to be influenced by each video. As expected, people said that the subliminal video would change their attitudes significantly more than the speech video. Further, they said that they were equally unwilling to have either tape change their attitudes; the mean ratings of willingness were 2.89 for the subliminal video and 3.00 for the speech video, on a nine-point scale on which 1 = very unwilling and 9 = very willing (this difference did not approach significance). Further, when asked which video they would like to see, 74% preferred the speech video and 26% preferred the subliminal video, replicating the results of Study 1. These results reinforce our conclusion that most people preferred to see the speech video because they thought it would change their attitudes less than the subliminal video.

An even more severe critic, however, might argue the following: Before seeing the speech video, people were unwilling to change their minds in response to what they imagined were weak or specious arguments. Once they watched the speech video, however, they might have found the arguments so compelling that they were perfectly willing to change their minds. That is, if we had questioned people *after* listening to the speech, they might have said, "Well, yes, at first I couldn't believe that arguments from a group like NORML would be compelling, but once I heard how helpful marijuana can be to people suffering from cancer and glaucoma, I changed my mind – quite deliberately and willingly." We will refer to this as the "rational believer" argument: That people weighed the arguments on the speech tape consciously and logically and decided which ones to accept or reject, and thus did not end up with contaminated beliefs. They changed their attitudes precisely as much as they wanted to.

We have already seen evidence that is inconsistent with the "rational believer" argument, such as Gilbert's (1991) work on the automatic acceptance of beliefs and evidence that people sometimes change their attitudes without knowing it. Nonetheless, there may be times when we discover that arguments we expected to be completely invalid in fact have some merit, and thus we willingly change our beliefs. To see if this was the case in the Wilson et al. (in press) study, we conducted what was perhaps the most stringent test of our hypothesis about contamination. We showed people both the speech and the subliminal videos (in counterbalanced order), measured their attitudes after they watched each tape, and asked them how willing they had been to change their minds in response to each video. Further, we asked them to estimate what their attitude had been when we measured it in a pretesting session a few weeks before, to see if they recognized how much their attitudes had changed.

The "rational believer" argument would predict the following: People should recognize exactly how much their attitude changed in response to each video and they should report that they were willing to have their attitude change this amount. We predicted, however, that people would not recognize how much their attitude changed and would be relatively unwilling to have their attitudes changed by either tape – even if their attitudes had, in fact, changed.

As seen in Figure 10.7, the speech video changed people's attitudes significantly more than the subliminal video: Those who saw the speech video first became significantly more in favor of the legalization of marijuana, whereas those who saw the subliminal video first did not.[2] This result replicates Wilson, Houston, and Meyers' first study, in which the speech video also caused more attitude change (see Figure 10.6, p. 193). Did people

sufficient control over their mental processes to undo the damage. They reviewed a substantial amount of evidence that each of these conditions often goes unmet. Another option, as we have discussed, is exposure control; we can prevent potential contaminants from entering our minds. Although there are clear costs to this strategy in some cases (Gilbert, 1993; Wilson & Brekke, 1994), there may be times when we should adopt a more humble attitude toward our minds and be more careful about the information we admit. Once we open the mind's gates we may not know how much our beliefs change or how to control this change.

Notes

1. It is possible, of course, that the difference between desired and actual ratings of influence is due entirely to the few people who said they wanted to be influenced by the stimuli. For example, everyone who said they did not want to be influenced by the gender of a job candidate may have reported that they would not be at all influenced, and everyone who said they did want to be influenced by the gender of a job candidate may have reported that they would be very much influenced. To examine this possibility we looked at the ratings of people who said that they did not want to be influenced at all by each stimulus (those who gave a "1" on the 9-point scale). For every stimulus, their ratings of actual influence were significantly higher than their ratings of desired influence.

2. Once people had seen one of the tapes, it is difficult to assess how much the other one changed their attitudes; thus, we assessed attitude change by comparing the attitude of people who saw the speech video first with the attitude of people who saw the subliminal video first.

References

Asch, S. (1952). *Social psychology*. New York: Prentice-Hall.

Bem, D.J. & McConnell, H.K. (1970). Testing the self-perception explanation of dissonance phenomena: On the salience of premanipulation attitudes. *Journal of Personality and Social Psychology, 14*, 23–31.

Breckler, S.J. (1984). Empirical validation of affect, behavior, and cognition as distinct components of attitude. *Journal of Personality and Social Psychology, 47*, 1191–1205.

Bruner, J.S. & Tagiuri, R. (1954). The perception of people. In G. Lindzey (Ed.), *The handbook of social psychology*. Cambridge, MA: Addison-Wesley.

Carlston, D.E. & Smith, E.R. (1996). Principles of mental representation. In E.T. Higgins & A.W. Kruglanski (Eds), *Social psychology: Handbook of basic principles* (pp. 184–210). New York: Guilford.

Catanzaro, S.J. & Mearns, J. (1990). Measuring generalized expectancies for negative mood regulation: Initial scale development and implications. *Journal of Personality Assessment, 54*, 546–563.

Chaiken, S. (1987). The heuristic model of persuasion. In M.P. Zanna, J.M. Olson, & C.P. Herman (Eds), *Social influence: The Ontario Symposium* (Vol. 5, pp. 3–39). Hillsdale, NJ: Erlbaum.

Crites, S.L., Fabrigar, L., & Petty, R.E. (1994). Measuring the affective and cognitive properties of attitudes: Conceptual and methodological issues. *Personality and Social Psychology Bulletin, 20*, 619–634.

DePaulo, B.M. (1992) Nonverbal behavior and self-presentation. *Psychological Bulletin, 111*, 203–243.

Flavell, J.H. (1979). Metacognition and cognitive monitoring: A new area of cognitive-developmental inquiry. *American Psychologist, 34*, 906–911.

Fletcher, G.J.O. (1984). Psychology and common sense. *American Psychologist, 39,* 203–213.

Frey, D. (1986). Recent research on selective exposure to information. In L. Berkowitz (Ed.), *Advances in experimental social psychology* (Vol. 19, pp. 41–80). Orlando, FL: Academic Press.

Furnham, A. (1983). Social psychology as common sense. *Bulletin of the British Psychological Society, 36,* 105–109.

Furnham, A. (1988). *Lay theories: Everyday understanding of problems in the social sciences.* New York: Pergamon Press.

Gilbert, D.T. (1991). How mental systems believe. *American Psychologist, 46,* 107–119.

Gilbert, D.T. (1993). The assent of man: Mental representation and the control of belief. In D.M. Wegner & J.W. Pennebaker (Eds), *Handbook of mental control* (pp. 57–87). Englewood Cliffs, NJ: Prentice-Hall.

Gilbert, D.T., Krull, D.S., & Malone, P.S. (1990). Unbelieving the unbelievable: Some problems in the rejection of false information. *Journal of Personality and Social Psychology, 59,* 601–613.

Gilbert, D.T., Pinel, E.C., Wilson, T.D., Blumberg, S.J., & Wheatley, T.P. (1997). Immune reglect: A source of durability bias in affective forecasting. Under editorial review.

Gilbert, D.T., Tafarodi, R.W., & Malone, P.S. (1993). You can't not believe everything you read. *Journal of Personality and Social Psychology, 65,* 221–233.

Goethals, G.R. & Reckman, R.F. (1973). The perception of consistency in attitudes. *Journal of Experimental Social Psychology, 9,* 491–501.

Greenwald, A.G. & Banaji, M.R. (1995). Implicit social cognition: Attitudes, self-esteem, and stereotypes. *Psychological Review, 102,* 4–27.

Heider, F. (1958). *The psychology of interpersonal relations.* New York: Wiley.

Hsee, C.K. & Abelson, R.P. (1991). The velocity relation: Satisfaction as a function of the first derivative of outcome over time. *Journal of Personality and Social Psychology, 60,* 341–347.

Ichheiser, G. (1949). Misunderstandings in human relations. *American Journal of Sociology, 55,* 2, Part 2.

Jacoby, L.L., Lindsay, D.S., & Toth, J.P. (1992). Unconscious influences revealed: Attention, awareness, and control. *American Psychologist, 47,* 802–809.

Kelley, H.H. (1992). Common-sense psychology and scientific psychology. *Annual Review of Psychology, 43,* 1–23.

Kelly, G.A. (1955). *The psychology of personal constructs.* New York, Norton.

Koriat, A. (1993). How do we know that we know? The accessibility model of the feeling of knowing. *Psychological Review, 100,* 609–639.

Kruglanski, A.W. (1989). *Lay epistemics and human knowledge: Cognitive and motivational biases.* New York: Plenum.

Lewin, K. (1943). Defining the "field at a given time." *Psychological Review, 50,* 292–310.

Liebert, R.M. & Sprafkin, J. (1988). *The early window* (3rd ed.). New York: Pergamon.

Linville, P.W. & Fischer, G.W. (1991). Preferences for combining or separating events: A social application of prospect theory and mental accounting. *Journal of Personality and Social Psychology, 60,* 5–23.

Lodish, L.M., Abraham, M., Kalmenson, S., Livelsberger, J., Lubetkin, B., Richardson, B., & Stevens, M. (1995). How TV advertising works: A meta-analysis of 389 real world split cable TV advertising experiments. *Journal of Marketing Research, 32,* 125–139.

McGuire, W.J. (1964). Inducing resistance to persuasion. In L. Berkowitz (Ed.), *Advances in experimental social psychology* (Vol. 1, pp. 192–229). New York: Academic Press.

Nelson, T.O. (1996). Consciousness and metacognition. *American Psychologist, 51,* 102–116.

Newcomb, T.M. (1947). Autistic hostility and social reality. *Human Relations, 1,* 69–86.

Nisbett, R.E. & Wilson, T.D. (1977a). The halo effect: Evidence for unconscious alteration of judgments. *Journal of Personality and Social Psychology, 35,* 250–256.

Nisbett, R.E. & Wilson, T.D. (1977b). Telling more than we can know: Verbal reports on mental processes. *Psychological Review, 84,* 231–259.

Parrot, W.G. (1993). Beyond hedonism: Motives for inhibiting good moods and for

11

The Metacognition of Bias Correction: Naive Theories of Bias and the Flexible Correction Model

Duane T. Wegener, Richard E. Petty and Meghan Dunn

In many situations, we want to assess the "true" qualities of some target person, object, or issue. Is Sally really the best job candidate? Is the National Bank the right choice for my mortgage? Is George truly guilty of bank robbery? Unfortunately, making accurate or otherwise appropriate judgments can often turn out to be rather difficult because many kinds of biasing factors – such as being in a bad mood – can unduly influence our perceptions. Especially when attempting to be accurate, people would presumably want to prevent such biasing factors from having an impact on their judgments. If people attempt to remove the influence of biasing factors, how do they do so? What metacognitive processes do people use to ensure that their assessments of and feelings toward targets are "accurate" or "legitimate?"

In brief, we believe that corrections (i.e. attempts at removing bias from assessments of targets) are often the result of people consulting their naive theories (beliefs) of how potentially biasing factors have influenced (or might yet influence) their views of the target. As we explain later in the chapter, this Flexible Correction Model (FCM) differs from previous models of bias correction in that a view of corrections based on perceivers' naive theories of bias allows for a more flexible set of adjustments to one's assessment of targets.

Corrections have been discussed or studied in a variety of areas including attribution, context and priming effects, mood and judgment, impression formation, and stereotyping (see Wegener & Petty, 1997, for a review). When work on the FCM began in 1990 (reported in Wegener & Petty, 1992; Petty & Wegener, 1993), correction phenomena had been discussed in general terms and for certain isolated research domains, and conceptual developments were generally aimed at explaining the phenomena in those particular domains (for a good example, see the work on attributional correction processes, Gilbert, Pelham, & Krull, 1988). In the context-effect (priming) literature, however, some rather explicit and detailed models of correction phenomena were developed (e.g. Martin's 1986 set–reset model). Because of this, we begin our discussion of correction phenomena by reviewing the models developed to account for context effects. Then, we outline the postulates of the Flexible Correction Model (Petty & Wegener, 1993; Wegener, 1994; Wegener & Petty, 1995, 1997), which is a general theory of correction – applicable to the multitude of situations in which corrections occur (for a comprehensive review, see Wegener & Petty, 1997). In outlining the FCM, we first review in brief some of the initial experiments that tested that flexible correction view. Next, we present the details of some new experiments guided by the FCM framework. We conclude by discussing some directions for future work on correction processes in general and theory-based corrections in particular.

Priming/context effects and correction: initial models of correction

Corrections have recently played a prominent role in the area of context effects on impression formation and social judgment. Many kinds of factors are objectively irrelevant to the true qualities of targets (e.g. mood states of the perceiver, unrelated information that serves to activate concepts in memory, etc.), but such factors have often been found to influence ratings of targets (e.g. Forgas & Moylan, 1987; Higgins, Rholes, & Jones, 1977; Petty, Schumann, Richman, & Strathman, 1993; Srull & Wyer, 1980).[1] In this literature, the direction of effects created by irrelevant contexts is described as either *assimilation* (i.e. making judgments of targets *more* like reactions to the context) or *contrast* (i.e. making judgments of targets *less* like reactions to the context).

Many discussions of assimilation and contrast focused on the distribution of contextual stimuli as an explanation for these distortions of judgment (e.g. Helson, 1964; Parducci, 1965; Sherif & Hovland, 1961; see also Herr, 1986; Herr, Sherman, & Fazio, 1983). Recently, however, researchers have found evidence of both assimilation and contrast effects even when using the same contextual stimuli. For example, Newman and Uleman (1990) primed subjects with either positive or negative traits and later tested whether traits consistent or inconsistent with those primes provided better cues to recall of sentences containing material related to the primes. When people could remember any of the priming (contextual) stimuli, traits *inconsistent* with the initial primes made the best recall cues for the sentences; but when people could *not* remember the same priming stimuli, traits consistent with the primes made the best recall cues. This suggests that perceivers initially made assessments of the targets that were contrasted to the primes when there was memory of the primes, but that were assimilated to the primes when there was no memory for the primes (see also Lombardi, Higgins, & Bargh, 1987). Strack, Schwarz, Bless, Kübler, and Wänke (1993) showed the same type of effect using a judgment task and a manipulation of awareness of the priming episode. When Strack et al. (1993) reminded participants of the priming task before an impression-formation task, impressions of targets were contrasted away from the primes, but when

both of these models, effortful corrections (i.e. resetting or exclusion) lead to target judgments *less* like the context than in no-correction settings. Also, within both of these models, contrast effects are conceptualized as more effortful than assimilation effects (because the contrast effects are due to corrections whereas the assimilation effects are not). The inclusion/exclusion model adds the feature that excluded (subtracted) information can then be used to construct a standard of comparison (which also leads to contrast effects to the extent that the excluded information is extreme; see Schwarz & Bless, 1992a, pp. 238–241; see Petty & Wegener, 1993, Wegener & Petty, 1997, for additional discussion).

The Flexible Correction Model: corrections guided by naive theories of bias

Although work guided by the partialling models has been quite useful in determining when priming effects would or would not occur (or might even be reversed), some of the assumptions of these models (e.g. that contrast effects were more effortful than assimilation, and that corrections always make assessments of targets less like reactions to the contextual stimuli) seemed to be unduly limiting (especially if attempting to apply the models outside the priming domain). Thus, the goal of the initial work on the FCM was to develop a perspective that was more flexible than these "partialling" views. That is, in the FCM corrections are driven by respondents' naive theories of how any given factor(s) have influenced (or might yet influence) their perceptions of the target, and these naive theories can be of very different biases across different contexts, targets, settings, and perceivers.

Basically, the FCM (Petty & Wegener, 1993; Wegener, 1994; Wegener & Petty, 1995, 1997) holds that corrections are aimed at removing the bias that social perceivers believe is associated with the factor(s) at hand. Consider, for example, a situation in which a person realizes that a bias might be operating (e.g. because the person has learned about a given judgmental bias in a psychology class). If the perceiver believes there is a small (or no) bias in a given situation, he or she attempts to adjust assessments of the true qualities of the target less than if he or she believes that there is a large bias. If the perceiver believes that the bias is to make the target seem higher on a dimension of judgment than would normally be the case, the perceiver attempts to adjust assessments of the target to be lower; if the perceiver believes that the bias is to make the target seem lower on a dimension of judgment than would normally be the case, the perceiver attempts to adjust assessments of the target to be higher than his or her initial reactions. If the person is warned of a bias (or realizes the potential for bias) before encountering the target, the person might engage in theory-based corrections on-line during exposure to the target, or the person might use theories of bias to guide exposure choices so as to avoid perceived or expected biases (see Wegener & Petty, 1995, 1997; Wilson & Brekke, 1994;

Wilson, Houston, & Meyers, in press). The greater the perceived or expected bias, the more vigilant the perceiver might be in correcting on-line or in avoiding the biasing factor. Although theorists have noted for some time that people are likely to possess or generate naive theories about how various contextual factors might influence or have influenced their perceptions of targets, most of the emphasis regarding these theories has been on how incorrect they often are (e.g. Nisbett & Wilson, 1977; Wilson, Laser, & Stone, 1982). Empirical evidence regarding the role of theories of bias in correction phenomena has only recently begun to appear (e.g. Petty & Wegener, 1993; Wegener & Petty, 1995).

The Flexible Correction Model

There are a variety of issues and assumptions surrounding the use of naive theories as a basis for a model of bias correction. In the sections to follow, we present the basic postulates of the FCM presented by Wegener and Petty (1997) along with some explication of the reasons underlying the postulates and the implications of those views.

> Postulate 1: Across judgment targets, perceivers, and situations, there is variation in the direction and magnitude of default (i.e. "uncorrected") effects.

According to the FCM, there is variation in the direction and magnitude of uncorrected effects of target-related, personal, and situational variables. That is, in contrast to the partialling models (which assumed a default direction for context effects – "assimilation"), such an assumption is explicitly rejected in the flexible correction framework.[2] Thus, the first form of flexibility that is evidenced in the FCM concerns the various types of effects and processes that can occur in the absence of corrections.

> Postulate 2: There are individual and situational differences in motivation and ability to identify potential sources of bias. If a person is unmotivated or unable to search for potential sources of bias, then his or her assessment of the qualities of the target will reflect his or her initial reaction to the target.
>
> To the extent that the perceiver is motivated and able to search for potential sources of bias, however, he or she will evaluate the potential biasing effect(s) of salient factors in the judgment setting (including factors external and internal to the perceiver). This is accomplished by consulting naive theories of the bias(es) associated with the salient factor(s).

The second form of flexibility in the FCM concerns individual and situational differences in motivation and ability to identify potential sources of bias. If a person lacks either the motivation or the ability to search for potential sources of bias, then corrective attempts are unlikely and his or her assessment of the target is more likely to correspond to his or her initial reaction(s) to the target – regardless of whether this initial reaction is based on effortful scrutiny of the target or on more cursory analyses (see Postulate 1; see also Petty & Cacioppo, 1986; Petty & Wegener, 1998). If motivation and ability to search for potential sources of bias are high, however, the

People can become aware of a potential bias before, during, or after judging (or even encountering) the target. Accordingly, corrections for bias need not occur only after reacting to the target, but people might also anticipate a bias and attempt to avoid it by changing how information about the target is gathered or scrutinized. We regard such attempts at avoidance of bias as "preemptive corrections" (see Wegener & Petty, 1997, for example). Especially before people have a great deal of experience with attempts to correct for a given biasing factor, such attempts would likely depend on some level of conscious awareness of the potential bias. However, with more experience of the factor and of the correction process, less conscious awareness of the bias might be sufficient for instigating the correction process (and the correction process itself might become less effortful, that is, to a certain extent, routinized; Wegener & Petty, 1997; cf. Smith, 1989). In fact, even in those cases where rather conscious awareness of the biasing factor occurs, we would not generally expect the whole of the correction process to be consciously reportable (consistent with Nisbett & Wilson, 1977). Rather, even if people are able to directly report the content of a given theory of bias, those same people might be unable to report which theory(ies) were used most in a correction, for example (i.e. even if content of a theory of bias is "explicit," there can still be "implicit" effects of the theory, Wegener & Petty, in press; see also Petty, Wegener, & White, in press).

As noted earlier (see Postulate 1), within the FCM, no assumptions are made concerning the direction of the default (i.e. "uncorrected") effect of potential biases. For example, within the context-effect domain, a factor might make initial reactions to the target more like reactions to the context (assimilation), might make initial reactions less like reactions to the context (contrast), or might have no effect at all. Regardless of the uncorrected effect, corrections are driven by the *perceptions* of the bias in that judgment setting. That is, corrections are aimed at removing *perceived* rather than actual bias. Although perceived and actual bias might coincide in certain circumstances, the two elements are conceptually distinct from one another. That is, a person might believe that a particular bias exists (and might attempt to remove that perceived bias) when no bias exists or even when a bias in the opposite direction is objectively present.

Postulate 5: Theory-based corrections can be undermined by a variety of factors that undermine the extent to which the theory of bias is viewed as applicable to the judgment target and setting, the extent to which the theory serves the perceiver's judgment goals, and the extent to which the theory is accessible.

A variety of factors might determine the nature of theories of bias and the likelihood that those theories guide corrective attempts. A theory of bias could be learned through experience and stored in memory, or it could be generated on-line to address a particular judgment and/or setting. Stored theories are likely to have a greater basis in past experience (with the biasing agent, the target, or both); but a theory of bias generated for the specific target and setting might be more likely to be viewed as applicable to the particular corrective attempt. In many settings, the theory of bias that is used is probably some combination of a theory stored in memory along with adjustments to the theory based on the perceiver's subjective experience of the context and target to be judged.

Perceived applicability of a theory of bias to a given setting and target is likely to depend on a variety of factors. For example, a theory of bias is more likely to be viewed as applicable to a given setting if the perceived biasing factor in that setting "matches" the theory well (i.e. if the biasing factor in the setting has a close resemblance to the "prototype" or representation of the biasing factor within the theory of bias). The "strength" of the theory in terms of its integration with related knowledge structures and its accessibility in memory would also help to determine the perceived applicability of the theory of bias, as would the "breadth" of the theory in terms of the situations and targets across which the theory is viewed as applicable. One could also view the notion of "breadth" as the globality versus specificity of the theory of bias. That is, some biasing factors might be viewed by some people as only having effects on certain kinds of targets or in certain kinds of settings, whereas other factors (or the same factors considered by other people) might be viewed as having effects across many kinds of targets and/or settings. Perceived applicability could also be influenced by the extent to which the perceiver experiences reactions to the target that are consistent with the reactions predicted by the theory of bias. If reactions to a target are quite different from those expected based on a theory of bias, it might seem less likely that the biasing factor is having an effect. Of course, a lack of reactions consistent with the theory might not undermine corrections if the theory of bias is relatively "strong" or "global" (or if the theory includes the possibility of decreasing typical reactions to the target rather than just increasing "biased" reactions). Thus, if a theory of bias is perceived as applicable to the judgment setting, serves the judgment goals of the perceiver, and is accessible when the perceiver assesses the target's qualities, that theory is likely to guide efforts at removing the perceived bias. To the extent that any or all of these properties are lacking, the theory becomes less likely to guide corrections, and the person might construct a new theory to account for this instance.

> Postulate 6: Although corrections generally require more motivation and ability (i.e. more cognitive effort) than lack of corrections (unless corrections become routinized), both corrected and uncorrected assessments of targets can vary in effort put into that assessment.

> Postulate 7: Just as differences in effort for uncorrected judgments create differences in persistence, resistance, etc., corrected assessments based on greater effort persist longer over time, are more resistant to attempts at changing assessments of the target, and are more likely to guide additional judgments and behavior toward the target than are corrected assessments based on lower levels of effort.

more effort than default (no-correction) contrast (though at the time we postulated this, correction-based assimilation had never been demonstrated; see Petty & Wegener, 1993). In comparison, according to a partialling view "the emergence of contrast effects requires extra processing steps, and more effort, than the emergence of assimilation effects" (Schwarz & Bless, 1992a, p. 240).

For a comparison between theory-based corrections and partialling (subtraction) views, the case of corrections driven by a theory of uncorrected contrast is a crucial case (because the theory of bias would lead one to correct in a direction opposite to a "removal of overlap" process). Thus, our early work on the FCM focused on this and related questions. For example, Petty and Wegener (1993, Study 1) showed that people do, in fact, believe that some contexts lead to biases that are contrastive in nature.[5] Using one of the contexts for which a "contrastive" theory of bias was held (i.e. rating the desirability of exciting vacation locations was believed to make perceptions of typical midwestern American cities less desirable), Petty and Wegener (1993, Study 2) showed that corrections made ratings of targets *more* (rather than less) like ratings of the context (consistent with theory-based corrections). Moreover, Petty and Wegener (1993) found that these corrections were not attributable to scale anchoring effects (Study 3) and that similar corrections occurred using more subtle instigations of corrections (Study 4).

Of course, according to the FCM, corrections guided by judges' naive theories of bias can go in opposite directions to the extent that the judges' theories of bias are that opposite biases are at work. One possible case would be when people hold opposite theories about how a given context influences judgments for different targets. For example, a person might believe that thinking about the qualities of vacation locations would make average locations seem *less* desirable, but might also believe that thinking about the vacation locations would make a job in one of those vacation spots seem *more* desirable (Wegener & Petty, 1995, Study 1). Some previous models of assimilation and contrast might predict that different *effects* on target judgment would occur for the same context (e.g. for some targets, the context might be "included" in the representation of the target – leading to assimilation – but the same context might be "excluded" from the representation of another target – leading to contrast; Schwarz & Bless, 1992a; cf. Herr et al., 1983). However, only a theory of correction based on judges' naive theories of bias predicts different *corrections* (i.e. away from and closer to the context) for these different targets.

Consistent with these notions, Wegener and Petty (1995, Studies 2 & 3) showed that opposite corrections occur for different targets judged within the same context when those different targets were associated with opposing theories of bias. Within this pattern, corrections for perceived contrast were also shown for the first time to potentially lead to "corrected assimilation" – in which corrections for perceived contrast led to target ratings that were even closer to ratings of the context than when no context was present.

These opposite corrections for the effects of the same context on different targets present a unique problem for correction models based on partialling or subtraction processes because contextually activated reactions (which are supposed to be "subtracted" in order to correct assessments of targets) are the same for each set of targets. Thus, according to "partialling" models, unless the contextual reactions are quite mixed rather than consistent, subtraction of overlap would tend to move assessments of each target in the same rather than opposite directions.

Whereas theories of bias were associated with different targets in the Wegener and Petty (1995, Studies 2 & 3) opposite-correction studies, Wegener and Petty (1995, Study 4) also found some evidence of opposite corrections when theories varied across people. In this study, participants' individual theories of bias were measured, and participants were later exposed to target judgments within conditions that would encourage corrections. Theories of bias significantly predicted shifts in target ratings, indicating that as theories of bias became more negative, shifts in target ratings became more positive. Within the overall effect, there was evidence of correction associated with both direction and magnitude of the perceived bias. That is, a dichotomous variable denoting direction of perceived bias accounted for significant variance in the positivity of shifts in target ratings, consistent with the opposite corrections found with shared theories varying across targets. In addition, participants corrected to a greater extent as people's theories of bias become more extreme, controlling for the direction of bias (see Wegener & Petty, 1995, p. 47 for descriptions of the various magnitude analyses).

Thus, in some of the correction studies, shared theories of bias were identified and corrections consistent with those theories were found (Petty & Wegener, 1993). In other studies, documented differences in theories predicted the direction of corrections (Wegener & Petty, 1995). In some of these studies, theories of bias varied with the target of judgment (Wegener & Petty, 1995, Studies 2 & 3). In other studies, theory varied across perceivers (Wegener & Petty, 1995, Study 4). A full triangulation of theories of bias could be achieved by showing that theories also guide corrections when theories of bias vary with different contexts (across people and with the same target). That is, to the extent that corrections are found that are consistent with theories of bias, regardless of whether those theories of bias are associated with different judgment targets, different perceivers, *or* different contexts, this makes it rather difficult to reasonably account for the data by making reference to non-theory qualities of the judgment setting. In the sections to follow, we describe two studies that complete this triangulation by demonstrating opposite corrections of perceptions of the same target within different contexts (that are consistent with measured theories of bias). In addition, these studies utilized contexts that were quite different from the contexts that had been used in the Petty and Wegener (1993) and the Wegener and Petty (1995) work (thereby increasing the breadth of the evidence supportive of theory-based corrections).

Theories of bias Twelve undergraduate psychology students received a questionnaire describing two contexts and judgments to be made, and were asked to provide their perceptions of how each context would affect the respective judgment. Instructions explained that a number of kinds of situations have been found to reliably influence people's judgments, but that little work had investigated the extent to which people are aware of the biases that situations create. Participants were asked to provide their best estimate of *how* each situation would or would not direct people's perceptions of the targets discussed.

For the first estimate of bias, participants responded to the question "If you were asked to rate how violent people like George Foreman or Arnold Schwarzenegger are, how would rating a number of *extremely violent* people (like Adolf Hitler or Josef Stalin) affect perceptions of George or Arnold?" Responses were made to the root "would make George and Arnold seem" on a nine-point scale anchored with "*less* violent than if no violent people were considered" (–4) and "*more* violent than if no violent people were considered" (+4). The second estimate of bias was for a different context but the same ratings of the same targets. That is, participants responded to the question "If you were asked to rate how violent people like George Foreman or Arnold Schwarzenegger are, how would rating a number of *extremely non-violent* people (like Gandhi or Jesus Christ) affect perceptions of George or Arnold?" Responses were made to the same root as noted earlier and on a similar scale [anchored with "*less* violent than if non-violent people weren't considered" (–4) and "*more* violent than if non-violent people weren't considered" (+4)].

Ratings of the perceived judgmental effects of each context were analyzed by testing the difference between the average rating for each context and the zero-point of the scale (i.e. no perceived influence of the context) using the Student's t statistic (each with df = 11). Participants believed that rating extremely violent people before rating George Foreman and Arnold Schwarzenegger would make George and Arnold seem *less* violent than usual ($M = -1.92$; $t = -2.82$, $p < 0.017$). Also, participants believed that rating extremely non-violent people before rating George Foreman and Arnold Schwarzenegger would make George and Arnold seem *more* violent than usual ($M = +1.67$; Student's $t = 3.86$, $p < 0.0027$). Thus, it should be possible to find opposite corrections of target judgments based on the opposite theories of bias associated with the different judgment contexts.

Opposite theory-based corrections Ninety-four undergraduate psychology students received experimental packets that were randomly assigned to a 2 (Theory of influence: more violent than usual, less violent than usual) X 2 (Correction: instruction, none) between-subjects design. Participants were told that the following ratings concerned people's perceptions of violence and that, for the following people, the question to be answered was "How violent do you think this person is?"

Participants first rated either three extremely violent people (i.e. Adolf Hitler, Josef Stalin, and Saddam Hussein – a context expected by participants in the theory-identification portion of the study to make perceptions of targets *less* violent than usual) or three extremely non-violent people (i.e. the Pope, Jesus Christ, and Gandhi – a context expected by participants in the theory-identification study to make perceptions of targets *more* violent than usual) on a scale anchored at 1 = "not at all violent" and 10 = "very violent." Then, research participants either immediately rated two target people (i.e. Arnold Schwarzenegger and George Foreman) on the same scale (no-correction condition), or were first asked not to let perceptions of the next two people be influenced by perceptions of the people they had just rated (correction-instruction condition).

Ratings of the two targets were averaged to form the primary dependent measure. This measure was submitted to a 2 (Theory of influence: more violent than usual, less violent than usual) X 2 (Correction: instruction, none) between-subject ANOVA. Results showed only the expected Theory X Correction interaction, $F(1, 90) = 11.81, p < 0.0009$. For participants who rated the targets in the extremely violent context (and expected that perceptions of targets would be biased toward *less* violence than usual), target ratings were *more* violent when a correction instruction was given ($M = 4.98$) than when no correction instruction was given ($M = 3.58$); $p < 0.027$, one-tailed. However, for participants who rated the targets in the extremely non-violent context (and expected that perceptions of targets would be biased toward *more* violence than usual), target ratings were *less* violent when a correction instruction was given ($M = 3.87$) than when no correction instruction was given ($M = 5.99$); $p < 0.003$, one-tailed.

Thirteen additional people also participated in the study who received the target ratings before receiving any ratings of context items. Thus, responses in this control condition could be used to determine when biases were actually operating and when corrected ratings were moved toward or away from context-independent ratings. Responses in this control condition ($M = 5.575$) showed that bias was only present under no-correction conditions when targets were rated after the extremely violent people ($p < 0.02$). When targets were rated after the extremely non-violent people, ratings did not differ from context-independent ratings ($p > 0.62$). Thus, corrections away from initial perceptions of targets following the non-violent context represents another case in which participants corrected according to a theory of bias even though no demonstrable bias was operating. In addition, corrections in the non-violent context condition led target ratings to be lower than context-independent ratings ($p < 0.06$). Because of this, the results of this study cannot be easily accounted for by response language effects (see also Petty & Wegener, 1993).[7]

Recently, opposite theory-based corrections of ratings of the same target were also obtained by Martin (1996). In Martin's study, participants rated context people who had been pretested to be either attractive or unattractive and then rated moderately attractive targets either with or without a

possesses, the importance to the person of arriving at an unbiased assessment of the target, time pressures for judgment, etc.).

Additional interesting areas for future work concern the generation of theories of bias and the ways in which stored theories of bias might be modified in specific judgment settings. For example, as we noted earlier, it might be possible to undermine a stored theory of bias (at least in certain circumstances) if reactions to the target seem inconsistent with the theory. Consider a situation in which a person possesses a stored theory that feelings induced by a sad movie would make perceptions of unfamiliar people more negative than usual. If such a person were to meet a new person and really like him or her, the perceiver might question the applicability of the theory of bias to this target or to this situation. If so, the person might question whether the movie affected him or her the way other sad movies do, or the person might question whether sad moods in fact have the effects that were expected. If such a "disconfirmation" of the theory were to happen again, the person might begin to revise the theory or develop beliefs about when the theory is or is not appropriate. It could also be that a well-developed "strong" theory of bias (or a theory that itself includes numerous settings and/or targets for which the bias occurs) might withstand reactions to the target that are inconsistent with the theory. Such a theory might then continue to guide corrections (i.e. the perceiver would view the new person as especially likeable, because the sad movie would make impressions less positive than they would otherwise be – even though the uncorrected impression was already quite positive). This might also depend on whether the perceiver could imagine having a view of the target that was more favorable (or unfavorable) than his or her experienced reactions (which would also depend on additional knowledge about the target). These and other interactions between stored theories and experienced reactions (which might give rise to generated theories based on salient aspects of the judgment setting) should receive future research attention.

Finally, within the FCM perspective, it will also be important to investigate the many personal and situational factors that might induce a motive to be "accurate" (and to link those factors with other determinants of when corrections will and will not occur). One important aspect of the FCM in this regard is that a motive to be "accurate" is not sufficient for corrections to take place. That is, if no potential bias is perceived, corrections are unlikely no matter how much "accuracy motivation" might exist (see Wegener & Petty, 1997). Therefore, some factors that probably increase motivation to be "accurate" (e.g. perceiving the target as personally relevant, Petty & Cacioppo, 1979) might not induce corrections in many settings. This was recently demonstrated by Petty et al. (in press, Study 2). In this study, biasing effects of a peripheral cue to persuasion (i.e. likeability of the source) were found to be eliminated when the policy was personally relevant to message receivers. Yet, when an instruction was given not to be influenced by perceptions of the source, significant corrections occurred (even though no effect of source perceptions had been observed without the correction instruction). This suggests that the original elimination of the impact of the source under high processing conditions had not been due to explicit attempts at correction (or else there would have been less need for additional correction when the instruction was given under high rather than low processing conditions). Instead, under high processing conditions, message recipients might have focused on the merits of the arguments in the message and might not have paid attention to the potential source-based bias (until the instruction directed them toward the source). In future work, linking correction outcomes directly to the theories of bias held by perceivers might help to determine when lack of a biasing effect is due to corrections and when it is not.

It is our hope that correction processes based on theories of bias can provide a bridge for studying corrections in many domains of psychology. To this end, the FCM provides a unifying perspective from which such corrections can be conceptualized, studied, and (hopefully) understood. We look forward to further development of flexible correction notions and to investigations of the untested portions of the flexible correction framework.

Notes

1. Although effects of mood, especially removal of effects of mood, have typically been conceptualized using non-corrective models (e.g. the mood-as-information view, Schwarz, 1990; Schwarz & Clore, 1983), we believe that becoming aware of mood-based biases might instigate correction processes much like those activated by perceiving biases associated with any other kind of stimulus (see Petty & Wegener, 1993; Wegener & Petty, 1997).

2. This is not to say that "partialling" models would predict that only one type of context effect can occur without corrections, but the processes postulated by these models would not be applicable when other kinds of uncorrected effects occur. The FCM is equally applicable, regardless of the qualities of the observed uncorrected effects.

3. This does not mean that perceivers can necessarily consciously report the correction processes that they undertake, but people should often be able to report their perceptions of the bias associated with a given context and target (though there are many potential difficulties with such assessments – e.g. that in retrospective reports, a person might report lack of an effect of the biasing factor because of *corrections* rather than because of a lack of perception of potential bias).

4. Even though corrections might generally require more effort than a lack of corrections, this should not be taken as suggesting that "corrected" assessments of targets should necessarily persist over time or resist changes more than "uncorrected" assessments. Because "uncorrected" assessments are more directly based on reactions to the target (and such reactions might be recalled or recur upon additional presentations of the target), there might be a variety of settings in which "uncorrected" assessments tend to persist and resist change to a greater extent than "corrected" assessments (see Petty & Wegener, 1998, for similar comments regarding comparison of changed and unchanged attitudes).

5. At the same time, this study also showed that people hold theories of bias that are "assimilative" for such biasing factors as priming tasks and mood. Effects of each of these factors have been "corrected" in previous work by making ratings of targets less like the context – which, given these theories of bias, was consistent with both a theory-based correction and a "partialling" view.

Schwarz, N. (1990). Feelings as information: Informational and motivational functions of affective states. In R. Sorrentino & E.T. Higgins (Eds), *Handbook of motivation and cognition: Foundations of social behavior* (Vol. 2, pp. 527–561). New York: Guilford Press.

Schwarz, N. & Bless, H. (1992a). Constructing reality and its alternatives: An inclusion/ exclusion model of assimilation and contrast effects in social judgment. In L.L. Martin and A. Tesser (Eds), *The construction of social judgments* (pp. 217–245). Hillsdale, NJ: Erlbaum.

Schwarz, N. & Bless, H. (1992b). Scandals and the public's trust in politicians: Assimilation and contrast effects. *Personality and Social Psychology Bulletin, 18,* 574–579.

Schwarz, N. & Clore, G.L. (1983). Mood, misattribution, and judgments of well-being: Informative and directive functions of affective states. *Journal of Personality and Social Psychology, 45,* 513–523.

Schwarz, N., Strack, F., & Mai, H.P. (1991). Assimilation and contrast effects in part-whole question sequences: A conversational-logic analysis. *Public Opinion Quarterly, 55,* 3–23.

Sherif, M. & Hovland, C.W. (1961). *Social judgment: Assimilation and contrast effects in communication and attitude change.* New Haven, CT: Yale University Press.

Smith, E.R. (1989). Procedural efficiency: General and specific components and effects on social judgment. *Journal of Experimental Social Psychology, 25,* 500–523.

Smith, E.R., Stewart, T.L., & Buttram, R.T. (1992). Inferring a trait from a behavior has long-term, highly specific effects. *Journal of Personality and Social Psychology, 62,* 753–759.

Srull, T.K. & Wyer, R.S. (1980). Category accessibility and social perception: Some implications for the study of person memory and interpersonal judgments. *Journal of Personality and Social Psychology, 38,* 841–856.

Strack, F. (1992a). The different routes to social judgments: Experiential versus informational based strategies. In L.L. Martin and A. Tesser (Eds), *The construction of social judgments* (pp. 249–275). Hillsdale, NJ: Erlbaum.

Strack, F. (1992b). "Order effects" in survey research: Activation and information functions of preceding questions. In N. Schwarz and S. Sudman (Eds), *Context effects in social and psychological research* (pp. 23–34). New York: Springer-Verlag.

Strack, F. & Hannover, B. (1996). Awareness of influence as a precondition for implementing correctional goals. In P.M. Gollwitzer & J.A. Bargh (Eds), *The psychology of action* (pp. 579–596). New York: Guilford Press.

Strack, F., Martin, L.L., & Schwarz, N. (1988). Priming and communication: Social determinants of information use in judgments of life satisfaction. *European Journal of Social Psychology, 18,* 429–442.

Strack, F., Schwarz, N., Bless, H., Kübler, A., & Wänke, M. (1993). Awareness of the influence as a determinant of assimilation versus contrast. *European Journal of Social Psychology, 23,* 53–62.

Tesser, A. & Martin, L.L. (1996). The psychology of evaluation. In E.T. Higgins & A.W. Kruglanski (Eds), *Social psychology: Handbook of basic principles* (pp. 400–432). New York: Guilford Press.

Thompson, M.M., Naccarato, M.E., & Parker, K.E. (1989). Assessing cognitive need: The development of the Personal Need for Structure and Personal Fear of Invalidity scales. Paper presented at the annual meeting of the Canadian Psychological Association, Halifax, Nova Scotia, June.

Thompson, W.C., Fong, G.T., & Rosenhan, D.L. (1981). Inadmissible evidence and juror verdicts. *Journal of Personality and Social Psychology, 40,* 453–463.

Wegener, D.T. (1994). *The flexible correction model: Using naive theories of bias to correct assessments of targets.* Doctoral dissertation, Ohio State University, Columbus, OH.

Wegener, D.T. & Petty, R.E. (1992). Correction for contrast: Thoughtful processes can wipe out or create contrast effects. Paper presented at the annual meeting of the Midwestern Psychological Association, Chicago, May.

Wegener, D.T. & Petty, R.E. (1995). Flexible correction processes in social judgment: The role of naive theories in corrections for perceived bias. *Journal of Personality and Social Psychology, 68,* 36–51.

Wegener, D.T. & Petty, R.E. (1997). The flexible correction model: The role of naive theories of bias in bias correction. In M.P. Zanna (Ed.) *Advances in experimental social psychology* (Vol. 29, pp. 141–208). New York: Academic Press.

Wegener, D.T. & Petty, R.E. (in press). The naive scientist revisited: Naive theories and social judgment. *Social Cognition.*

Wegner, D.M. (1994). Ironic processes of mental control. *Psychological Review, 101,* 34–52.

Wilson, T.D. & Brekke, N. (1994). Mental contamination and mental correction: Unwanted influences on judgments and evaluations. *Psychological Bulletin, 116,* 117–142.

Wilson, T.D., Houston, C.E., & Meyers, J.M. (in press). Choose your poison: Effects of lay beliefs about mental processes on attitude change. *Social Cognition.*

Wilson, T.D., Laser, P.S., & Stone, J.I. (1982). Judging the predictors of one's own mood: Accuracy and the use of shared theories. *Journal of Experimental Social Psychology, 18,* 537–556.

Wyer, R.S. & Budesheim, T.L. (1987). Person memory and judgments: The impact of information that one is told to disregard. *Journal of Personality and Social Psychology, 53,* 14–29.

Zeigarnik, B. (1938). On finished and unfinished tasks. In W.D. Ellis (Ed.), *A source book of Gestalt psychology* (pp. 300–314). New York: Harcourt, Brace, & World. (Reprinted and condensed from *Psychologishe Forschung,* 1927, *9,* 1–85.)

12

Correction and Metacognition: Are People Naive Dogmatists or Naive Empiricists during Social Judgments?

Leonard L. Martin and Diederik A. Stapel

Let's start with the obvious: (1) people can enact behaviors and (2) people can provide explanations for their behaviors. Now, the less obvious: What is the relation between the two? Do people consciously consider various features of the situation, weigh the pros and cons, develop a conscious intention, and then act upon that intention (cf. Fishbein & Ajzen, 1975)? Or do people initiate behaviors for reasons of which they may not be entirely aware, and only later attempt to piece together why they might have behaved as they did (cf. Bem, 1967; Nisbett & Wilson, 1977)?

In this chapter, we address this general issue in the area of social judgment. Obviously, people can make judgments and, obviously, people can provide rationales for their judgments, but what is the relation between the two? To paraphrase our opening question: Do people consciously consider various features of the judgment situation, weigh the positive and negative features of the context and target, develop a conscious understanding of the effects of these features, and then make judgments based upon that understanding? Or do people arrive at judgments for reasons of which they may not be entirely aware, and only later attempt to piece together why they might have made the judgments they did?

Each of these positions has its proponents in current social judgment theorizing. In this chapter, we compare and contrast these alternate views. First, we discuss the view that people's attempts to make their judgments accurate (i.e. remove bias from their judgments) are guided by their naive, metacognitive theories (Strack, 1992; Wegener & Petty, 1995; Wilson & Brekke, 1994). Then, we discuss the view that people's accuracy attempts are guided by non-conscious processes initiated by features of the general judgment setting (Martin & Achee, 1992). After presenting these two views, we discuss our own research on judgmental correction processes, and conclude from this work that people's conscious theories of social judgment are generally not causal, a priori, or accurate. Rather, these theories are descriptions of what people think they observed themselves doing while forming a judgment, and these theories influence judgments primarily when people are sensitized to (e.g. warned about) a particularly salient bias.

The initial judgment models

It has generally been assumed that all judgments are relative to some context (see Eiser, 1990). We cannot describe an object as large or small, for example, without having some sort of standard in mind (i.e. large or small compared to what?). Consistent with this context-dependent view of judgment, a great deal of research has explored the effects of various contexts on people's judgments. This research can be divided roughly into two categories based on the nature of the contextual stimuli typically used. In research following the tradition of social judgment theory (Sherif & Hovland, 1961), the contextual stimuli have typically been exemplars that are obviously relevant to the target judgment, and that are judged along the same dimension as the target stimulus. For example, researchers in this tradition might ask participants to judge the size of a dog after having judged the size of an elephant or a mouse (cf. Herr, 1986; Herr, Sherman, & Fazio, 1983).

In priming research, on the other hand, the context has been construed not as another external stimulus to be judged, but as the cognitive concepts that are accessible to the judge at the time of the target judgment. The accessibility of these concepts has typically been manipulated in subtle, disguised ways (e.g. having participants read a series of words in what is ostensibly a color perception task in what is ostensibly an experiment unrelated to that in which the participants subsequently form their impression of the target). One consequence of these unobtrusive manipulations is that participants in priming studies typically do not realize that the contextual stimuli are in any way related to their target judgment (Martin, 1986; Stapel, Koomen, & Van der Pligt, 1997; Strack, Schwarz, Bless, Kuebler, & Waenke, 1993). In fact, priming can influence judgments even when participants are not aware of having been exposed to the contextual stimuli (Bargh & Pietromonaco, 1982; Winkielman & Schwarz, 1996).

Despite these (and other) differences (see Stapel et al., 1997), the social judgment research and the priming research make similar predictions regarding the conditions that lead to different types of context effects. Specifically, the initial theoretical models in both areas suggested that people assimilate their judgments of the target toward the implications of the context when certain context and target features overlap, but contrast their target judgments away from the implications of the context when the context and target do not show overlap (Herr et al., 1983).

The case for correction

The hypothesis that the degree of feature overlap between the context and target is crucial in determining the direction of context effects can take us far in understanding the effect of various contexts on judgments. Within the last 10 or so years, however, a number of studies have been published that point to limitations on this hypothesis. These studies have shown that either assimilation or contrast can occur with a given degree of similarity between the target and the context (e.g. Martin, 1986; Martin, Seta, & Crelia, 1990; Strack et al., 1993). To account for such results, a number of investigators have begun to hypothesize that social judges may engage in more active processing than the initial models gave us reason to believe. Martin and Achee (1992), for example, suggested that a filter metaphor might be useful in explaining the occurrence of both assimilation and contrast to the same context-target configuration. The argument was that people have a wide range of information they could bring to bear on a judgment. This includes not only concepts or exemplars as suggested by the initial models, but also previously stored judgments, attitudes, moods, and emotions, non-mood bodily states such as arousal or confusion, scripts, communication rules, and more. For any given judgment, however, people bring only a subset of these into play. People may even fail to bring into play information that is highly accessible and applicable to the target. They may fail to do so because use of this information would be inappropriate in light of their current processing objectives. In short, the filter metaphor suggests that people are sensitive to the appropriateness of using a contextually induced response in addition to being sensitive to the response's similarity to the target response.

Conceptually similar positions have been proposed by others. Higgins (1989), for example, suggested that people judge the relevance of the context as well as its similarity to the target. According to Strack (1992), people assess neither relevance nor appropriateness; they assess representativeness. From this perspective, people do not use a contextually induced response in their target evaluation if that response does not appear to have been elicited by the target. Yzerbyt, Schadron, Leyens, and Rocher (1994) described a social judgeability model in which people do not use information in their judgments if they do not feel justified in doing so (e.g. characterizing someone in terms of a stereotype is unjustified). Wilson and Brekke (1994) suggested that people engage in correction processes in an attempt to avoid mental contamination, and Wegener and Petty (1995) suggested that people engage in correction processes in an attempt to avoid perceived bias.

Despite their differences, each of the models just described are based on the assumption that people are in some way actively influencing the effect of the context on their target judgment. Social judgments are not merely a function of the similarity between the target and the contextual stimuli. They are a function of the target, the contextual stimuli, the judge, and the judgment setting. One reasonable way to categorize these models is in terms of the amount of credit they accord to people's naive theories (i.e. people's verbal reports of the effect of the context on the target judgment). The most credit is accorded by Wegener and Petty (1995) who suggested not only that people's theories determine the direction and extent of their corrections but also that a consideration of people's naive theories may be useful in "organizing correction findings across different paradigms and domains"

(p. 39). Similar, though somewhat less expansive positions, have been taken by Wilson and Brekke (1994) and by Strack (1992).

Even less credit is accorded to people's naive theories by Martin and Achee (1992). Although these investigators described the possibility of both assimilation and contrast arising from people's use of theories (pp. 212–213), they qualified this possibility by suggesting that "the answer lies, in part, in people's theories" (p. 212). They suggested instead that most of the variance in correction is attributable to the general judgmental setting, or more precisely, to the implicit processing objectives activated by features of the setting. In discussing these models, we have divided them into two categories: Those that view correction as guided primarily by people's naive theories and those that view correction as guided primarily by features of the judgmental setting.

Theory-driven correction

There are at least three models that explicitly suggest that people's corrections for contextual influences are based primarily on people's naive theories (Strack, 1992; Wegener & Petty, 1995; Wilson & Brekke, 1994). Although these models differ from one another in certain respects, they share the following four assumptions: To correct for contextual influences, people must (1) be aware of being biased by the contextual stimuli; (2) be aware of the direction and magnitude of this bias; (3) be motivated to correct for this bias; and (4) have sufficient control over their responses to be able to correct. Unless all four of these conditions are satisfied, people will not correct. We present this general view by discussing one model in detail, namely Wegener and Petty's flexible correction model. The assumptions and predictions of this model are representative of the other models of theory-based correction, yet the flexible correction model has been empirically tested more than the other models. Consequently, it can be spoken about in more detail.

According to the flexible correction model (Petty & Wegener, 1994; Wegener & Petty, 1995), people possess a store of naive theories that specify the effects that various stimuli exert on various judgments. These theories are verbalizable, exist in a person's memory prior to the time of the target judgment, and play a causal role in the person's judgments. Before a research participant ever enters a psychology lab, for example, is placed in a positive mood, and asked to evaluate his or her life satisfaction, the participant could articulate the possible effect of his or her mood on his or her life satisfaction judgment. The participant may theorize, for example, that he or she will be predisposed to render a more favorable evaluation when in a positive as compared to a negative mood.

Of what use is this insight? Does it help people in their attempts to make their judgments more accurate? According to the flexible correction model, when people suspect that their target judgment may be in danger of being biased, they retrieve their naive theories relevant to the judgment and the particular context in which they are making this judgment (e.g. a theory of the effects of mood on life satisfaction judgments). These theories allow people to determine the likely direction and extent of the effect of the context on their judgment. Armed with this information, people can attempt to remove the contextually induced bias from their judgment. They do this by adjusting their final target ratings in a direction opposite to the theorized bias and in an amount commensurate with the theorized amount of bias. Thus, people who suspect that a context might be exerting an assimilative effect on their ratings will adjust their ratings of the target in a direction away from the value of the context (i.e. contrast), whereas people who suspect that a context might be exerting a contrastive influence will adjust their ratings of the target back toward the context (i.e. assimilation).

It should be noted that the flexible correction model does not assume that people's theories are necessarily accurate. A person's theory might suggest assimilation, for example, when the context is actually biasing their judgments toward a contrast effect. In such cases, people's corrections follow their theories because corrections are aimed at removing the theorized bias, not the actual bias. As a result, "people may overcorrect, undercorrect, or even correct for a bias that does not exist" (Wegener & Petty, 1995, p. 38)

What are the conditions that make people access their theories and attempt to remove bias from their judgments? Unfortunately, the flexible correction model is mute on this point. The initial research has been concerned primarily with showing that when people correct for perceived bias, they do so in accordance with their naive theories. Thus, in the initial studies, participants were essentially instructed to correct (i.e. Don't let your rating of the context influence your rating of the targets). Wegener and Petty have suggested, however, that theory-based correction will only occur when people are willing and able to exert a sufficient amount of cognitive effort. This is because it is presumably more difficult to complete the correction process than it is to use one's initial reaction to the target as one's judgment (see Martin et al., 1990).

To summarize, the flexible correction model, like the other models of theory-based correction (Strack, 1992; Wilson & Brekke, 1994), is based on the assumption that people correct for unwanted influences on their judgments only when they are aware of the influence, aware of the direction and magnitude of the influence, and are motivated to engage in the correction process. Awareness of the direction and magnitude of the bias is assumed to come from people's naive theories which are verbalizable and in existence prior to the correction. Without these theories, people could be induced to correct but would not know exactly how to do so. With the theories, people at least have a direction in which to head. They may not succeed in their debiasing efforts, however, because their theories do not always accurately reflect the actual contextual influence.

Correction induced by the judgment setting

One alternative to the view that people's corrections are guided by a priori, verbalizable theories is the view that people's corrections are determined by processes that are beyond their introspective capabilities. We discuss this possibility in terms of Martin's set–reset model (Martin, 1985, 1986; Martin & Achee, 1992; Martin et al., 1990). Like the theory-based models of correction, the set–reset model assumes that people attempt to correct for biases in their target judgments and that this correction demands the expenditure of cognitive effort. The set–reset model also assumes that the direction and extent of some corrections can be influenced by people's naive theories (Martin & Achee, 1992, pp. 212–213). The model differs from the theory-based correction models, however, in according a much smaller role to these theories.

The overriding principle behind the set–reset model is that in making any judgment, people must (1) retrieve information that is pertinent to locating the target accurately on the dimension of judgment and (2) discard or fail to retrieve information that does not satisfy this objective. Although these processes may be triggered by conscious and verbalizable theories, it may often be the case that these processes are triggered relatively spontaneously by features of the judgment setting that may not be open to articulation. If we are asked to judge how tall a person is, for example, then it would be inappropriate for us to report that the person has blue eyes or is left-handed, because these features do not allow us to locate the target on the tallness dimension. It is unlikely, however, that we would be conscious of our decision to exclude eye color and handedness from our judgment. Phenomenologically, we make our judgments of tallness simply by noting how tall the person is. Similarly, if we are asked to judge our life as a whole, then it would be inappropriate for us to respond by considering only our social life. Although evaluation of our social life is relevant to judging our life as a whole, it is not the sole focus of a "life as a whole" judgment. But this reasoning may not come explicitly to mind as we make our life satisfaction judgment.

Correction in the absence of verbal reports of a contextual influence make sense if one keeps in mind the distinction between declarative and procedural knowledge (Anderson, 1982; Smith & Lerner, 1986; Gazzaniga, 1985). Roughly, declarative knowledge is knowledge of descriptive features, knowledge that can be verbalized. Procedural knowledge, on the other hand, is reflective of skills and abilities. It cannot be verbalized either because it has become automatized as a function of repeated practice or because of its inherent inaccessibility. By analogy, people may be able to declare that one object is farther away than another, but they cannot report on the extent to which they relied upon convergence, accommodation, and retinal disparity in making this judgment.

One useful characterization of procedural knowledge is in terms of implicit *if-then* rules or production systems (Anderson, 1982; Smith & Lerner, 1986). According to this characterization, if values of the stimulus information match values in the *if* statement, then specified operations are initiated. Moreover, the assessment of the value match and the performance of the operations can take place beyond the person's awareness (Anderson, 1982; Smith & Lerner, 1986). Martin and Achee (1992) proposed that such a system might be involved in some corrections in social judgments. Their hypothetical reset production system was depicted as follows:

If my reaction to the target is <INAPPROPRIATE> then <RESET>.

The inappropriate slot is construed as an implicit filtering process that initiates a correction when it detects aspects of the target reaction that belong to something other than the target ("I like the target because I am in a good mood") or that are part of the target but a part that should not be included in the particular judgment the person is making ("I know the target is attractive but this has nothing to do with whether she is honest"). A number of factors that seem to satisfy this inappropriateness constraint have been identified. For example, people are unlikely to use contextual responses in forming their target judgments if the context is perceived as belonging to a different category than the target (Schwarz & Bless, 1992; Seta, Martin, & Capehart, 1979; Tajfel & Wilkes, 1963). People also fail to use contextual responses if those responses are attributed to a non-target source (Schwarz & Clore, 1983), or if the judge has adopted a communication rule that implicitly suggests that the contextual response be excluded from their judgment (Strack, Martin, & Schwarz, 1988). Explicit warnings or requests to exclude the contextual response also lead people to exclude that response (Leach, 1974; Stapel, Martin, & Schwarz, in press; Wegener & Petty, 1995). People are also less likely to incorporate their context response into their target judgment when they rate the context and the target in sequence rather than simultaneously (Martin & Seta, 1983; Byrne, Lamberth, Palmer, & London, 1969). And people attempt to avoid target-related reactions if those reactions violate social norms, as might be the case with stereotypes (Devine, 1989; Yzerbyt et al, 1994).

According to the set–reset model, once a reaction has been categorized as inappropriate, people may attempt to partial this reaction from their true reaction to the target (see Figure 12.1). In the context of the set–reset model, this type of correction is called resetting, and is thought to be accomplished by focusing on features of the target reaction that distinguish it from the context reaction, and then using these distinctive features to generate a new reaction. The result is a shift in the target judgment away from the implications of the contextually induced reaction. Because correction involves the disuse of the initial reaction and the generation of another, correction is assumed to demand the expenditure of more cognitive effort than does going with the initial reaction (Martin et al., 1990).

When the overlapping contextual reaction is not instantiated as inappropriate, people incorporate the reaction into their target judgment. The result is assimilation of the target judgment toward the contextually induced reaction.

A. Initial representation of ambiguous target person

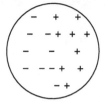

B. Representation after priming with a positive concept

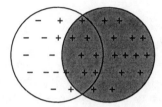

C. Representation after resetting

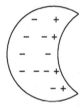

Figure 12.1 *Metaphorical representation of the set–reset process*

Dogmatists vs. empiricists

Both the theory-based models of correction as well as the set–reset model suggest that people try to place the target accurately on the dimension of judgment, and that they do this by removing what they perceive to be biasing contextual influences. The models differ, however, in their depiction of this debiasing process. According to the theory-based view, people have conscious theories of the direction and extent of the contextual bias, and use these theories to guide their corrections. It is in this sense that the theory-based correction models portray people as naive dogmatists. People have a priori theories of how the context influences their judgments and they use these theories to guide their corrections regardless of the accuracy of the theories.

The alternate view is that features of the judgment situation activate production systems which, in turn, initiate various judgment operations, including corrections, beyond the judge's awareness. Having observed themselves experiencing the conscious thoughts and feelings that are the output of the production systems, however, people can make inferences about the probable influence of the contextual factors. In this way, people's theories and explanations come after the judgment to be explained (Bem, 1967; Griffin & Buehler, 1993). To the extent that this is true, people can be characterized as naive empiricists. They wait to see the conscious effects of various contextual factors before developing a theory to explain these effects.

Is there a way to tease these two views apart? In other words, can we tell if people act more like naive dogmatists or naive empiricists during social judgments? We think so.

Predicting the uncorrected reaction

One potentially interesting way in which the flexible correction model and the set–reset model differ from one another is in their treatment of uncorrected reactions (i.e. the effects of a context when judges do not correct for the contextual influence). The flexible correction model does not include factors that allow it to predict the uncorrected effect of any given context. From a flexible correction perspective, we can know the uncorrected effect only by exposing participants to a context and observing the resultant judgments when participants have not been induced to correct. A concrete example of this logic can be seen in a study by Wegener and Petty (1995). They began by providing participants with a series of context-target configurations and asked the participants to say what the effect of the context might be on the target. They found, for example, that most participants believed that their ratings of a product would be biased toward desirability if the product was endorsed by attractive as compared to unattractive women (i.e. an assimilation effect). On the other hand, most participants also believed that their ratings of moderately attractive women would be biased away from their ratings of extremely attractive or extremely unattractive women (i.e. a contrast effect).

After establishing that there were sets of stimuli for which participants held theories of either assimilation and contrast, Wegener and Petty (1995) had participants rate these stimuli. Half of the participants were asked, without further elaboration, to rate the context and target items. The remaining participants were given an explicit warning not to let their judgments of the context influence their judgments of the target. Although this warning informed participants of a possible bias, it did not specify the direction or magnitude of that bias. It was assumed that this information would be gleaned by participants from their naive theories. The results were consistent with this hypothesis.

When participants simply rated the context and target stimuli, their target judgments reflected assimilation when participants rated stimuli they had earlier theorized would lead to assimilation, but reflected contrast when they rated stimuli they had earlier theorized would lead to contrast. When participants had been instructed to remove the contextual bias, however, their judgments showed the opposite pattern. There was assimilation when participants rated stimuli they had earlier theorized would lead to contrast, but contrast when they rated stimuli they had earlier theorized would lead to assimilation.

According to Wegener and Petty (1995), when participants were not instructed to remove the contextual bias, their target judgments reflected the uncorrected effect of the context. When participants were instructed to correct, however, their target judgments reflected an effortful correction in a direction opposite to the contextual influence suggested by their theories. Thus, we can conclude that contrast is the uncorrected effect of rating moderately attractive women after rating either extremely attractive or extremely unattractive women because participants who rated these stimuli produced contrast when they had not been instructed to correct.

The set–reset model, on the other hand, suggests that aspects of the stimulus configuration can influence the uncorrected reaction. As can be seen in Figure 12.1, p. 235, the Venn diagram typically used to depict reset contrast depicts an overlap between the representation of the target and the representation of the context (e.g. priming with an applicable concept). This overlap is crucial because, according to the set–reset model, failure to remove this overlap results in assimilation, whereas reset contrast occurs only when people partial out this overlap. So, if we know the degree of overlap, we can predict the likely uncorrected effect. Assimilation will be the uncorrected effect when there is overlap between the context and the target, whereas contrast will be the uncorrected effect when there is no overlap between the context and the target. A consideration of these set–reset assumptions suggests an alternate interpretation of Wegener and Petty's (1995) results.

From a flexible correction perspective, we assume that contrast is the default effect of rating moderately attractive women in the context of either extremely attractive or extremely unattractive women because judgments of participants who rated such stimuli showed contrast. From a set–reset perspective, however, contrast is not the default with these stimuli. This is because with these stimuli, there is an overlap between the representations of the target and the context. Specifically, the extremely attractive women possessed attractive features, the extremely unattractive women possessed unattractive features, and the moderately attractive women possessed some attractive and some unattractive features. So, according to the set–reset model, there should be assimilation when participants do not correct for the contextual influence (i.e. partial out the overlap). If this is true, then why did Wegener and Petty (1995) obtain contrast with these stimuli when participants were not instructed to correct for the contextual bias?

Recall that the set–reset model allows for implicitly initiated correction (i.e. production systems). This means that participants need not be able to verbalize the contextual influence nor do they need to be aware of having engaged in correction. These assumptions leave open the possibility that participants may correct implicitly or spontaneously even when they have not received explicit instructions to correct. The result would be a contrast effect that would appear to arise in the absence of a correction. It follows, therefore, that when participants are explicitly instructed to correct in such a case, their ratings would reflect assimilation because these participants would be correcting for the output of the earlier, implicit reset (i.e. a contrast effect).

Obviously, this interpretation is speculative. And, although it allows the set–reset model to account for the Wegener and Petty data, it also raises two questions. First, is it possible to find evidence of implicit resetting in the Wegener and Petty paradigm? Second, why would participants warned about a contextual bias correct if they had already corrected implicitly? We address each of these questions in turn.

Cognitive effort and implicit corrections

Both the flexible correction model and the set–reset model suggest that judgments rendered with little cognitive effort are likely to reflect the initial, uncorrected effect of a context. The models differ, however, on what they expect this effect to be when participants rate moderate stimuli in the context of more extreme stimuli (i.e. moderately attractive women in the context of either extremely attractive or extremely unattractive women). Wegener and Petty found that the uncorrected effect with such stimuli was contrast. According to the set–reset model the uncorrected effect with such stimuli is assimilation, but this assimilation should show up only when participants exert sufficiently little cognitive effort that they do not engage even in implicit correction.

To test these ideas, Martin (1997) had female participants rate the attractiveness of moderately attractive males in the context of either very attractive or very unattractive males (stimuli for which these participants held theories of contrast). Half of the participants were run under conditions similar to those of Wegener and Petty (1995). Specifically, some participants were asked merely to rate the contextual and target stimuli, whereas others, when asked to rate these stimuli, were instructed to keep their ratings of the context stimuli from influencing their ratings of the targets. Although the results in these conditions cannot tease the two models apart, they can tell us if we captured the same phenomena as Wegener and Petty. If we did, then we should see judgments of the unwarned participants reflecting contrast, but judgments of the warned participants reflecting assimilation.

It is the judgments of a second group of participants that are useful in testing the predictions about the uncorrected effect of the context. In this second group, all participants rated the contextual and target stimuli without receiving any mention of the contextual bias. Half of these participants, however, were induced to exert little cognitive effort in forming their judgments, whereas half were induced to exert considerable cognitive effort (Martin et al., 1990). Specifically, participants in the low effort condition were told that the experimenter was interested in "top of the head" judgments and that they were to exert little effort in forming their judgment, respond with the first thoughts that came to them, and put no name or other identifying mark on the paper. Participants in the high effort condition, on the other hand, were told to put their name on their papers and be as accurate as possible, so that later in the experiment they could justify their ratings.

According to the flexible correction model, when participants do not exert sufficient cognitive effort, their judgments should reflect the uncorrected effect of the context. Because contrast was reflected in the judgments of the unwarned participants in the Wegener and Petty study (and presumably what would be obtained in our parallel conditions), the flexible correction model leads us to conclude that judgments of the low effort participants will reflect contrast (i.e. the default, uncorrected effect).

The high effort participants, on the other hand, might exert sufficient effort to retrieve their theories and use them in correcting for the theorized bias. Because participants held theories of contrast for these stimuli, the corrections of these participants should produce assimilation, a shift away from the theorized bias. In sum, the flexible correction model leads us to expect that judgments of the low effort participants will reflect contrast, whereas judgments of the high effort participants will reflect assimilation.

The set–reset model, on the other hand, is based on the assumption that, with these stimuli, there is some overlap between the representations of the context and the target. Participants who do not exert much effort may not partial out this overlap, whereas participants who exert high effort may partial it out. Thus, the set–reset model predicts the mirror image of the flexible correction model: assimilation among the low effort participants, but contrast among the high effort participants.

As can be seen in Figure 12.2, the results supported the set–reset hypotheses. When participants did not exert cognitive effort, they rated the target as more attractive in the positive context than in the negative context (assimilation). When participants exerted effort, however, they rated the target as more attractive in the negative than in the positive context (contrast).

These results suggest that the judgments of Wegener and Petty's unwarned participants did not reflect the uncorrected effect of the context. Their unwarned participants, like ours, showed contrast in their judgments. Our low effort participants, on the other hand, showed assimilation. This pattern suggests that even though the unwarned participants were not alerted to a contextual bias, they nevertheless completed an implicit correction process. Our results fit with the flexible correction assumption that the uncorrected effect of a context can be observed when people do not exert sufficient cognitive effort, but they suggest that the no-warning condition used by Wegener and Petty did not produce a low enough level of cognitive effort to reveal the true uncorrected effect. Without a sufficiently low level of effort, participants (even unwarned ones) may complete an initial, implicit correction.

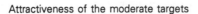

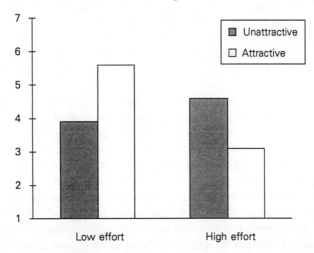

Figure 12.2 *Ratings of target persons as a function of level of effort and the attractiveness of the context persons*

What are the implications of the results in the high effort, accuracy condition? Participants given accuracy instructions clearly performed a reset. Their judgments reflected contrast, not the uncorrected assimilation seen among the low effort participants. This contrast was not a correction in the direction recommended by the participants' a priori, verbal theories, however. Participants had indicated in pilot testing that they thought the context would have a contrastive influence. So, if participants were correcting away from the bias suggested by their theories, then they would have corrected in the direction of assimilation. The accuracy participants, however, corrected away from the true uncorrected effect (low effort assimilation), toward the theorized uncorrected effect.

In fact, the only participants to correct in a direction recommended by the a priori theories were those given Wegener and Petty's blatant warning. It may be that the flexible correction process holds only when people are explicitly instructed to correct and are conscious of the output of their initial judgmental processes.

In sum, the data suggest that people act more like naive empiricists than naive dogmatists. Exposure to the context-target configurations seemed to engender an implicit correction process (i.e. resetting). Participants were unaware of this process, but were aware of its output. When asked what the effect of the context might be on their judgments (i.e. when asked their theory), they reported contrast, not the original uncorrected assimilation effect. Similarly, when given a blatant warning to correct, they corrected for contrast (i.e. the output of the initial correction process), not assimilation (i.e. the low effort default effect).

Correction or communication?

If the set–reset interpretation just described is correct, then the blatantly warned participants corrected for a judgment they had already corrected. Specifically, they performed an implicit correction followed by an explicit correction. Why would participants engage in this kind of double correction? There are at least two reasons why this might be the case. First, participants may have been unaware of having made the first correction. If this initial correction was indeed implicit, then participants would have been aware only of its output. This possibility is consistent with participants' self-reported theories. As noted earlier, when participants reported what the effect of the context would be, they reported contrast (i.e. the output of the initial, implicit reset), not the actual, uncorrected effect (i.e. assimilation). A second factor that might make people correct after having already corrected lies in the correction instructions themselves. Note that the blatant warning used by Martin and Wegener and Petty conveys a strong demand to correct. Following the rules of communication (Grice, 1975), participants may ask themselves "Why would the experimenter tell me to correct for the influence of the context unless there was in fact such an influence?" (see Leach, 1974; Schwarz, Strack, & Mai, 1991; Strack et al., 1988). In short, participants may have corrected twice because, in a sense, they thought they were being asked to do so.

Would participants show the same tendency to correct if the warning was less demanding? Suppose, for example, that participants were told to correct only if they actually detected a bias. With this warning, there is no implication that a bias exists, so there is no demand to correct. Thus, participants receiving a conditional warning might correct only if they actually detected a bias. This hypothesis can be tested by having participants receive either a blatant or a conditional warning while rating context-target configurations in which the biasing effect of the context is either subtle or obvious. If the demand hypothesis is valid, then conditionally warned participants may correct only when the bias is obvious, whereas blatantly warned participants may correct regardless of the level of bias.

This hypothesis was tested by Stapel, Martin, and Schwarz (in press). Following Wegener and Petty, they had participants rate exotic vacation spots (e.g. Hawaii) before rating the desirability of the weather in some less desirable midwestern US cities (e.g. Indianapolis). Some participants rated these vacation spots on the same dimension on which they subsequently rated the cities (i.e. desirability of weather). Other participants rated people's job satisfaction in the vacation spots, and then rated the desirability of the weather in the midwestern cities. It was assumed that the biasing effect of rating the vacation spots would be more apparent when participants judged the vacation spots and cities on the same dimension (cf. Brown, 1953).

Within each of these two conditions, some participants received the blatant warning used by Wegener and Petty (1995), whereas some received

Favorableness of target cities

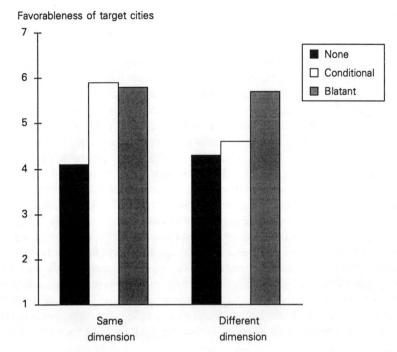

Figure 12.3 *Rating of target cities as a function of correction instruction and dimension of judgment*

a more subtle warning. The blatantly warned participants were instructed to keep their perceptions of the contextual stimuli from influencing their target judgments. The conditionally warned participants were instructed as follows: "Please try to make sure that your ratings of the desirability of the weather in the locations below reflect your true response. When you feel there is something that may have an unwanted influence on your ratings, please try to adjust for that influence." A third group of participants, the control group, received no warning at all.

If the blatant warning acts as a communication demand to alter one's target judgment, then we would expect to see participants given the blatant warning correcting regardless of the dimension on which they rated the cities and vacation spots. If the conditional warning, on the other hand, makes people sensitive to contextual influences, then we would expect to find that participants given the conditional warning would correct when they rated the cities and vacation spots on the same dimension, but not when they rated the two on different dimensions.

As can be seen in Figure 12.3, the results supported these hypotheses. Note, first of all, that participants in the control condition (i.e. those given no warning) did not correct for the implicit contrast. They judged the weather in the midwestern US cities to be undesirable relative to the vacation spots regardless of the dimension on which the vacation spots had been judged. Participants asked to correct only if they detected a bias, however, corrected for the initial contrast when they rated the vacation spots and cities on the same dimension, but not when they rated these on different dimensions. Specifically, they judged the weather in the midwestern cities favorably after having rated the weather in the vacation spots, but rated it unfavorably after having rated people's job satisfaction in the vacation spots. Finally, participants who had received the blatant warning corrected for the initial contrast regardless of the dimension on which the vacation spots had been judged. Regardless of the context judgment, these participants rated the weather in the midwestern US cities as relatively desirable, an assimilative shift away from the initial contrastive effect of the context.

These results seem to suggest that the corrections obtained with the blatant warning used by Wegener and Petty (1995) do not reflect the operation of a spontaneous correction process. Rather, such corrections seem to reflect a compliance with communication demands. Participants correct because they think they are being asked to. This insight makes it easier to understand why participants might correct after having already made an implicit correction. They are essentially following the demands of the experimenter's communication. Unlike the conditionally warned participants, those receiving the blatant warning showed no sensitivity to the level of bias coming from the context.

Conclusions

In this chapter, we have explored the extent to which people are aware of what they are doing while making social judgments. Awareness, for us, referred to the extent to which people guide their judgment processes by use of verbal, a priori theories. Stated differently, can people give verbal accounts of the effects of various contexts on their judgments and do these verbal accounts subsequently influence their judgments? Our studies found little evidence that this was the case. Participants did not use their theories in the unwarned conditions of any of our studies, nor did they use their theories in either the low effort condition or the high effort condition in the Martin study.

The only participants whose judgments were suggestive of theory use were those who were either explicitly instructed to correct or who were conditionally warned in the presence of a blatant bias. The theory-based models of correction (see Wilson & Brekke, 1994 for a summary) tell us that people correct only when they are (1) aware of being biased, (2) aware of the direction and magnitude of this bias, (3) motivated to correct for this bias, and (4) have sufficient control over their responses to be able to correct.

The judgments of the conditionally warned participants fit nicely with these assumptions. These participants were instructed to correct only if they detected a bias, and they did, in fact, correct only when the influence of the context was obvious. That these participants did not correct when the contextual stimuli were presented more subtly suggests that they did not detect a bias coming from the subtle context. In other words, they had no theory indicating that subtle presentation of the contextual stimuli could bias their judgments.

If the participants indeed had no theory of bias for the subtle context, then what induced the blatantly warned participants to correct for the subtly presented contextual stimuli? Our suggestion was that the blatant warning (i.e. don't let your ratings of the context influence your ratings of the target) induced compliance with a communication rule. The blatantly warned participants corrected because they were essentially being asked to do so.

Not only was correction by means of verbalizable, a priori theories rare in our studies, but we also found evidence that people can sometimes correct in a direction opposite to these theories. Specifically, the high effort participants in the Martin study rendered judgments reflective of contrast. This was clearly a correction relative to the assimilative default of the low effort participants. Because the participants' theories suggested that the context was exerting a contrastive bias, if participants had used these theories to guide their corrections, then they would have corrected in the direction of assimilation. The high accuracy participants, however, showed contrast relative to the low effort participants.

We should also note that to the extent that verbalizable theories came into play, they did not do so with an a priori status. The results suggest that participants developed their theories after engaging in an implicit correction process and reading off the output of this process. This is evidenced by the fact that participants' theories reflected contrast, not the default assimilative effect of the context. Similarly, when participants used their theories to guide their corrections, they corrected back in the direction of the initial default assimilation.

So, what implications do our results have for theory-based models of correction? Consistent with these models, we found that sensitizing participants to a bias can lead them to correct in a direction away from their verbal theories (the conditionally warned participants in the Stapel et al. studies). And we showed that people's theories are not always accurate. Participants had theorized that the effect of the context was contrast, whereas the actual default was assimilation.

Qualification of the theory-based view, on the other hand, came with the possibility that the blatant warning instructions often used in tests of theory-based models of correction may reflect simple compliance with communication demands. And there was at least one finding that seemed genuinely inconsistent with a theory-based view of correction. Participants in the high effort, accuracy condition of the Martin study corrected in a direction opposite to the a priori theories.

In sum, we see our results as more supportive of an empiricist view of social judgment than a dogmatist view. Exposure to the judgment situation (i.e. context, target, processing objectives) seemed to induce participants to perform certain judgment operations (e.g. resetting) and seemed to do so in a way that was beyond the participants' awareness. After observing the conscious output of these operations, however, participants were able to develop post hoc theories of how the contextual stimuli may have influenced them. Participants appeared to have done this, however, only when they received a warning to watch out for contextual biases.

At first blush, this empiricist view might seem to paint a rather negative portrait of social judges. One could conclude from our summary that social judges operate as mindless automatons, engaging in processing of which they are unaware, and rationalizing their actions after the fact. There is a more flattering interpretation, however. What the data indicate is that people's automatic processes are quite good at doing what they were developed to do. If people exert at least some minimal degree of cognitive effort, then their filtering processes can detect bias in their judgments and correct for that bias. Only after the filter has done its job does it provide people's conscious minds with the "unbiased" output. One implication of this arrangement is that people's verbal, conscious minds are free to pursue matters more interesting than scrutinizing each of their thoughts for bias. The general conclusion is that we may want to start placing more trust in our implicit processes. These processes may be more efficient than our verbal, a priori theories would lead us to believe.

References

Anderson, J. (1982). Acquisition of cognitive skill. *Psychological Review, 89*, 369–406.

Bargh, J.A. & Pietromonaco, P. (1982). Automatic information processing and social perceptions: The influence of trait information presented outside of awareness. *Journal of Personality and Social Psychology, 43*, 437–449.

Bem, D.J. (1967). Self-perception: An alternative interpretation of cognitive dissonance phenomena. *Psychological Review, 74*, 183–200.

Brown, D.R. (1953). Stimulus-similarity and the anchoring of subjective scales. *The American Journal of Psychology, 66*, 199–214.

Byrne, D., Lamberth, J., Palmer, J., & London, O. (1969). Sequential effects as a function of explicit and implicit interpolated attraction responses. *Journal of Personality and Social Psychology, 13*, 70–78.

Devine, P.G. (1989). Stereotypes and prejudice: Their automatic and controlled components. *Journal of Personality and Social Psychology, 56*, 5–18.

Eiser, J.R. (1990). *Social judgment.* London: Open University Press.

Fishbein, M. & Ajzen, I. (1975). *Belief, attitude, intention, and behavior: An introduction to theory and research.* Reading, MA: Addison-Wesley.

Gazzaniga, M. (1985). *The social brain.* New York: Basic Books.

Grice, H.P. (1975). Logic and conversation. In P. Cole & J.L. Morgan (Eds), *Syntax and semantics: Vol. 3. Speech acts* (pp. 41–58). New York: Academic Press.

Griffin, D. & Buehler, R. (1993). Role of construal processes in conformity and dissent. *Journal of Personality and Social Psychology, 65*, 657–669.

Herr, P.M. (1986). Consequences of priming: Judgment and behavior. *Journal of Personality and Social Psychology, 51*, 1106–1115.

Herr, P.M., Sherman, S.J., & Fazio, R.H. (1983). On the consequences of priming: Assimilation and contrast effects. *Journal of Experimental Social Psychology, 19*, 323–340.

Higgins, E.T. (1989). Knowledge accessibility and activation: Subjectivity and suffering from unconscious sources. In J.S. Uleman & J.A. Bargh (Eds), *Unintended thought* (pp. 75–123). New York: Guilford Press.

Leach, C. (1974). The importance of instructions in assessing sequential effects in impression formation. *British Journal of Social and Clinical Psychology, 13*, 151–156.

Martin, L.L. (1985). *Categorization and differentiation: A set, re-set, comparison analysis of the effects of context on person perception*. New York: Springer-Verlag.

Martin, L.L. (1986). Set/reset: Use and disuse of concepts in impression formation. *Journal of Personality and Social Psychology, 51*, 493–504.

Martin, L.L. (1997). Manuscript in preparation. University of Georgia.

Martin. L.L. & Achee, J.A. (1992). Beyond accessibility: The role of processing objectives in judgment. In L.L. Martin & A. Tesser (Eds), *The construction of social judgments* (pp. 195–216). Hillsdale, NJ: Lawrence Erlbaum Associates.

Martin, L.L. & Seta, J.J. (1983). Perceptions of unity and distinctiveness as determinants of attraction. *Journal of Personality and Social Psychology, 44*, 763–772.

Martin, L.L., Seta, J.J., & Crelia, R.A. (1990). Assimilation and contrast as a function of people's willingness to expend effort in forming an impression. *Journal of Personality and Social Psychology, 59*, 27–37.

Nisbett, R.E. & Wilson, T.D. (1977). Telling more than we can know: Verbal reports on mental processes. *Psychological Review, 84*, 231–259.

Petty, R.E. & Wegener, D.T. (1994). Flexible correction processes in social judgment: Correcting for context-induced contrast. *Journal of Experimental Social Psychology, 29*, 137–165.

Schwarz, N. & Bless, H. (1992). Constructing reality and its alternatives: An inclusion/exclusion model of assimilation and contrast effects in social judgment. In L.L. Martin & A. Tesser (Eds), *The construction of social judgments* (pp. 217–245). Hillsdale, NJ: Lawrence Erlbaum Associates.

Schwarz, N. & Clore, G.L. (1983). Mood, misattribution, and judgments of well-being: Informative and directive functions of affective states. *Journal of Personality and Social Psychology, 45*, 513–523.

Schwarz, N., Strack, F., & Mai, H.P. (1991). Assimilation and contrast effects in part-whole question sequences: A conversational analysis. *Public Opinion Quarterly, 55*, 3–23.

Seta, J.J., Martin, L.L., & Capehart, G. (1979). The effects of contrast and generalization on the attitude similarity-attraction relationship. *Journal of Personality and Social Psychology, 37*, 462–467.

Sherif, M. & Hovland, C.I. (1961). *Social judgment: Assimilation and contrast effects in communication and attitude change*. New Haven, CT: Yale University Press.

Smith, E.R. & Lerner, M. (1986). Development and automatism of social judgments. *Journal of Personality and Social Psychology, 50*, 246–259.

Stapel, D.A., Koomen, W., & Van der Pligt, J. (1997). Categories of category accessibility: The impact of trait versus exemplar priming on person judgments. *Journal of Experimental Social Psychology, 33*, 44–76.

Stapel, D.A., Martin, L.L., & Schwarz, N. (in press). The smell of bias: What instigates correction processes in social judgments? *Personality and Social Psychology Bulletin*.

Strack, F. (1992). The different routes to social judgments: Experiential versus informational strategies. In L.L. Martin & A. Tesser (Eds), *The construction of social judgments* (pp. 249–300). Hillsdale, NJ: Lawrence Erlbaum Associates.

Strack, F., Martin, L.L., & Schwarz, N. (1988). Priming and communication: The social determinants of information use in judgments of life-satisfaction. *European Journal of Social Psychology, 18*, 429–442.

Strack, F., Schwarz, N., Bless, H., Kuebler, A., & Waenke, M. (1993). Awareness of the influence as a determinant of assimilation versus contrast. *European Journal of Social Psychology, 23*, 53–62.

Tajfel, H. & Wilkes, A.L. (1963). Classification and quantitative judgment. *British Journal of Psychology*, *54*, 101–114.

Wegener, D.T. & Petty, R.E. (1995). Flexible correction processes in social judgment: The role of naive theories of corrections for perceived bias. *Journal of Personality and Social Psychology*, *68*, 36–51.

Wilson, T.D. & Brekke, N. (1994). Mental contamination and mental correction: Unwanted influences on judgments and evaluations. *Psychological Bulletin*, *116*, 117–142.

Winkielman, P. & Schwarz, N. (1996). Contrast and assimilation with and without awareness: A test of the inclusion/exclusion model. Paper presented at the 68th annual meeting of the Midwestern Psychological Association, Chicago, IL, May.

Yzerbyt, V.Y., Schadron, G., Leyens, J.-P, & Rocher, S. (1994). Social judgeability: The impact of meta-informational cues on the use of stereotypes. *Journal of Personality and Social Psychology*, *66*, 48–55.

Index